SPEARHEADS FOR REFORM

SPEARHEADS
FOR REFORM

The Social Settlements
and the Progressive Movement
1890–1914

ALLEN F. DAVIS

RUTGERS UNIVERSITY PRESS

NEW BRUNSWICK, NEW JERSEY

Second paperback printing, 1991

This edition first published in 1984 by
Rutgers University Press
under agreement with author.

Library of Congress Cataloging in Publication Data

Davis, Allen Freeman, 1931–
Spearheads for reform.

   Bibliography: p.
   Includes index.
   1. Social settlements—United States—History.
2. Progressivism (United States politics)   3. Cities
and towns—United States—History.   I. Title.
HV4194.D38   1984   362'.973   84-13471
ISBN 0-8135-1072-4
ISBN 0-8135-1073-2 (pbk.)

Contents

*To My Father and
the Memory of My Mother*

Preface

This is a study of a group of idealists who believed that they could solve some of the problems of the sprawling, crowded city by going to live in a working-class neighborhood. It is the story of optimists who were convinced that reform was not only necessary, but also possible, in an age when rapid industrialization and a deluge of immigrants exaggerated the social and economic differences in America and challenged the very tenets of democracy. Some of the settlement workers were naïve; others were little more than kindergarten teachers and recreation directors; but a group of men and women who centered their activities in the social settlements in Boston, Chicago, and New York became initiators and organizers of reform in the progressive era.

This is primarily a story of a group of men and women, of their ideas and their actions, rather than a study of institutions or organizations. It is an attempt to explore the impact of settlement workers on the reform movements of the progressive era rather than an internal analysis of the settlement movement or a collective history of four hundred settlement houses. I have tried to show development and change within the settlement movement, but my major concern has been with its influence and impact. For this reason

I have directed most of my attention to settlements in Boston, Chicago, and New York, where the movement was strongest and most concerned with reform. For the same reason my primary scheme of organization is topical rather than chronological. Within each section, however, I have tried to chart development and change in ideas and action, and to show how the settlement workers organized reform—first in the neighborhood, then in the city, the state, and the nation.

Throughout the study I have been concerned with what settlement workers thought, wrote, and did, and how thought and action were interrelated. Robert Bremner notes the important role social workers played in communicating to the public the great need for reform.[1] This, of course, they did; but they also played a large part in the practical task of getting bills passed in Springfield, Albany, and in Washington. Arthur Schlesinger, Jr., describes the "subtle and persistent saintliness of the social workers." "Theirs," he says, "was the implacability of gentleness";[2] but behind the gentleness, many settlement workers were tough-minded realists who understood how the American political system operated. Of course it is true that they were also idealists who sometimes came perilously close to believing that if they gathered enough statistics and enough information on the social evils in America, the solution would follow naturally. A large number of settlement workers, however, became expert not only at collecting statistics, but also at using them to influence both public opinion and elected officials.

In tracing the impact of the settlements on the progressive movement I have profited, as will become obvious, from the work of many historians who have explored one aspect or another of this fascinating period. The settlement workers were progressive with a vengeance; unlike some who committed themselves to reform only ideologically, they actually became involved, to the extent of going to live in the slums. As a group they were optimists who fit Henry May's description of people who "wanted to make a number of sharp changes because they were so confident in the basic rightness of things as they were."[3] A few did join the

Socialist Party; but most of them believed in and supported the American system of government, though they were determined to improve it. They were "practical idealists"—a term used by Henry May and by settlement workers themselves. Leaders in what Arthur Link has called "the social justice movement," they were also part of Robert Bremner's "factual generation," though they went beyond statistics to try to understand the men, women, and children who were their neighbors.[4]

As compared to progressives described by Samuel Hays, George Mowry, and others, the settlement workers were less paternalistic and more genuinely sympathetic to the cause of organized labor.[5] In addition, they were less prejudiced and more active in working for Negroes and immigrants.[6] They were also more genuinely committed to the city in their attitudes and action than were the progressives pictured by Mowry and Morton White.[7] They were indeed influenced by Darwin's theories, yet not to the extent that the progressives portrayed by Eric Goldman would suggest.[8] They were pragmatists, though not often relativists, and although they were engaged in a "revolt against formalism," in the phrase of Morton White, they were concerned with much more than that.[9] The settlement workers were progressives driven by complex needs, but their motivation cannot be explained as simply the product of a "status revolution" as defined by Richard Hofstadter.[10]

Settlement workers were actively involved in and working for reform on the local level in the 1890's; for them the progressive era did not begin on that day in 1901 when an assassin's bullet made Theodore Roosevelt President. Yet World War I marked the end of an era. For, while they continued to work for reform throughout the war, and on a limited basis during the 1920's and after, the spirit was different and their movement had changed.

The settlement workers do not fit many of the sweeping generalizations made by historians about the progressive movement. Yet they were reformers who served as initiators and organizers and helped to extend the social welfare function of government in the city, the state, and the nation.

In the 1960's the Peace Corps and the civil rights movement

have some of the same appeal to a generation of young idealists that the settlements had in the 1890's. Today's youth are perhaps less motivated by religious concern. They do not talk of "Christianizing the Social Order," though a part of the civil rights movement, at least, finds its rhetoric and its songs in a brand of Christianity not far removed from the social gospel of the earlier period. The young reformers of the 1960's have less confidence in human nature, less faith that the American people will rise up and change things if told the truth documented with statistics. But they still do believe that change is possible and that they can play a part in it. Today's reformers—whether in Africa, in Chicago, or Mississippi—go with the blessings of a large portion of public opinion and frequently with a government paycheck in their pockets. The settlement pioneers got neither pay nor support in their crusades, at least not in the beginning.

Despite differences between the two generations of reformers, they have much in common in spirit and tactics. The settlement worker who went to live in a working-class neighborhood in the 1890's, the peace corpsman who settled in an African village, the SNCC member who moved into a Mississippi hamlet, the Southern Christian Leadership Conference worker who lived in a slum tenement in Chicago in the 1960's all began their reform efforts from the inside: they went to the people, to the neighborhood, and started there. The settlement worker—and the best of the young reformers in the 1960's—tried, sometimes with limited success, to be more than missionaries from the outside, to become part of the community they sought to change.

The conditions of the slums and of the poor, it has been argued, are in some respects worse now than in the 1890's; Michael Harrington has suggested that today's poor are without hope.[11] They do not participate in the "culture of aspiration" that made the pre-World War I slums bearable, at least to the ambitious who were on their way out. It was this group, "the transfigured few" as Jane Addams called them, with which the early settlements were most successful. Yet Harrington exaggerates, for the slums of the 1890's and the 1960's have much in common: poor housing, poor sanitation, inadequate education, unemployment, ignorance, prejudice, and limited opportunity and initiative. And many of the urban poor of the 1890's were at least as hopeless and pathetic as those trapped in the slums today.

The settlement movement was in the vanguard of reform in the progressive era, but settlement workers today have not, as a rule, been leaders in the fight on poverty and the drive for civil rights. True, they have co-operated with many reform programs, but the leadership in the 'sixties has come from elsewhere, and the settlements, when compared with the new movements, seem thoroughly accredited and professional. In part this is the penalty for being established and successful, but it is also the product of trends within the broad field of social work which, in the decades after World War I, put more emphasis on professional standing and individual adjustment and less on social action. Many settlements became institutions to serve the neighborhood rather than levers for social change.[12] With a shifting population, and the increased role of the federal government, the settlement's task became more difficult, and its purpose, blurred. Of course there were always a few who kept the faith and saw reform as the settlement's major task, and beginning in the late 1950's there seemed to be a renewed commitment to social action within the movement and a rededication to meet the massive challenge of the "exploding metropolis."

At that time, settlements in various cities set up recreation and community centers within public housing developments to try to stimulate neighborhood organization in the cold and dreary apartment houses. Others helped to rehabilitate older neighborhoods and to find new homes for those displaced by urban renewal; they developed special projects to deal with the problems of the aged poor, the mentally ill, and the juvenile delinquent. A few settlement workers remained experts in the art of influencing elected officials and in mounting campaigns for legislative action. Settlement workers in the 1960's were not often leaders and initiators, but they did co-operate with the new movement for social reform.[13] Helen Hall, whose career began in the progressive period and continued into the 1960's, summed up some of this continuing concern with social action when she announced: "The main point is that you see what's wrong in your neighborhood and find a way to do something about it, whether that means you start in Washington or City Hall or at the State Capital." [14] In just that way a large group of settlement workers made important contributions to the movements for social reform and social justice during the progressive era and after.

A. F. D.

Columbia, Missouri
March 15, 1967

Acknowledgments

This study has developed over a period of time longer than I sometimes care to recall, and in the process I have incurred more debts than I can ever discharge. Research and writing are essentially lonely occupations made bearable by the intellectual companionship of other scholars along the way. My first obligation is to Merle Curti in whose seminar the idea for this project was first formulated. He has been a sympathetic critic and a warm friend. A number of other historians have aided me at one time or another; Arthur Mann, Lawrence Cremin, Robert Bremner and Mark Haller read portions of early drafts and offered valuable comments. A great many others too numerous to mention, including students and friends, have made suggestions and criticisms even though they perhaps did not realize it. My colleague Richard Kirkendall read the entire manuscript at one point, an act beyond the call of friendship. I owe a special debt to Louise and Richard Wade, who recognized the importance of my settlement workers when some others did not. The American Philosophical Society supported my research during one summer, and the Research Council of the University of Missouri granted me a summer fellowship and funds to pay for typing the manuscript.

Like all historians I have been dependent on a large number of librarians and curators of manuscripts. I encountered a few who seemed to prefer that their material remain on the shelves, but most went out of their way to aid me in my search. Most helpful were the people at the Wisconsin State Historical Society, the Chicago Historical Society, the Newberry Library, the New York Public Library, the Library of Congress, the Radcliffe Women's Archives (recently renamed the Arthur and Elizabeth Schlesinger Library), the Peace Collection at Swarthmore College, the Sophia Smith Collection at Smith College, the libraries at Harvard University, and the library of the University of Missouri. Several settlement workers helped me locate indispensable records and manuscripts; especially I want to thank Charles Fraggos of South End House in Boston, Margaret Berry, Executive Director of the National Federation of Settlements and Neighborhood Centers, and Helen M. Harris, Executive Director of the United Neighborhood Houses of New York. Several settlement workers have also read and criticized the last chapter and have given me insight into a still vital movement; these include Lea Taylor, Margaret Berry, Susan Brown, and Helen M. Harris. Richard Wade and Sheldon Meyer have been patient and understanding critics; both have improved the style of the book.

I cannot adequately thank my wife Roberta, who typed one draft of the manuscript and who has lived with this project in its various stages without complaining. Finally I should mention my sons, Gregory and Paul; without them this book might have been completed sooner, but more probably it would never have been written at all.

Portions of this study, in quite different form, have appeared in various periodicals. For permission to reuse this material I want to thank: the *American Historical Review,* the *Journal of The Illinois State Historical Society, Labor History, Mid-America, Review of Politics,* and *Social Service Review.*

Introduction to the
1984 Edition

Publishing a book freezes the ideas, assumptions, even the writing style of the author at a particular point in time. Those who never publish but only lecture and teach always can deny that they once held a controversial position or supported an unfashionable point of view. Those who publish are stuck with their views as written. I am pleased that *Spearheads for Reform* has held up reasonably well after seventeen years, and I am happy that a new edition is appearing on the 100th anniversary of the settlement movement. But as I reread the book I cringed at certain statements. I wanted to rewrite and revise paragraphs and bring them into line with my current thoughts and the most recent research. Fortunately the publisher will not allow me to make major changes. I say fortunately because scholars should not spend time rewriting and revising a book anymore than artists should repaint the same picture constantly. But I do welcome the opportunity to explain what I would do differently and what I would leave the same if I could do it over again.

Fashions change and contemporary movements force us to readjust our thinking and the way we express our thoughts. For example, if I were rewriting I would use "black" rather than "Negro." I also would avoid the unconscious sexist attitudes that are betrayed throughout the book. I discover that I used "Miss" or "Mrs." when referring to women, but very rarely "Mr." when referring to a man. I use "he" and "him" when now I simply would use the plural. I would resist writing about the settlement "ladies," and the spirit of "fraternity."

I concentrated on the settlements in Boston, Chicago, and New York, but I now know that I certainly could have added Philadelphia, where settlements also played important roles in a variety of reform movements. There are probably many other cities where the settlement movement fit the pattern that I described. But I tried to point out that many of the larger and more famous settlements were exceptions. By adding a number of smaller cities, and by including many of the lesser known settlements, community centers and missions, the movement can be made to appear narrow, bigoted and paternalistic, as a number of scholars have pointed out.

Spearheads for Reform was researched and written as a dissertation in the late 1950's and then expanded and rewritten in its current form in the early 1960's. It was influenced by the optimistic spirit of the New Frontier and the Great Society. These political movements had nothing to do with my selection of the settlement movement to write about, but the Peace Corps, Vista and SNCC seemed to represent some of the same commitment to change that led an earlier generation of reformers to live for a time in settlement houses. In the early 1960's, before the bitterness and divisiveness of the war in Vietnam destroyed most of the idealism, it seemed possible that a new generation of urban reformers was going to solve some of the problems of the city wilderness. The spirit of the times in which I wrote influenced the tone of the book. By the time I published my biography of Jane Addams in 1973, my outlook was much less optimistic about the possibilities of urban reform in America.

More important than political movements, however, in influencing my interpretation of the settlement movement was the progressive historiographical tradition. This school of history took reformers seriously and thought their causes, with some exceptions, worthwhile. My book was written more particularly in opposition to the consensus school, which denied conflict in American history and de-emphasized the importance of reform movements. It was written especially in opposition to the work of Richard Hofstadter, George Mowry and others who found a "status revolution," or some internal psychological need, rather than conditions in society, as the best explanation for the motivation of the progressive reformers. In my book I tried to take the settlement workers seriously and on their own terms. I recognized the complex nature of their motivation, as Jane Addams and others did as well. I was critical of many of their ideas and some of their activities. I pointed out their limitations, their tendency toward paternalism, their inability to get beyond racial stereotypes, and their exaggerated faith in statistics. Still I was sympathetic to their cause, and that sympathy came through in my interpretation.

The same year that *Spearheads for Reform* appeared, Robert Wiebe published his influential *The Search for Order* (1967). While I emphasized the social justice crusade as well as the moralism and the religious commitment of a group of reformers, Wiebe saw professional men searching for efficiency as well as new forms of community and bureaucracy. The next year James Weinstein, in *The Corporate Ideal in the Liberal State* (1968), called progressivism "corporate liberalism" and argued that the progressive period marked a new phase of business-government cooperation. Together with Gabriel Kolko's earlier book, *The Triumph of Conservatism* (1963), Weinstein provided the basis for a "New Left" interpretation of progressivism that depicted reform legislation as originated by business leaders for their own advantage. In the light of the search for order, efficiency, and the corporate liberalism interpretations I might alter my story to some extent. I certainly would emphasize more than I did that the social settlements were training grounds for professionals and experts of all kinds. Sometimes they cooperated with business leaders, and often in their municipal reform efforts their reforms were taken over and subverted by the business community. Sometimes the settlements' industrial education projects trained young men and women who then were employed as strikebreakers, and occasionally the legislation they pushed turned out to profit the businesses they had hoped to regulate. This was true of the meat packing and pure food and drug bills. But unlike Kolko I would not argue that this legislation was originated by businessmen to strengthen capitalism and improve profits. Like most progressive-era legislation it was supported by a variety of groups for many purposes.

The settlement workers thought that they could promote justice and efficiency at the same time. But to emphasize only efficiency and order is to overlook the commitment of the reformers to justice. It is to ignore the moralism and the religious zeal with which they sought to create a better world. Order and efficiency and the promotion of capitalism do not explain the campaigns against child labor and prostitution, nor those for better housing and womens' rights. They also do not explain the rhetoric of the progressives that stressed truth, justice, democracy, and the faith that it was possible to build a better world.

Closely related to the "New Left" critique of liberal reform was the social control thesis. In many ways the key book here was Frances F. Piven and Richard A. Cloward's *Regulating the Poor: The Functions of Public Welfare* (1971), written by a political scientist and a sociologist—social worker. They did not deal with the settlement movement explicitly but charged that all welfare movements have no humanitarian or philanthropic motivation. Reform movements are designed, according to Piven and Cloward, by elite groups seeking to control and manipulate the poor in order to benefit the upper class and promote economic and social stability. Two years earlier Anthony M. Platt, in *The Child Savers: The Invention of Delinquency* (1969), charged that the upper-class women who sought to help children and prevent delinquency simply were using children to promote their own careers. He left no room for humanitarian concerns, but argued that the juvenile reformers, many of them settlement workers, sought only to control lower class children and to make them behave in a manner less threatening to the upper class. These books set the tone for much of the historical writing on reform in the 1970's. Social control rather than social reform seemed to be the dominant interpretation.

More recently Paul Boyer, in *Urban Masses and Moral Order in America, 1820–1920* (1978), has developed a more subtle and important argument. He suggests that a moral or social control tradition dominated reform for a century. It was fear of the immigrants, distrust of the city, and the threat of class violence that united reformers in their efforts to improve urban life, he argues. But during the progressive period he sees the movement dividing into what he calls negative and positive environmentalism. The first resulted in battles against the brothel and the saloon, while the second, led by settlement workers and their allies, included campaigns for parks, playgrounds, and better housing.

In light of all the writing and controversy over social reform versus social control I now would modify some parts of *Spearheads* and emphasize more than I did the upper-class paternalism and the social control aspects of many of the settlement crusades. I would point out, for example, how the settlement workers had little sympathy or understanding for the families who were in desperate need of the wages their working children brought home. In trying to pass laws to prohibit child labor the settlement workers looked at the big picture and failed to see the pathos in individual situations. I also would stress more than I did the way that the reformers tried to promote their own middle class values and failed to understand the ethnic customs and culture of their neighbors. The settlement workers, for example, often tried to encourage Italians, East European Jews, and other recent immigrants to live in uncluttered rooms, and to separate the functions of living into clearly defined spaces. But many of the recent immigrants were much more comfortable mixing sleeping, eating, and working in the same space, and they did not mind clutter. To live neat and ordered lives in overcrowded tenements often was impossible in any case. I also would indicate more clearly that the settlement workers failed to comprehend the importance of alcohol in the social life of many immigrant groups, though they did realize that the saloon was a social center. And I would stress, in describing the campaigns against prostitution, that the settlement workers utterly failed to comprehend that some women became prostitutes willingly and that the attempts to wipe out prostitution were inspired, at least in part, by upper-class fear of lower-class sexuality.

The settlement workers tried to promote both social justice and

social control, and they saw no contradiction between the two. They
thought it necessary to intervene in the lives of the poor, or to pass
laws to allow the government to intervene, because they believed
that this was the only way that the poor could be helped. They were
convinced that they knew what kind of help the poor needed. They
wanted to transform the state into a parent, in David Rothman's
phrase. And they were much more concerned with the needs of the
urban poor than they were in the rights of the disadvantaged. The
settlement workers at their best tried to understand the problems
they observed in their urban neighborhoods, and they tried to comprehend the alien ways of those around them. But they were bound
by their own culture and their own time. Their solutions were not
perfect, nor their motives always pure. There was a great deal of
irony and ambiguity in the settlement workers' reform efforts. Still,
in interpreting the settlement movement today I would come down
more on the side of social reform than social control.

Another historiographical movement of the 1970's that sometimes
is connected with the "New Left" and social control positions (but
that extends beyond them) is the new social history and the attempt
to write the history of ordinary Americans. *Spearheads for Reform*
focuses on the reformers and uses sources largely generated by
them. Even though I tried to discuss immigrant and neighborhood
reactions to the settlements, I could get only a glimpse now and
then of the other side. It is obvious that the settlements only appealed to a small minority of the immigrant community. A Catholic
church a few blocks from Hull House and a Jewish club down the
street from Henry Street Settlement probably had a greater impact
on the neighborhood, and on a majority of the immigrants, than did
the settlements. But the settlements and their residents had a
greater impact on the nation. Yet, if I were doing it over again, I
would make a greater effort to understand the point of view of the
Italians, Greeks, and East European Jews who visited the settlements, and those who stayed away. The sources for this kind of study
are not easily available, and it would make a different kind of book
than the one I wrote. Yet it is a book that badly needs to be written.
The history of social welfare and reform have been written from the

top down for too long. We need to have the story from the point of view of the client, the inmate, the tenement dweller, and the factory worker.

Nothing has changed the writing of history more in the last decade and a half than the emergence of women's history. Looking at the past through the eyes of women has forced American historians to reexamine their categories and their assumptions. Using the new women's history and the insights I gained from writing about Jane Addams, there are a number of things I would alter and expand in *Spearheads for Reform*. I set out to write a book on the impact of the settlements on a variety of reform movements. I was not much concerned with settlements as institutions. But now I certainly would discuss in some detail the important role that settlements played as centers of cooperative living. Hull House, for example, in 1910 had thirty-one women residents and twenty men. They lived in a variety of apartments and rooms throughout the settlement complex. Some were married but most were single, and they all shared a common dining room. Especially for the unmarried women the settlement provided an acceptable alternative to living alone or with family. The maid service and the public kitchen freed the professional women from the task of keeping house. But more than that, the living arrangement often provided stimulating companionship and close personal relationships. The female support networks and the possibilities of social housekeeping also led to cooperative reform efforts that might not have happened otherwise. At Hull House, for example, Jane Addams and the other residents established a cooperative apartment house for working women. Many of the settlement-led reform movements, from wage and hour legislation for women to parks, playgrounds, and better housing, were influenced by the living arrangements at the settlements and the long discussions and planning sessions around the dining room table.

The settlements also became training grounds for new administration careers in government, industry, and the universities. I make this point in *Spearheads for Reform*, but now I would emphasize how important this function was, especially for women settlement workers. Jane Addams, Lillian Wald, Mary Simkhovitch, and a few others made careers in the settlement houses, but many more moved

on to other positions. Many careers for women were literally in-
vented in the settlements. Again Hull House is the best, but not
the only, example. Florence Kelley left Hull House to become head
of the National Consumers' League. Julia Lathrop, who honed her
administrative skills as a settlement resident, became the first
head of the Children's Bureau. Grace Abbott was the director of
the Immigrants' Protective League before replacing Lathrop at the
Children's Bureau. Alice Hamilton became the first woman professor
at Harvard Medical School and a leading expert on industrial medicine. Sophonisba Breckinridge and Edith Abbott became leaders in
the new field of social work at the University of Chicago. Frances
Perkins, Crystal Eastman, Frances Kellor, Charlotte Perkins Gilman,
and a great many other women were influenced strongly by their
settlement experience. For the first generation of college women the
settlements not only provided a convenient and stimulating place to
live, but they also laid the ground work for new professional careers.

If I were to revise and rewrite I would change the tone of the
book in several spots and occasionally expand a subject or alter the
emphasis. But I would not change the major thrust of the study.
Despite their limitations, the young men and women who went to
live in the social settlements during the progressive era are still
worth studying today. If anything, their example is even more relevant in 1984 than it was in 1967.

SPEARHEADS FOR REFORM

1

The Settlement Idea

On Christmas eve 1884, two Oxford University students slept in a half-completed building in the slums of East London. They did not come for a brief visit to an exciting underworld, nor did they intend to dole out charity to the needy. They expected to become residents of the neighborhood, and to learn as well as to teach. They were the first settlement workers, and the half-completed Toynbee Hall, the first settlement.[1]

The founding of Toynbee Hall was a beginning; it was also the culmination of a diverse reform movement, closely allied with Romanticism, that sought to preserve humanistic and spiritual values in a world dominated by materialism and urban industrialism. The tangled web of influence that eventually led to the development of the settlement idea begins with Frederick Denison Maurice and Charles Kingsley, two dedicated and idealistic Christian Socialists. Influenced by Hegel, and more directly by Carlyle, they believed in the organic unity of life, abhorring the class differences they saw all around them. Both were clergymen as well as professors, who set as their goals the replacement of competition by co-operation, and the establishment of the Kingdom of God on earth. They were joined, especially after 1848, by a group of energetic young men who

3

worked to improve sanitation and housing while testing their ideas on the local level. Kingsley himself promoted Christian socialism in his essays, articles, and novels; Maurice, on the other hand, who was determined to wipe out class distinctions through education, opened the Working Men's College in London in 1854.[2]

A number of men offered to help Maurice in this experimental attempt to bring culture to the laboring man. The most important of these was the writer, art critic, and social reformer, John Ruskin, who influenced the ideas of the early settlement workers in both England and America. Ruskin, a professor of fine arts at Oxford, taught drawing and art history at the Working Men's College. More important, however, his lectures and his strange and compelling books had a great impact on a generation of young men and women searching for a means of rebelling against the drab and overpowering industrial city. Ruskin believed that all aspects of society—art, religion, morality—were interrelated, and that a corrupt society could not produce great art. He desired beauty in all things and felt that not only beauty, but meaning, had been driven from the city.

Ruskin hated industrial cities; indeed, he often seemed to want to destroy them and return to a more pastoral age. Some of this anti-urbanism was transmitted to his followers. He also hated industrialism and the division of labor. The trouble, he declared at one point, "is not that men are ill fed, but that they have no pleasure in the work by which they make their bread." The industrial process, as he observed it, made some men less than men and separated them from culture and beauty, and from the few who had power and influence and controlled the culture. Ruskin, as a teacher in the Working Men's College, led groups of students in manual labor projects. He went further and suggested that a group of college men live in the slums; he argued for a return to a pre-industrial society, and even tried to revive handicrafts. Yet in his book on reform, *Unto This Last,* he suggests: a program of government vocational schools to set national standards of workmanship, a social security system, public works projects, minimum wage laws, public ownership of transportation, old age benefits, improved housing, and other programs to make the city bearable. His reforms turned out to be less influential than his identification of the problems. Most of all, Ruskin's moral indignation at the squalor and abuses of the industrial city inspired others to find solutions.[3]

One of the many who learned from Ruskin was the poet and artist William Morris, a blond, ruddy-faced giant of a man. He, too, combined art with social criticism but he was more outspoken than Ruskin. "The cause of art is the cause of the people," he announced. "Nothing should be made by man's labour which is not worth making, or which must be made by labour degrading to the makers." Like Ruskin, Morris dreamed of a pre-industrial age of handicrafts and pastoral villages; although in looking back, he challenged the system that had produced ugly, gray cities devoid of art. His poems, books, and lectures inspired a generation on both sides of the Atlantic to act.[4]

Octavia Hill, a gentle young woman with considerable artistic talent, was another moved by John Ruskin. Encouraged by him, she experimented with model tenements in order to improve the housing of the urban poor; she also bought vacant lots and made them into parks. She planted trees and flowers and tried to bring meaning and beauty back to the city, but she was best known and most influential as a housing reformer.[5]

In addition, Ruskin profoundly influenced a sensitive, frail young man named Edward Denison. While waiting for his father to arrange a seat in the House of Commons for him, Denison volunteered to work for the London Society for the Relief of Distress. He became discouraged by the methods of relief, however, and by what he saw in the slums of East London. In 1867 he took a room in a depressed neighborhood and set out to help the workingmen in the area, but his health gave out and in 1870 he died.

Arnold Toynbee also came under the same strange spell of John Ruskin. Though studying industrial history, he was more deeply concerned with the lot of the ordinary workingman, and he became convinced that a way must be found to share the benefits of culture and education with those who worked with their hands. Toynbee helped Ruskin in the manual labor projects and even joined a labor union. Still not satisfied, he followed Denison's example and moved to the slums, where in an atmosphere of "bad whisky, bad tobacco, bad drainage," he sought to teach workingmen and to learn from them. But, like Denison, he was not strong. He died in 1883 at the age of thirty-two.[6]

One of Toynbee's closest friends was Samuel A. Barnett, a somber and intense, but immensely able, Anglican clergyman married to Henrietta Rowland, one of Octavia Hill's co-workers. Barnett in 1873 became the vicar of St. Jude's, "the worst parish in London," and it was here that Toynbee lived during his sporadic attempts to settle in the slums. Through Toynbee, Barnett and his wife met the group of young men from Oxford and Cambridge who were searching for something meaningful and useful. These young men thus came under the influence of Ruskin and the examples of Denison and Toynbee. They were appalled, as was much of London in 1883, by a pamphlet written by the Reverend Andrew Mearns, *The Bitter Cry of Outcast London*, which described the many horrors of life in the East London slums. Some of them were active in the growing university extension movement, and were ripe to be enlisted for reform.[7]

It was Samuel Barnett who recognized the needs of the restless college students, and also the needs of the workingmen in his parish, and acted to bring the two together. In 1883 he read two papers to the students, "Our Great Towns and Social Reform" and "Settlements of University Men in Great Towns." In these he spelled out the ideas which became the foundation of the first university settlement. At Mrs. Barnett's suggestion, it was named Toynbee Hall after the young man who had lived with them in the "worst parish in London." Thus in 1884 was the settlement movement born.[8]

The university settlement idea, as Barnett explained it, and as he put it into operation at Toynbee Hall, was deceptively simple; to bridge the gulf that industrialism had created between rich and poor, to reduce the mutual suspicion and ignorance of one class for the other, and to do something more than give charity, university men would live in a poor neighborhood of a great city. They would make their settlement in the slums an outpost of education and culture. Like Ruskin and Morris, Barnett believed that social reform had to begin with the individual, but more than many reformers of his day, he willingly admitted "the power of circumstances over character." Yet it was spiritual poverty that concerned him more than economic want. "The poor," he wrote, "need more than food; they need also the knowledge, the character, the happiness which are the gifts of God to this Age." [9] The settlement movement was part of the larger Romantic revolt against the vulgarization of society, and its ultimate goal was the spiritual reawakening of the whole man—and not just the laborer, but the university man also. Barnett hoped that the settlement resident would obtain an "education by permeation." He also hoped that the settlement would become a rallying point for the neighborhood and that laborers and intellectuals would co-operate in promoting social reform. Though they did not enter politics directly, the settlement workers did try to make politicians aware of the people's needs. They got a library for their district. They promoted parks, playgrounds, and cleaner streets; and several of the residents served on the school board.

Barnett called his program of government responsibility, "Practicable Socialism," but the emphasis at Toynbee Hall was on education, for he believed that the greatest need was to bring some of the advantages of college to the workingmen. He sought to restore communication between classes and to revive the humanistic and aesthetic aspects of life. The settlement promoted picture exhibitions, university extension classes, and special lectures. "Toynbee Hall is essentially a transplant of university life in Whitechapel," an American visitor observed. "The quadrangle, the gables, the diamond-paned windows, the large general rooms, especially the dining room with its brilliant frieze of college shields, all make the place seem not so distant from the dreamy walks by the Isis or the Cam." Indeed it was the college atmosphere of the settlement as well as the feeling of doing something useful that made it so attractive to the university graduate.[10]

Toynbee Hall had many critics. Octavia Hill, who had played a small part in inspiring the venture, thought that the strain of living permanently in a squalid section of the city would be too depressing and discouraging to most educated men. It would be better, she argued, to spend only a few hours a week in the slums. Others laughed at trying to reform with "picture parties and pianos," and scoffed at the idea of undergraduates regenerating workingmen. But the settlement idea spread. A few weeks after Toynbee Hall opened its doors, another group at Oxford, who objected to the nonsectarian nature of Barnett's enterprise, established Oxford House, a settlement that was connected to a parish and was openly a project of the Anglican Church. Women's University Settlement, Mansfield House, and many others followed until in 1911 there were forty-six settlements in Great Britain.[11]

II

The settlement idea and the example of Toynbee Hall inspired many Americans. Suddenly confronted by the overwhelming problems of urbanism and industrialism, a number of young men and women looked to England and the social awakening there for a solution. Robert A. Woods, a tall, serious, young graduate of Amherst and Andover Theological Seminary, may have been right when he suggested that Americans were more impressed and more disturbed by a drive through East London than by a tour of an American slum because in London they saw not Italian or Polish or Irish poor, but familiar English faces. Unconsciously, they saw themselves in tatters.[12]

Stanton Coit, a moody and idealistic graduate of Amherst with a Ph.D. from the University of Berlin, who had spent three months at Toynbee Hall in 1886, was the first American to borrow the settlement idea. Though critical of its haphazard methods, lack of democracy, and small emphasis on social reform, he returned to America excited about the possibilities of neighborhood organization. Coit, who was strongly influenced by Felix Adler and the Society of Ethical Culture, decided that the first step toward social reform in the city should be "the conscious organization of the intellectual and moral life of the people." He believed that the key to this was a system of neighborhood guilds. Each would contain about one hundred families and would depend largely on the natural leadership in the neighborhood to promote "all the reforms, domestic, provident or recreative which the social ideal demands." Coit had great hopes for his experiment: he expected that guilds would multiply, and that within ten years they would provide the foundation for a civic renaissance in America.[13] He moved to the Lower East Side of New York in August 1886, and invited a workingmen's club to meet in his apartment. A short time later he acquired a small building and gathered a strange group of reformers, ministers, and labor leaders. Among the first to join him were Charles B. Stover and Edward King.[14]

Stover, "learned eccentric, full of passionate zeal for human rights," was a graduate of Union Theological Seminary. He had been a mission worker in the Bowery before going to the University of Berlin to study theology. On his return to New York in 1885 he became a director of a model tenement house erected by the Ethical Culture Society and patterned after those begun by Octavia Hill. He organized clubs and classes in the tenement, becoming something of a settlement worker without a settlement. Only a few weeks after Coit organized Neighborhood Guild, Stover joined forces with him at the first settlement in America.[15]

Edward King, a self-styled intellectual, was an Englishman by birth, but the influence of the writings of Auguste Comte led him to New York, where he sought to promote a society based on reason and natural law. King settled on the Lower East Side about 1880; taught classes in Greek and Roman history to the working people; encouraged their labor organizations; and argued about philosophy and socialism with Stover or anyone else who would disagree with him. To King the settlement seemed to represent the same goals that he had been fighting alone to accomplish and he, too, became a settlement worker at Neighborhood Guild.[16]

Others quickly joined the group on the Lower East Side. Morrison Swift, utopian socialist and later a leader of one contingent of Coxey's Army, stayed for a short time. Elmer S. Forbes, an idealistic young minister, remained for a few months before moving to

Boston to take over a Unitarian Church. Gregory Weinstein, a Russian Jew who had come to the United States at seventeen and tried farming and printing before he met Stover and King, decided to become a resident at Neighborhood Guild. He remembered that educated Russians sometimes went to live in the villages to bring the peasants culture and education, and he saw nothing strange about the settlement idea. Few Americans, however, were influenced by this Russian movement; for most, the English example and their American experiences were more important.[17]

The idealistic and varied group at Neighborhood Guild immediately became an influence on the Lower East Side, but unfortunately Coit moved to England in 1887, and his grandiose plans for a civic renaissance collapsed. Edward King later blamed the failure on Coit's "excessive, almost poetic, overconfidence in the possibilities of self-help and generosity among the overworked, underpaid and underfed working peoples. . . ." In 1891 King, Stover, and a few others reorganized Neighborhood Guild and renamed it University Settlement.[18] A few years later John Lovejoy Elliot, another follower of Felix Adler, tried to apply some of Coit's ideas in modified form in New York at a settlement he called Hudson Guild. Coit's visionary scheme of neighborhood regeneration had only indirect influence on the movement, but in the next decade many young men and women followed his example and went to live in a poor area of a great city.

The settlement movement in America did not collapse with the failure of Neighborhood Guild. From the beginning it was more than a one-man crusade, for it appeared almost simultaneously in several cities. In the fall of 1887, just a year after Coit's move to the Lower East Side, a small group of Smith College graduates gathered at Northampton, Massachusetts, for a reunion. Among them was Vida Scudder, a sensitive and impassioned young English instructor at Wellesley, who had returned two years before from Oxford, where John Ruskin and others had "awakened her to the realities of modern civilization," and kindled "the flame of social passion." For two years she had been brooding and reading, but like many of her contemporaries, she longed to do something concrete to solve social problems. She was joined by Jean Fine and Helen Rand, who also had seen the settlement idea in operation in England. These young women knew nothing of Neighborhood Guild and had not heard of Ellen Gates Starr and Jane Addams, but suddenly they decided to found a settlement. To Vida Scudder and the other women graduates the idea seemed to be a way to solve the overwhelming problems created by the industrial city. It also seemed a means "to rouse the coming generation to know and feel that justice could only be won at cost of a tremendous crusade of social upheaval. . . .[19] Katherine Coman, Katherine Lee Bates, Cornelia Warren, Jane Robbins, Helena Dudley, and many others excitedly joined the original group; together they organized the College Settlements Association. Smith, Wellesley, Vassar, Bryn Mawr, and Harvard Annex (Radcliffe) began chapters, but it was two years before the women could establish their first settlement in New York.

Seven young women hired a bleak tenement building not far from Neighborhood Guild in the fall of 1889, calling it College Settlement. Their first visitor was a policeman, who could not imagine what the well-dressed young women were doing in the slums if not opening another house of prostitution. He stopped by to let them know that he would leave them alone if they made a regular monthly contribution to his income. The college girls may have been shocked, but they decided to stay. "Seven Lilies have been dropped in the mud," a New York newspaper dryly reported, "and the mud does not seem particularly pleased." [20] Many college women were intrigued and fascinated with the idea of living in the slums, for more than eighty applied for residence at College Settlement during the first year. But not all women who became settlement workers in the 1890's had college degrees. Leonora O'Reilly was a frail little Irish girl who had been forced to go to work in a textile mill when she was only eleven years old. By the time she was twenty-six, however, she had joined the Knights of Labor and helped to organize a group of working women into a club that met regularly to discuss working conditions and social problems. Through this group she met Edward King, who advised her on

many things ranging from shorthand to Positivism, and he talked
her into bringing her club to Neighborhood Guild.[21]

Lillian Wald, a slender, dark-haired young girl of German-Jew-
ish background, was also influenced by Edward King, but her decision to become a settlement worker was her own. Together with
Mary Brewster, also a graduate of a training school for nurses, she
set out in 1893 to find an apartment on the Lower East Side to use
as a base from which to treat the sick and infirm in the area. They
had never heard of a settlement, but they soon learned that Stover
and King knew more about the area than anyone else. When they
happened upon College Settlement they found it a convenient
place to stay while looking for the house that was to become Henry
Street Settlement.[22]

Lillian Wald had not heard of Jane Addams in 1893; they later
became close friends and allies in the movement to humanize the
industrial city. Four years before Lillian Wald began Henry Street
Settlement and only a week after the founding of College Settlement, Jane Addams and her Rockford College classmate, Ellen
Gates Starr, moved into an old mansion on South Halsted Street,
near the corner of Polk Street in Chicago, and began what was to
become the most famous social settlement in America. Jane Addams had visited Toynbee Hall in 1888, but she had decided even
before that to do something concrete to promote social justice in
America. The founders of Hull House believed that they were establishing an instrument for social, educational, humanitarian, and
civic reform. They wanted "to make social intercourse express the
growing sense of the economic unity of society and to add to the
social functions of democracy," but in the beginning they were not
quite sure how to proceed.[23]

Indeed, none of the settlement pioneers knew exactly how to
begin. Nevertheless, the idea spread. In 1891 there were six settlements in the United States; in 1897 there were seventy-four. By
1900 the number jumped to over one hundred settlements, to over
two hundred, five years later, and by 1910 there were more than
four hundred.[24] The settlement idea was especially appealing to a
number of Protestant clergymen, who had been influenced by the

social gospel movement, or by what William Jewett Tucker called "a stirring progressive movement in religion and social ethics." [25]

Tucker, a Congregational minister and follower of Horace Bushnell, was himself a leader in the social gospel movement. In his courses at Andover Theological Seminary he emphasized "the new and enlarged functions of the church in modern society," and taught one of the first sociology courses ever offered at a theological school. He looked to England in order to find material for his unorthodox courses and encouraged his students to go abroad to study new forms of church work. In 1890 he sent Robert Woods to England to have a look at the English settlement movement. Woods collected enough material for a book, *English Social Movements,* and returned to become the new head resident of Andover House, which Tucker founded in 1891 in Boston.[26]

Graham Taylor was one of the first to introduce sociology or social ethics into the curriculum of a theological school, and, like Tucker, he also moved on to found a social settlement. It was not surprising that Graham Taylor should have chosen the ministry as a career; four generations of Taylors before him had been ministers in the Dutch Reformed Church, but after he was ordained in 1873, he did not merely follow in the steps of his ancestors. Even while serving as pastor of a little church in Hopewell, near Poughkeepsie, New York, Taylor emphasized Christian responsibility to serve the community. The twelve years he spent in Hartford, Connecticut, both as minister of a Congregational church and as professor at Hartford Theological School, marked the maturation of Taylor's belief that the Church must play an active role in social reform. He learned about Toynbee Hall, and about Hull House and Andover House. Furthermore, he saw the social settlement as both an outpost for Christian social reform in the city and a training ground for young ministers and reformers. When Taylor accepted a position at the Chicago Theological Seminary in 1892, one of the conditions of his appointment was permission to found a social settlement. Two years later he opened the doors of Chicago Commons.[27]

In Pittsburgh, George Hodges, a young minister who became the rector of Calvary Episcopal Church in 1889, was troubled by the contrast of wealth and poverty he saw all around him, and concerned because most of the people he knew in Pittsburgh—layman and minister alike—accepted or ignored the constrast. He felt a great desire to do something. At first he was satisfied to add a reading room, a baby clinic, and a lecture series to the regular activities of his church, to the horror of some of his parishioners. He learned of the settlement movement in England, where he spent a summer, and discovered its counterpart in America. And in the summer of 1893, "when the weather thermometer was very high and the financial thermometer was very low," Hodges founded Kingsley House in Pittsburgh.[28] The settlement movement was "absurdly inadequate," he decided, but it was at least a step in the right direction.[29]

Everett P. Wheeler, a New York publicist, civil service reformer, and lawyer, had more confidence than Hodges in the settlement idea. He had visited Toynbee Hall and met Canon Barnett in the summer of 1889; he had also been influenced by reports of the work of Neighborhood Guild and College Settlement in New York. He was, in fact, so impressed with the idea that he persuaded the Church Club, an association of Episcopal laymen, to organize East Side House in New York in 1891.[30] The settlement soon abandoned its Episcopal connections, but under Clarence Gordon, for many years head resident, East Side House remained essentially a religious settlement. "Humanitarians, socialists, philanthropists, may do settlement work and do it well . . ." Gordon decided, "but only on the foundation of Christ . . . and His example, and grace to inspire and direct, can the settlement realize its highest possibilities."[31]

III

Many ministers and many settlement workers agreed with Clarence Gordon, and churches and religious organizations soon adapted the idea to their own uses. The Episcopal Church, with its strong parish and diocesan organization, easily adjusted to the idea of neighborhood reconstruction and was the first to make widespread use of settlement work.[32] But it was soon joined by the Congregationalists,

Presbyterians, and Methodists. The Jewish settlements—four in 1895 and twenty-four by 1910—often became important influences for reform in their neighborhood.[33] And the Catholic Church borrowed the settlement idea for use in the urban mission field. St. Rose's in New York, started in 1898, was one of the first and the most successful of this type. In 1908 Marion F. Gurney, a convert, founded a new order, the Sisters of Our Lady of Christian Doctrine, to promote settlement work, especially on the East Side, with Catholic laywomen directing most of the work. One of the best workers was Grace O'Brien, who organized several settlements for Italians in Brooklyn. A great many of the Catholic settlements were founded with the hope of reviving the religious faith of the Italian immigrants; indeed, the Catholic settlements, which in 1915 numbered 2500 by one count, were more like missions than settlement houses and contributed very little to social reform.[34]

It was often difficult to distinguish between religious settlements and missions or institutional churches, whether Protestant or Catholic. A mission did not become a settlement merely by adding clubs and classes or residents, John Gavit, editor of the *Commons*, declared in 1898. "A mission, in the ordinary sense of that word comes from *outside* to a neighborhood or community which it regards as 'degraded.' . . . The settlement bases its existence, its hope, its endeavor on the firm foundation of Democracy—on the thesis that the people must and can and will *save themselves*." Almost without exception, the settlements that became important centers of social reform attempted to avoid anything that might give the impression of proselytizing.[35] Settlement workers like Graham Taylor, Robert Woods, and Jane Addams realized that in predominantly immigrant Catholic or Jewish neighborhoods the settlement sacrificed its chance to become an instrument for reform if it had a religious label. Robert Woods decided to change the name of Andover House in 1895 to South End House "in order to release the settlement from certain restraints which the old name placed upon its natural progress." For the same reason, Eleanor McMain, the head resident of Kingsley House in New Orleans, divorced her settlement from its Episcopal connections in 1900.[36]

The nonsectarian nature of the most important American settlements was in direct contrast to the development of the movement
in England. With the exception of Toynbee Hall, Mansfield House,
and perhaps one or two others, the English settlements were little
more than modified missions.[37] The two movements diverged in
other ways. American settlement workers, unlike their English
counterparts, had to deal with the problems of the immigrants, and
that more than anything else caused the American settlement
workers to alter the English model. Some of the essentials of Barnett's ideas remained, however; the one indispensable requirement
was residence in a poor section of a great city. And Americans continued to emphasize the necessity of restoring communication
among the diverse and isolated groups in society. The settlement,
one American suggested, was "a great modern protest against the
heresy that wealth makes character, that education can establish an
aristocracy, that one can rise to a social pinnacle without obligation
to those who have contributed to that rise. . . ." "What a blessing
it would be to Fifth Avenue to have a settlement of mechanics
there," Robert Woods remarked.[38]

American settlement workers quickly revised Barnett's idea that
reform must begin with the individual; they came to view the social
environment as the starting point. They were interested in education and social research, and were especially concerned with reviving the neighborhood in the city. But more than the English they
thought their responsibility extended beyond the neighborhood.[39]

Yet most American settlement workers remained conscious of
their debt to England. They corresponded with Canon and Mrs.
Barnett, and other leaders in England, inviting them to their conferences and visiting them when they traveled abroad. Although
communication remained good, the movements diverged of necessity, and even Mrs. Barnett admitted that of the two, the American
movement was more important and a much greater force for reform.[40]

In part because of their separation from the English movement,
the American leaders felt called upon to define the nature of their
task. Self-conscious and defensive, they wrote volumes attempting

to clarify their vague purposes and goals. However, they could not agree among themselves. A committee of Chicago settlement workers met in 1898 to draft a workable definition of aims, but gave up after several hours: all that the most important settlement workers could agree on was that the settlement ought to become a "Social Center for Civic Cooperation" and a rallying point for reform in the city.[41]

The flexibility and pragmatic nature of the settlement movement left it open to the charge that it was too vague to be meaningful. The settlement seemed to some "an attempt to paint the wound of poverty with a camel's hair brush dipped in a weak solution of Ruskin, Prince Kropotkin and Florence Nightingale." To others it suggested "young ladies with weak eyes and young gentlemen with weak chins flittering confused among heterogeneous foreigners, offering cocoa and sponge cake as a sort of dessert to the factory system." Thorstein Veblen, a caustic social critic, remarked that "the solicitude of settlements . . . is in part directed to enhance the industrial efficiency of the poor and to teach them the more adequate utilization of the means at hand; but it is also no less consistently directed to the incubation, by precept and example, of certain punctilios of upper-class propriety in manners and customs." Much later Sinclair Lewis made a character in one of his novels denounce settlements as little more than "cultural comfort stations, rearing their brick Gothic among the speakeasies and hand laundries and kosher butcher shops, and upholding a standard of tight-smiling prissiness. . . ." There was an element of truth in all the charges; there were also elements of exaggeration and paradox: settlements were attacked as being too radical and not radical enough, also, too religious and not religious enough. Especially annoying to many settlement workers were the people who confused settlements with missions, or those who assumed that settlements and charity organizations were somehow connected, even synonymous. The latter carried special irony because in one sense the settlement movement began as a protest against the very methods and philosophy of organized charity.[42]

IV

The charitable impulse is as old as poverty itself, but the organization of efficient charity was largely the product of the nineteenth
century and the industrial revolution, which made the problems of
poverty more acute and more conspicuous. Even before the Civil
War, Robert Hartley had founded the Association for Improving
the Conditions of the Poor in New York, and Charles Loring Brace,
the Children's Aid Society. Although these organizations promoted
incidental reforms that helped in some ways to improve living conditions in the city, both Hartley and Brace considered the major
cause of poverty to be the laziness, lack of application, and moral
decay of the people living in the slums. Ironically, Hartley was one
of the first to maintain that better living conditions must be provided before the morality and ambition of the people in the slums
could be improved, yet both men believed that the ultimate solution for the problems of the city lay in the migration of the poor to
the farms.[43]

The Charity Organization Society Movement, which began in
England in 1869 and was quickly introduced into America, brought
business efficiency to the administration of charity and eliminated
some of the duplication of effort caused by a rapid increase in organizations designed to help the poor. The endless examinations,
reports, and investigations used to separate the worthy from the
unworthy poor served to make charity more efficient, but less
human.[44]

The differences in approach were crucial. To begin with, charity
workers emphasized the individual causes of poverty, while settlement workers stressed the social and economic conditions that
made people poor. Charity organizations sought primarily to help
paupers and the unemployed; settlement workers, on the other
hand, believed that they could work best with the working class
above the poverty line. It was not so much the "poverty of clothes,"
as the "poverty of opportunity" that concerned settlements. There
were other striking contrasts. Unlike charity societies that were

built on the assumption that the upper class had a responsibility to help the needy, the settlement movement was based, as Jane Addams expressed it, "on the theory that the dependence of classes on each other is reciprocal." Thus, the philosophy of the charity organization movement led to philanthropy, and the philosophy of the settlement movement, to reform.[45]

Robert Hunter, an itinerant political radical who lived in settlements while working for charity societies, observed in 1902 that there was a striking difference in temperament between settlement workers and those employed by charity organizations. The charity worker was hesitant about becoming involved in reform: he had a philosophy of "don't, don't" and was constantly troubled by the fear that relief would destroy the independence of the poor. By contrast, the settlement worker was more often the victim of unbounded enthusiasm rather than of moral questioning. "He is constantly doing, urging; he is constantly pressing forward, occasionally tilting at wind mills, at times, making mistakes, often, perhaps, doing injury, but filled with enthusiasm, warmth and purpose and without much question." [46] Hunter exaggerated, and his generalizations were more adequate descriptions of the younger settlement workers than of settlement leaders like Jane Addams, Graham Taylor, and Robert Woods, who certainly tempered their reform impulse with moral questioning. Yet the contrasts in temperament and philosophy were real, and despite growing co-operation between the two groups in the twentieth century, they remained.[47]

These differences often led to open antagonism. The settlement workers tried desperately to disassociate their movement from charity in the public mind. "There can hardly be anything more opposed to conventional charity than the social settlement," a member of the 1897 Conference on Charities and Correction declared. "What every conscientious settlement worker is anxious to have understood by the public," Leonora O'Reilly wrote in 1899, "is that the neighborhood work is not charity, but a recognition of a sociological fact that we are, none of us, mere atoms independent and apart from each other. . . ." [48]

Settlement workers and sympathetic friends took pleasure in

comparing methods. William Jewitt Tucker called the settlements
"the higher philanthropy" and charity organization the "lower philanthropy." Jacob Riis, a constant friend and ally of the settlement
workers, enjoyed describing the improvements wrought by the
movement: "We have substituted for the old charity coal chute,
that bred resentment . . . the passenger bridge which we call settlements, upon which men go over not down to their duty." In part,
the settlement workers' criticism of charity was caused by a self-
conscious desire to establish their own *raison d' être;* in part it was
also the sincere belief that their movement was the best way to
improve conditions in the cities.[49]

Charity workers, during the first years of the settlement movement in America, were troubled by the fact that "the people who
have supported the charity organization work are now supporting
college settlement work." They were also annoyed at the criticism
of their methods. Publicly, charity workers dismissed the settlement
movement as sentimental and unscientific and too vague to be useful. One compared the settlement worker to a man who found a
drunkard lying in the gutter and said to him, "I can't help you my
friend, but I will sit down in the gutter beside you." Charity organizers also criticized the settlement workers as being too radical and
too easily "bowled over by the first labor leader, anarchist or socialist" who came into the settlement. Mary Richmond, general secretary of the Baltimore Charity Organization Society, was disturbed
because "under the name of settlement, the old-fashioned mission,
distributing a cheap and sprinkly sort of charity, can do more harm
than under the right name." Yet she had a great deal of respect for
settlements like Hull House and South End House, and believed
that all charity workers should listen to the ideas of the important
settlement workers.[50]

Settlement workers, for their part, soon learned how difficult it
was to avoid dispensing charity from the settlement house. It was
difficult to sponsor lectures and art exhibits or to promote reform
while people were starving. Especially after the depression of 1893,
they became "overwhelmed with the poor and the needy," and
forced to give charity whether they liked it or not. In Chicago Jane

Addams and the Hull House group helped to organize the Chicago Bureau of Charities, and most settlement workers co-operated by referring needy cases to them. Settlement workers sometimes served as friendly visitors for the local charity societies, and many charity workers discovered that a settlement house was a convenient and stimulating place to live. Growing co-operation on the local level, however, did not obliterate the basic differences between the two movements, and only in the twentieth century did a substantial number of charity workers join with the settlement movement to promote reform.[51]

The relationship between charity organizations and the settlements can be traced in the *Proceedings of the National Conference of Charities and Correction.* From open hostility in the early 1890's the relationship changed in two decades to close co-operation; at the same time the philosophy of the Conference shifted from correction to prevention, from charity to social reform. Julia Lathrop of Hull House was the first settlement worker invited to speak at the National Conference in 1894; she tried, without too much success, to explain what the settlement movement was trying to do in the slums. In 1896 the Conference devoted a whole section to se-tlements, and Mary McDowell suggested that the settlement worker could give "the scientific charity worker inside knowledge and keep a fresh vital flow of life into the organization, and thus prevent fossilization. . . ." The next year Jane Addams found it necessary to apologize for being at the Conference, because "Settlements are accused of doing their charity work very badly." By 1904, however, a new department was added to the Conference called "Neighborhood Improvement," and at least twelve head residents of settlements attended. Five years later, the department of "Needy Families" was renamed "Families and Neighborhoods," and Jane Addams, who no longer had to apologize for being there, was elected president of the National Conference of Charities and Correction.[52]

There were other indications at the time that settlements and the charity organizations were working more closely together. Emily Greene Balch and Mrs. Robert Woods were members of the committee that organized the first State Conference of Charities in Massachusetts in 1903. James B. Reynolds, of University Settlement, read a paper on the "Needs and Value of Settlement Work," and J. G. Phelps Stokes led the discussion of the paper at the first New York State Conference of Charities in 1900; and, in New York the settlements and the Charity Organization Society co-operated in promoting tenement house reform. In Illinois, Jane Addams and Julia Lathrop remained active on the board of the Chicago Bureau of Charities, which they had helped to organize. In New Jersey, however, it was not until 1914 that the settlements were officially represented at the New Jersey Conference of Charities and Correction. In November 1905 the *Commons,* the magazine of Chicago Commons and in effect the magazine of the settlement movement, merged with *Charities,* the official publication of the New York Charity Organization Society. This merger symbolized the growing trend.[53]

One reason for this co-operation was a widespread exchange of personnel. Edward T. Devine, of the New York Charity Organization Society, and Frederic Almy, of the Buffalo Charity Organization Society, were frequent residents for short periods at University Settlement and Greenwich House in New York. Francis McClean spent more than five years as a settlement worker at Northwestern Settlement, University Settlement in New York, and Asacog House in Brooklyn, before becoming associated with charity organizations in Brooklyn, Montreal, and Chicago.[54] J. G. Phelps Stokes, son of a wealthy New York family and a resident of University Settlement, was able to communicate a little of his enthusiasm for the settlement idea to others on the executive board of the New York Association for Improving the Condition of the Poor, and in 1897 the AICP established Hartley House. Most of the members of the society founded by Robert Hartley gave this venture in settlement work only grudging support, but Stokes was convinced that charity organizations could profit from adding settlement work to their other activities.[55]

V

A few settlements were founded by charity societies and others developed out of boys' clubs or kindergartens, but however they began, almost all were located in the large urban centers. Many early settlement workers, influenced by Ruskin and Morris, talked at times as though they wanted to restore the rural village; but few ever suggested that the solution to urban problems lay in a migration to the country. Most settlement workers had an ambivalent attitude toward the city: they hated it, were fascinated and appalled by it, and they loved it. Occasionally they denounced the city; but they elected to live in it. Their movement was an attempt to deal with the problems of the city, not to escape them.[56]

The great majority of the social settlements in America during the progressive era were located in the large cities of the Northeast and Midwest. The South had few, and except for Eleanor Mc-Main's Kingsley House in New Orleans, and Frances Ingram's Neighborhood House in Louisville, they were of very little importance. In addition, most of them were modified missions; religious settlements (mostly Methodist) comprised nearly 70 per cent of the total. The churches and the universities in the South were relatively untouched by the reform movements that transformed their northern counterparts in the last two decades of the nineteenth century, and this severely limited the impact of the movement there.[57] There were also but a few settlements on the West Coast; San Francisco residents had to abandon reform in favor of charity and relief after the fire of 1906.[58] The movement developed most rapidly in the large cities of the Midwest and the Northeast, particularly in Chicago, Boston, and New York.[59] Philadelphia had twenty-one settlements in 1911, but only one, College Settlement with head residents Katharine B. Davis (1893–98) and Anna Davies (1898–1942), was an important influence for reform in that city.[60]

The movement developed most rapidly and exerted most influence for reform in places where several strong settlements were established close together. Thus, the "picket line of settlements" on the Lower East Side in New York, the West Side in Chicago, and the South End in Boston, were able to co-operate in many local and city-wide reform ventures. Even so, only about 10 per cent of the total number of settlements in 1911 achieved the goal of becoming centers of civic co-operation, and those usually had a strong head resident and a sizable group of men residents. Cornelia Bradford at Whittier House in Jersey City, Eleanor McMain at Kingsley House in New Orleans, and Frances Ingram at Neighborhood House in Louisville made their settlements important factors for reform through the strength of their own dominant personalities. James B. Reynolds, Robert Woods, and Graham Taylor were able to multiply their influence by using a succession of young residents to carry out their reform ideas. The ladies at Hull House and Greenwich House were effective reformers, but they often had to depend upon the men residents to do many tasks connected with the practical application of reform.

A settlement could not hope to have much influence in its neighborhood or city for the first few years of its existence, and the small settlement with just a few residents and a tiny building was handicapped in its reform efforts. James B. Reynolds, recalling the history of University Settlement, placed the beginning of the settlement's influence at 1893 when it moved from Forsyth Street to Delancy Street, where a larger building allowed more residents to live in, made it possible to invite labor unions to meet in the building, and made the settlement a meeting place for reformers as well as for children. 1893 marked an important turning point for several of the early settlements, for the devastating depression that began in that year convinced many of the pioneers that more than kindergartens and art exhibits were needed to solve the desperate problems of urban America.[61]

The first settlement workers in America had the feeling that they were devoting their lives to an individual, informal effort for reform. In fact, they feared the development of a cult, but this feeling did not last long. As settlements began to multiply and expand, settlement workers gradually came to believe that they were not just residents lost in the slums of a city, but a part of a larger reform movement. They held conferences, published reports and journals, organized city-wide federations, and in 1911 formed the National Federation of Settlements. Long before they developed the trappings of a profession, however, they were promoting reform in the neighborhood, the city, and the nation.[62]

The settlements, of course, were not alone in working for social reform in the progressive era; indeed, there was such a proliferation of reform organizations, often with interchangeable memberships, that it was impossible to identify the group involved in a particular campaign. So many organizations had their offices in the so-called Charities Building on Twenty-second Street in New York that one day when Charles Spahr of the *Outlook* poked his head in the assembly room on the first floor and saw Edward T. Devine of the Charity Organization Society, Lawrence Veiller, the tenement house reformer, Samuel McCune Lindsay and Owen Lovejoy of the National Child Labor Committee, Florence Kelley of the Consumers' League, and Paul and Arthur Kellogg of *Charities*, he exclaimed, "Ah, what's this bunch call itself today?"[63] Whatever the reformers called themselves they rarely acted without utilizing the experience of settlement workers.

Because they actually lived in a working-class neighborhood, the settlement residents saw problems from a fresh and different perspective, and they often became initiators and organizers of reform. This is not to suggest that the settlements originated all the important social reform efforts, nor does it argue that all men and women were transformed by a few months in residence. Many settlements remained modified missions or elaborate boys' clubs, but others like South End House, Hull House, and University Settlement became spearheads for reform in the progressive era.

2

The Settlement Impulse

The social settlement in a working-class neighborhood of an American city was usually easy to spot. It was often the only house with flower boxes and a brass plate on the door; and it usually had a stream of children moving in and out. It was much more difficult to define the impulse that led a generation of young, well-educated Americans to spend a year or two—or a lifetime—living in a dreary section of an industrial city.

Jane Addams attempted to explain it shortly after she and Ellen Gates Starr had founded Hull House. She divided the motivation behind the movement into "the subjective necessity" and the "objective value." Though well aware that her generation was compelled by various personal influences, she also believed that a more important motivation was the genuine need for reform. She saw a growing number of well-educated men and women troubled by their uselessness and "shut off from the common labor by which they live and which is a great source of moral and physical health." She also appreciated the overpowering destitution of those forced to live in the overcrowded, industrial sections of Chicago and other cities. "The idea underlying our self-government breaks down in such a ward," she remarked.

"The streets are inexpressibly dirty, the number of schools inadequate, factory legislation unenforced, and hundreds of houses are unconnected with the street sewer." [1]

It has become fashionable to explain the reform impulse of the progressive era as the product of a "status revolution" or the result of the "alienation" of a group of potential leaders from the mainstream of American life. Jane Addams and some of the other settlement workers were more accurate in recognizing a dual and complementary process. Certainly a number of the reformers had a compelling need to do something important and useful; but they decided quite rationally to try to solve the pressing problems of urban America.[2]

A large part of the settlement impulse was religious. In 1905 William Dwight Porter Bliss, Christian socialist and reformer, polled 339 settlement workers and discovered that 88 per cent were active church members; furthermore, nearly all admitted that religion had been a dominant influence on their lives.[3] Despite a sizable number of Jewish settlement workers, especially in New York, and an occasional Catholic, the movement was predominantly Protestant. More than half of the settlement workers were Congregationalists or Presbyterians. There were also substantial numbers of Episcopalians and Unitarians, but very few Baptists and Methodists.[4] Many probably acquired a sense of personal responsibility, a sense of mission to do something about the world's problems, from their Calvinist upbringing. More important, however, was the influence of what Jane Addams described as "a certain renaissance of Christianity, a movement toward its early humanitarian aspects"; others called it simply, the social gospel.[5]

A sizeable group of the early settlement workers had theological training; and many others were directly influenced by the diverse but important effort to create a meaningful faith for an urban, industrial society. Robert Woods, for example, came from a devout Presbyterian family. Four years at Amherst College did not disturb his basic faith, although they did serve to make him uncomfortable about orthodox Presbyterian dogma. He then went on to Andover Theological Seminary, still intending to be a parish minister. There the impact of William Jewitt Tucker and his concern with the place of the church in the industrial city turned Woods into a settlement worker and reformer.[6]

Like Woods, James Bronson Reynolds seemed destined for the ministry. Born in the little town of Kiantone, New York, the son of a Congregational minister, he was known as one of the most devoutly religious men in the class of 1885 at Yale where he earned a B.D. He then studied in Paris and Berlin, and at Columbia University in New York, before taking a job with the Y.M.C.A. Impressed in part by what he saw in Europe, in part by the stirrings toward social reform in the Congregational Church in America, and by a desire to do something that seemed worthwhile, Reynolds decided to devote his life to social reform. He could have stayed with the Y.M.C.A., but the settlement movement seemed to him a better place to begin. Therefore, in 1893 he accepted the position of head resident of University Settlement in New York.[7]

J. G. Phelps Stokes never went to a theological school, but this sensitive and idealistic son of a wealthy and socially prominent New York family planned from early youth to become a medical missionary in Africa. Four years at Yale only increased this ambition. But when his father would not hear of it, Stokes went to work in his father's office and became instead a missionary to the Lower East Side and a resident of University Settlement.

Unlike most other settlement workers, Raymond Robins had little religious training as a child. He was a fruit-grower in Florida, a coal miner, prospector, storekeeper, lawyer, a wanderer, and political campaigner before joining the gold rush to Alaska. He found little gold, but he did find a meaningful religious faith. After an almost mystical conversion in the snowy wilderness he became an ordained minister, crusaded to clean up the boom town of Nome, and in 1901 became a settlement worker at Graham Taylor's Chicago Commons.[8]

The religious impulse took many forms. In an age when denomination and dogma meant less and less, the desire to serve remained strong. Jane Addams was moved by the simple Quaker faith of her father. Vida Scudder was inspired by the example of St. Francis and the work of John Ruskin. For Ellen Gates Starr, the co-founder of Hull House, the decision to become a settlement worker was closely related to her search for a meaningful faith that carried her from the Unitarian Society to the Episcopal Church and eventually to a Roman Catholic religious order. For John Lovejoy Elliot, Charles B. Stover, Stanton Coit, plus many others of the Jewish faith, the movement was closely related to the agnosticism of Ethical Culture.[9] For most, however, the decision to live in the slums was somehow related to the desire to apply the Christian idea of service to the new challenges and the new problems of the city.

After 1900 the religious impulse became less important as a motive for entering settlement work. When Mark A. DeWolfe Howe went to Andover House in Boston in 1893, he found that most of the other residents were young theological students or ministers. If he had returned in 1903, he would have discovered young graduate students in sociology and economics and a wide variety of reformers and writers interested in studying the city and its problems.[10]

II

The broadly religious desire to serve remained important, of course, but as the social settlement movement became well established other motives became increasingly significant. In the early 1890's, Jane Addams once remarked, young men and women came to the settlement saying, "We must do something about the social disorder." After the turn of the century they were more likely to come with just as much enthusiasm and say, "We want to investigate something." [11]

Writers and would-be writers of all types were also attracted to the settlements. The progressive era was the age of the muckraking article and realistic fiction, and a settlement house offered the perfect vantage point from which to observe and study the teeming city, and collect the necessary data for an article on child labor or crowded tenements or for a novel about strikes or an immigrant family. Ernest Poole went from Princeton to University Settlement to learn how to write about the problems of urban America and discovered that nearly all the residents were working on books and articles.[12] With Henry Moskowitz as a guide, he often toured the little cafes on the Lower East Side where Russian, Pole, German, and Rumanian mingled, and where socialists, anarchists, labor leaders, free thinkers argued with actors, poets, and social workers. Over beer or black coffee, Poole listened to the talk and took part in the discussion, then went back to the settlement to work half the night jotting down "chunks of life intensely real." [13]

He described the life he saw in several novels; he also wrote well-documented reports and articles. Others before him had studied and documented what they observed in the city. In fact, the publication of such pioneer studies as *City Wilderness* and *Hull-House Maps and Papers* advertised the settlements, called attention to their importance as sociological laboratories, and attracted many students who wanted to study urban life.[14] A few settlements even offered fellowships to lure some who otherwise might not have been interested. South End House, Greenwich House, and the College Settlements Association, especially after 1900, offered free room and board as well as a small stipend to college graduates interested in studying the city and living in a settlement.[15]

Many young men and women accepted a fellowship merely to advance their own careers. One young resident at South End House in Boston recalled that he had never heard of the settlement movement until one day during his senior year at Harvard when a professor in the Department of Education offered him a fellowship. He jumped at this chance to continue his education, even though he disapproved of much that the movement stood for. Others went to live in a settlement for a few years because they could not decide on a profession, and for some the settlement house was little more than a cheap place to live. Francis

Hackett, who made twenty-three dollars a week as literary editor of the *Chicago Evening Post,* remarked, "as my room and board at Hull House only came to $7 or $8, I had good cold reasons for being glad to live there." [16]

Yet many young men and women joined the movement because the best settlements were exciting, intellectually stimulating places to live. If the English settlements reminded many of a transplanted college, the American settlement often seemed like a misplaced fraternity. "It was startling to find the atmosphere of a college dormitory in the center of the slums," a character in Arthur Bullard's *A Man's World* remarks, "The books, the fencing foils, the sofa pillows in the window seat . . . made me homesick for my college fraternity house." Books, magazines, reports, and partially completed surveys were often stacked high in the rooms, and exciting conversations continued into the night. There was usually a gathering of the residents around the dinner table at night and a discussion of the day's activities. At Hull House, Jane Addams presided and used the occasion to read the day's correspondence, often asking other residents to answer individual letters. The food was never particularly good, but often there were interesting guests. Always there was a sense of purpose. The settlements turned the Lower East Side into what Arthur Bullard called an "Ethical Bohemia" that differed greatly from Paris and Greenwich Village; the settlement Bohemia, however, was just as exciting—and more meaningful.[17]

III

Henry Demarest Lloyd once called Hull House, "the best club in Chicago." He did not mean that it was the most elaborate, for like the settlement in Isaac K. Friedman's *By Bread Alone,* Hull House had a "plainness that just escaped barrenness and just touched the artistic." It began in an old run-down mansion on South Halsted Street and gradually expanded to include a dozen buildings that sprawled over more than a city block. Most settlements started in a strategically placed, available building. The

first home of the Neighborhood Guild was a dilapidated tenement no better looking than its neighbors. The police prohibited
dances in the University Settlement because the floors of their
old building could safely support only a few people at a time.

South End House, on the other hand, occupied an elegant,
curved-front townhouse on an attractive street opposite a small
park in an area that had once been an upper-class residential
district, but which was, by 1901, on the fringe of one of the
worst slums in the city. A few settlements hired architects to
construct a special building, and early in the twentieth century
Frank Lloyd Wright designed the Abraham Lincoln Center in
Chicago. But most settlements grew haphazardly. All settlements tried to create a home-like environment for their residents
and neighbors; few succeeded. But the best often combined a
"curious mixture of hope and frivolity, of casualness and constant endeavor." [18]

The residents—not the building—made most settlements interesting places to visit or to live in. They were often a diverse
lot, most not even engaged in full-time social work but rather
employed as teachers, writers, lawyers, even probation officers.
They lived at the settlement and devoted their spare time to club
and class work, and to work for social reform.

All kinds of people came to the settlements. One resident divided those at Hull House into the "noble" and "frivolous" sets.
There were a few like the "anemic young man, all glasses, no
nose and a feminine voice," described by Friedman in *By Bread
Alone*. There were also a number of women who, in the words
of one observer, were "sexually unemployed"; but most of the
men were masculine and most of the women were feminine, and
the majority tried to avoid anything sentimental. William English
Walling of University Settlement used to advise the new settlement workers to make friends with the tenement people, and
listen, listen all the time. "They've got a lot to teach us boys, so for
the love of Jesus Christ don't let's be uplifters here." On one occasion a newspaper reporter made Walling appear to be a sentimental

do-gooder. Angered, but still amused by the account, Walling collected a double quartet of East Side boys at University Settlement, and while they hummed "Fair Harvard," Walling, to the glee of the other residents, read solemnly from the newspaper that pretended to quote him: "It shall be my aim to live my life among the lowly and to bring a little sunshine to those whose lives are full of clouds." Then the settlement workers and the boys retired to a nearby cafe, where they drank, sang, and talked well into the night.[19]

IV

The settlement residents had many things in common. First of all, as a group they were young; the median age when one group of men and women entered settlement work was twenty-five. Jane Addams was only twenty-nine when she founded Hull House, Robert Woods was twenty-seven when he went to live at Andover House, and the women who organized the College Settlements Association were all under thirty. There were exceptions, of course, but youth was a characteristic of any group of settlement workers.

This was true partly because there was always a big turnover among settlement residents. The median number of years spent in settlement work was three. Many stayed only a year or two before moving on to another job or reform. Jane Addams, Mary McDowell, Lillian Wald, Robert Woods, and Graham Taylor, all of whom spent a lifetime in settlement work, were the exceptions rather than the rule. Each year a new group of young men and women, most of them in their twenties, came to the settlements, and the movement profited from their energy and enthusiasm even though it suffered from their inexperience.[20]

Apart from their youth, the most remarkable characteristic of the settlement workers was their education. Nearly 90 per cent had attended college; more than 80 per cent had earned a bachelor's degree or the equivalent; and over 50 per cent had done graduate work of one kind or another. Moreover, as a group they had an impressive list of advanced degrees; and more had studied abroad than had taken courses in social work.[21]

Most were also unmarried. Florence Kelley came to Hull House after she obtained a divorce from her Russian husband; and Graham Taylor had married long before he became a settlement worker, but they were the exceptions. Occasionally a critic would charge the settlements with being havens for "old maids," and there were even whispers of homosexuality. But although a number of the movement's leaders never married, the settlements served as marriage bureaus for the younger residents. South End House in Boston and Hull House in Chicago tried to provide apartments for married couples, but lack of pay and poor conditions for bringing up children prevented most couples from remaining for long. Graham Taylor and his family, however, resided at Chicago Commons, and Robert and Eleanor Woods lived near the South End House in Boston. For most of the settlement workers, however, marriage meant the end of active participation in the movement, leaving the young and unmarried to carry on as the typical settlement worker.[22]

Most workers came from old-stock American families. They had English or Scotch-Irish names, and could trace their ancestry back to colonial New England. After 1900 there was a growing tendency for the sons and daughters of immigrants, many of whom had belonged to settlement clubs, to return to the slums as settlement residents. But despite the influx of newcomers, English and Scotch-Irish names continued to dominate the settlement roster until after the First World War.[23]

An overwhelming percentage of settlement workers were born in the Northeast or Midwest, and the majority were brought up in a city. Thus the typical settlement worker was not a rural yokel who had moved to the city and was shocked into becoming a reformer by the massive social evils of the metropolis. However, few had any real awareness of the problems faced by the poor in large cities. Most grew up in pleasant residential neighborhoods in an urban environment far removed from the slum areas.[24]

Vida Scudder spent her childhood only a few blocks from the slums, in Boston's fashionable Back Bay district, not knowing that the "other half" existed until she was in college. J. G. Phelps Stokes grew up in New York City, but Madison Avenue was a long way from Rivington Street, and he knew nothing of the Lower East Side until he returned from Yale. Mary Kingsbury Simkhovitch, who lived in suburban Boston, suddenly discovered at the age of fourteen, while helping her Sunday school class deliver Thanksgiving turkeys, that some people in her city actually lacked food and clothing. Even Jane Addams, brought up in rural Illinois, recalled that before she was seven years old she had been shocked by the poverty and the squalor of the poor section of a neighboring city of 10,000, but this early experience had little connection with her later decision to establish Hull House. Probably most settlement workers had little idea while they were young of the extent or intensity of the social problems existing among a substantial proportion of urban dwellers.[25]

Most settlement workers came from families that were moderately well-to-do. The fact that they were able to enter settlement work at all, especially during the early years, was often an indication that they did not have to earn a living. There were some, however, like Raymond Fosdick, who endured many hardships in order to live at Henry Street Settlement. He made five dollars a week at a law office during the day, and had to pay it all for board at the settlement. He found it difficult to get back to Henry Street for lunch, so he haunted the saloons, paid a nickel for beer, and helped himself to cheese and sandwiches. Once he was forced to pawn his books and many of his clothes, and several times during the winter he made the long walk from Henry Street to Lenox Hill Settlement on Seventy-second Street to borrow money from his sister, who was a resident there.[26]

The settlements, like most of the other social and economic reform organizations in the progressive era, were filled with the sons and daughters of ministers. Many had fathers who were teachers in high school or college. A few were doctors, lawyers, or small businessmen. Whatever their occupation, many of the parents were actively involved in reform or concerned with aiding the poor. Ernest Poole's mother occasionally took him on her trips to the slums of Chicago, where she worked for various welfare agencies. Fosdick's father was a high school principal and teacher in a little town near Buffalo, New York. Raymond grew up in the same family environment that influenced his brother, Harry Emerson Fosdick, one of the most famous clergymen in America, and his sister Edith Fosdick, who had a career as teacher and social worker. He was strongly impressed by college and graduate school, but he was equally influenced by the hundreds of family discussions around the dining-room table after church on Sunday. Mary Kingsbury's mother disapproved of her living in the slums, but her father, who had devoted his life to philanthropy and public service, understood from the first why she wanted to become a settlement worker. There were some who entered a settlement against their parents' judgment, but the majority inherited a tradition of service.

They were not especially frustrated by their inability to achieve the same status and positions of leadership occupied by their parents. These young men and women simply chose to serve in a different way than their mothers and fathers. In some cases they felt they were rebelling against their parents, but more often they were simply translating an inherited impulse to fit a new situation and a new generation.[27]

Yet as a group they were a restless lot, often self-conscious about their decision to live in the slums. Many had tried several occupations before coming to the settlement. Some of the women had been teachers, several of the men had been ministers or lawyers. Even so, most remained settlement workers for only a few years before embarking on a wide variety of reform activities and occupations. Part of this restlessness was merely the product of youth, but some of it stemmed from a nagging sense of uneasiness about their relationship to the world's problems. "We have in America a fast-growing number of cultivated young people who have no recognized outlet for their active faculties," Jane Addams wrote in 1892. "They hear constantly of the great social maladjustment, but no way is provided for them to change it, and their uselessness hangs about them heavily." [28]

This sense of uselessness rested most heavily upon the growing numbers of college-educated women—the first generation of college women—who felt they had to prove their right to a higher education by doing something important. These middle- and upper-class young women were left "with a longing to know life at its barest and hardest, to grapple with cold physical facts, to stand on a common footing with those who have no special advantages." This was the impulse to "share the race life" that Jane Addams decided was one of the subjective reasons for social settlements. Vida Scudder called it "the dominant note of all modern social effort." Another motivation she suggested in her novel *A Listener in Babel,* where a college professor tells a young girl who has decided to become a settlement worker that "any woman feels restless unless she is taking care of somebody. You have no one near you to take care of so you want to take care of the poor." Women had been restless in other periods, but as one Chicago newspaper reporter commented in 1908, "twenty years ago . . . a young woman who was restless and yearned to sacrifice herself, would have become a missionary or married a drinking man in order to save him. Today she studies medicine or goes into settlement work." [29]

Years of study made both men and women "feel nervously the need of putting theory into action." One young Harvard graduate became so tired of studying economic and political theory at the University of Berlin that he gave up his idea of a career in teaching, went to East London to work at Toynbee Hall, and later became a settlement worker in America. Mark A. DeWolfe Howe, a Harvard graduate and son of a prominent Boston family, a member of the right church and all the right clubs, became a resident at Andover House in Boston (South End House) primarily because he was bored with the social whirl and yearned for a more simple existence. Like many other young settlement workers, he was con cerned more with what the settlement experience would do for him than with what he would be able to do for the poor. He became a resident even though his friends thought him a "quixotic crank" and his mother and father feared he would get some terrible disease in the slums that would inhibit his activities at the Cricket Club.[30]

Whatever the reasons for entering settlement work, nearly half of the settlement workers came directly to the movement from college or graduate school or before taking a job. For some, settlement work was merely an extension of graduate school, while for others it was a place to test the new ideas and theories discovered in college. The influence of a professor or a classmate, experience with a debating team or with the Christian association, or the impact of a book like Ruskin's *Unto This Last* or Riis's *How the Other Half Lives* set young college students aflame with a reforming zeal and sent them from the campus to the slums.

During the last two decades of the nineteenth century there was a current of change and reform on many college campuses. Revised curricula often included courses in sociology or courses like Philosophy II at Harvard (the Ethics of Social Reform) taught by Dr. Francis Peabody, and called "drainage, drunkenness, and divorce" by the students. It was in Dr. Peabody's course that many students first learned about charity organization societies, settlement houses, improved housing, and other attempts to solve the city's problems. These courses often inspired young men and women "to do something for suffering humanity." Frederick C. Howe summed up what such formal education often meant to the settlement worker. "My life began . . . at Johns Hopkins University," Howe recalled. "Under the influence of Richard T. Ely, Woodrow Wolson, Albert Shaw, James Bryce, I came alive, I felt a sense of responsibility to the world, I wanted to change things." [31]

Thus, there were many influences that moulded a generation of young men and women to make them want to change things. Some became settlement residents for very practical reasons, but as a group they were idealists who believed they were helping to solve the problems of urban and industrial America. Among the many influences that combined to create the settlement impulse, anxiety, alienation, and guilt were important; but much more significant was recognition of the authentic need for settlements.

3

The Settlement, the Public School,
and Progressive Education

Many early settlement residents were teachers by training or inclination. Some of them even had classroom experience, but rejected a career in high school or college teaching as too routine and narrow, and too far removed from the pressing problems of an urban, industrialized country. They came to the settlement as educational innovators, ready to cut down the barriers that separated learning from reality. "A settlement is a protest against a restricted view of education," Jane Addams once remarked, and like most settlement workers, she considered education a method of social reform.[1]

Jane Addams and the other settlement pioneers drew heavily on the English settlements and university extension movements. They planned to extend the advantages of a college education to workingmen in order to narrow the gulf between factory worker and college graduate through classes, lectures, and discussions. Stanton Coit patterned his Neighborhood Guild in part on Frederick Denison Maurice's Working Men's College in London, and in 1890 Morrison Swift planned a settlement in Philadelphia that would be a social university. Jane Addams and Ellen Starr began to teach and to lecture as soon as they unpacked at Hull House. Miss Starr organized a reading group to discuss George Eliot's *Romola,* which broadened to include Dante, Browning, and Shakespeare. Julia Lathrop started a Sunday afternoon Plato Club for the discussion of philosophical questions. Vida Scudder and Helena Dudley organized a Social Science Club at Denison House in Boston in 1893, and for a time forty or fifty businessmen, professionals, workingmen, and students gathered weekly to hear lectures and discussions on such topics as "The Ethics of Trade Unions" or "German Socialism." But attendance dwindled after a few months, and the club collapsed after the third year.[2]

Almost every settlement had its lecture series and its educational conferences, and a few like Hull House had university extension classes for college credit. John Dewey and Frank Lloyd Wright were among those who spoke at Hull House. George Santayana once gave a lecture on St. Francis and the beauty of poverty at Prospect Union in Cambridge that left most of the hearers aghast. Some of the lectures and discussions were exciting at least to the residents and students if not to the workingmen in the neighborhood. And although Sinclair Lewis exaggerated in *Ann Vickers* when he described the educational fare in his fictional settlement as composed mostly of "lectures delivered gratis by earnest advocates of the single tax, troutfishing, exploring Tibet, pacifism, sea shell collecting, the eating of bran, and the geography of Charlemagne's Empire," there was an element of the unreal and the esoteric about the early settlement workers' attempts to dispense the culture of the universities to workingmen.[3]

There was also something unrealistic about the attempt to turn settlements into art galleries. Many of the early residents, influenced in part by John Ruskin, were convinced that one way to bring meaning and hope into drab lives was by an introduction to things of beauty and good design. Ellen Starr and Jane Addams collected reproductions of great art in Europe before they founded Hull House and took pride in hanging the pictures in the settlement. Miss Starr was the leader in the "attempt of Hull House to make the aesthetic and artistic a vital influence in the lives of its neighbors." She taught classes in the history of art, patiently explaining the meaning of each picture. She also organized exhibitions gathered from the homes of wealthy Chicagoans with the hope of limiting the pictures to those which combined "an elevated tone with technical excellence." Edward Burchard, the first male resident of the settlement, was elected to guard the pictures at night and to carry placards up and down the streets and into the saloons to advertise the exhibitions.[4]

Burchard understandably hated his work, but thousands came to see the pictures. Most of them, however, were women and children who had little interest in "technical excellence." An Italian was impressed that there were some Americans interested in art and not just money. A Greek became homesick when he saw a picture of the Acropolis. Others, too, found something that reminded them of home in the exhibitions of European painters. Many, of course, came because it was a chance to meet friends and to escape the dreary tenement rooms. In Boston, Denison House and South End House co-operated in an exhibition. Fifteen hundred a day came to view the paintings and cast ballots for their favorite pictures. The men chose the "Village Smithy," while the women picked a painting of a nude child by Leon Perrault, called "Sleeping Innocence."

University Settlement in New York also held art exhibitions, but the men in the neighborhood were openly hostile. Edward King reported that many of his friends thought they were "a cleverly disguised trick on the part of the eminent mugwumps in the University Settlement Society to get a grip on the district in the ante-election months." The women were less suspicious. A young immigrant girl hung a reproduction of a Fra Angelico angel on the wall of her tenement.[5] Many workingmen and their families were genuinely interested in art, but they found nothing in the public schools to satisfy this interest; the schools did not even have pictures on their walls.

The first building especially constructed for Hull House contained a gallery and the settlement continued its art exhibits until the opening of the Chicago Art Institute made them unnecessary. Ellen Starr also led the movement to put art in the schools. She donated a series of reproductions to the school nearest Hull House and helped the Chicago Women's Club form a committee to exhibit pictures in all other schools in the city. Thus began the Chicago Public School Art Society. It was a small beginning that did not revolutionize public education in the city, but it was significant as the first of many experiments tried first in the settlements and then adopted by the public schools.[6]

II

Art exhibitions, lectures, and university extension classes were fine; they satisfied the desire of many settlement residents to make use of their college training. Moreover they provided intellectual stimulation for "the transfigured few" in the neighborhood capable of abstract thought. Men like Philip Davis, Meyer Bloomfield, Henry Moskowitz, and Francis Hackett found the programs stimulating and were thus inspired to continue their education. In addition, settlement lectures and classes served to bring the real world to a number of university professors (or at least they liked to think so). But it soon became obvious that the great majority of the people in the settlement neighborhood were not interested in extension classes. Although thousands attended art exhibitions they took little away that would vitally influence their lives.[7]

What most people in a working-class neighborhood needed was something useful and concrete, something closely related to their daily lives. This might mean courses in manual training, or homemaking; it might simply mean instruction in English or basic American government and history. Large groups of immigrants made both English-type university extention courses and American public schools inadequate in the urban setting, thus forcing settlement workers, whether they liked it or not, to experiment with new methods and techniques.

They quickly learned that among the most useful things were child care and kindergarten classes for young children whose mothers worked all day. Stanton Coit opened a kindergarten at Neighborhood Guild only a few months after the settlement was organized, and Hull House, New York College Settlement, Chicago Commons, and most other pioneer settlements, established them soon after opening their doors.[8]

The settlements, however, were not the first in this country to adopt kindergartens. German liberals, finding sanctuary here after the failure of the Revolution of 1848, brought the educational ideas of Friedrich Froebel to the United States. By 1890, his ideas of freeing little children from harsh discipline and fear and encouraging their natural development through creative play, nature study, art, and music had become popular in the United States, especially among a large group of idealistic women.[9] Froebel did not directly influence most of the early settlement workers, however. His ideas had not reached the colleges and theological schools by the last decade of the nineteenth century. And although some workers were familiar with G. Stanley Hall's writing on child development, most of the settlements founded kindergartens not out of any particular conviction, but merely to provide a needed service for their neighborhood. It was not long, however, before they were converted to the kindergarten ideal of developing the total personality of the child through a variety of group activities. The settlement workers were especially intrigued by the use of art and music to encourage creative self-expression and the appreciation of beauty. They had a similar goal in mind when they tried to introduce great literature and art to the adults in the neighborhood. Indeed, the kindergarten ideal of developing the whole personality seemed closely related to the settlement idea of making life more meaningful for those who lived in the overcrowded tenement districts.[10]

The goals of the settlements and the kindergartens seemed so similar that one kindergarten teacher labeled the social settlement "the kindergarten for adults." [11] Most settlements were more than that, but many had actually developed from kindergartens. In Boston a number of neighborhood kindergartens and day nurseries established by Mrs. Quincy A. Shaw in the late 1870's and early 1880's became settlements in the 'nineties. Also in Boston, a group of men and women who sought consciously to combine the principles of the kindergarten and the settlement established the Elizabeth Peabody House. Neighborhood House in Chicago, Kingsley House in New Orleans, and others scattered around the country, developed this same way. Mary McDowell was trained as a kindergarten teacher and directed classes at Hull House before becoming the head resident of the University of Chicago Settlement. Eleanor McMain, who had taught pre-school children became head resident of Kingsley House in New Orleans. Still others brought some of the kindergarten ideals to the settlement, and introduced a large number of college-trained men and women to Froebel and the possibilities of creative play. Many settlements trained kindergarten teachers in a more formal way. Amalie Hofer, the editor of *Kindergarten Magazine*, and her sister, Mrs. Bertha Hofer Hegner, directed the Pestalozzi-Froebel Kindergarten Training School at Chicago Commons. The Chicago Kindergarten Institute met for several years at the University of Chicago Settlement. Mrs. Alice H. Putnam's Kindergarten Training School used Hull House, and South End House had a kindergarten normal school after 1897.[12]

While the settlements did not originate the kindergarten idea, they played a significant part in popularizing it, especially since they often pressured the public schools to take over their work. Teaching little children could be a thankless occupation, but the idea of developing the whole child through art and music and creative play provided a challenge also to revise the whole educational system. It led to attempts to apply the same principles to adult education; for grown men and women could also learn by "playing." It led to a search for playgrounds, parks, and gymnasiums, and to campaigns against child labor. The kindergarten ideas of Froebel, taken seriously, could lead to reform. In the case of the settlement workers they often did.[13]

III

The kindergarten classes brought mothers and sisters as well as little boys and girls to the settlement and led naturally to attempts to provide them with something useful and meaningful. Usually this meant classes in homemaking, cooking, sewing, and shopping.

Some courses taught useless skills, such as the art of serving tea from a silver service or accepting a calling card on a tray. Many of the women settlement workers were appalled at the way their immigrant neighbors kept house. Their wastefulness and disorderliness bothered those brought up in neat middle-class American homes. Some settlement workers could never quite overcome their feeling of superiority, and these homemaking classes only made the immigrant woman more conscious of differences and deficiencies. But many newcomers, baffled by unfamiliar urban ways of household management, acquired helpful suggestions and new confidence at the settlement. Of course, the immigrants did not always listen; and, indeed, sometimes they knew more than the settlement workers. For example, Alice Hamilton, trained at the University of Michigan Medical School, told the women near Hull House to give babies nothing but milk until their teeth appeared. Then one day a young mother brought her healthy three-year-old son into the makeshift "baby clinic" and explained her difficulties when the boy was small. "I gave him the breast and there was plenty of milk," she recalled, "but he cried all the time. Then one day I was frying eggs and just to make him stop I gave him one and it went fine. The next day I was making cup cakes and as soon as they were cool I gave him one, and after that I gave him just whatever we had and he got fat and didn't cry any more." Alice Hamilton did convince the Italian mothers, however, that it was important to bathe babies, helping them to overcome their prejudice against water by anointing the babies with olive oil. Settlement workers soon discovered that they could get the attention of neighborhood women by setting up model flats and housekeeping centers similar to tenement apartments. There they taught cooking, cleaning, caring for children, and other household tasks, in a more realistic setting. In this way they tried to relate their teaching to the real problems that their neighbors faced. Eventually the public schools borrowed many of their techniques.[14]

The practical needs of the people in the neighborhood usually dictated the types of classes offered. Many settlements were located near textile factories where women and children could take out work. Skill and speed in making buttonholes or operating a sewing machine was vitally important and meant increased family income. Most settlements attempting to satisfy the real needs of their neighborhoods soon found themselves very much involved in manual training and industrial education. Hartley House in New York maintained a carpentry shop; Boston's South End House had a lace-making shop and, after 1903, a separate building equipped with a stage for plays; carpentry and clay-modeling rooms; and kitchen and kindergarten equipment. Hull House held classes in pottery, metalwork, enameling, wood carving, weaving, dressmaking, sewing, millinery, and cooking. Greenwich House in New York began a handicrafts school and shop in 1907 to teach young women how to make lace, pottery, and other articles, and also to employ the many immigrant women in the neighborhood who already had special skills. Settlement workers combined lectures and visits to museums with the teaching of practical skills in order that the newcomers might see that they were engaged in artistic work that had a long history and real importance. Greenwich House started the shop and school primarily to aid the people in the neighborhood, but after three years it was self-supporting and was taken over as a private enterprise by two young women.[15]

Most settlement workers wanted to do more than just teach practical skills to their neighbors. Borrowing from Ruskin and Morris, they also tried to preserve handicraft skills in an industrial age. Moreover, they were concerned with the wider implications of the teaching and learning process in an urban setting. They saw immigrant women who felt useless and out of place in a strange land. They observed sons and daughters employed in meaningless jobs and rebelling against their parents and the language and customs of the old country. When Jane Addams and Ellen Starr decided to establish the Hull House Labor Museum in 1900 they were anxious to preserve the spinning and weaving art of the Italian women. But they also saw a chance to help the younger generation appreciate this talent, and by teaching the girls something of the history of the textile industry, something of the relationship between raw material and the finished product, they hoped to transform their lives from drudgery to more meaningful activity.[16]

The Hull House Labor Museum, like many other settlement experiments, was in part a protest against the dull, formal, and abstract fare offered by the public schools. There, most teachers seemed oblivious to the backgrounds and daily experiences of their pupils and unaware that industrialism and urbanism had profoundly altered the experiences and educational needs of young and old alike. These same forces had also separated those who worked with their hands from those who worked with their minds. It was important to show the workingman that he was part of a larger process and to relate his education to his experience. But it was also important, Ellen Starr believed, to teach the man who no longer needed to work with his hands some kind of manual skill or handicraft. She spent fifteen months in England learning the art of bookbinding, then returned to Hull House to teach it to others. There were few people, however, in the Hull House neighborhood who had any use for the technical skill of binding fine books. Years later, the irony of her project struck her and she remarked, "If I had thought it through, I would have realized that I would be using my hands to create books that only the rich could buy." [17]

IV

Not all settlement workers were realistic in their educational experiments, and there was something romantic and nostalgic about their attempt to revive handicrafts in the face of increasing industrialism. But they were usually concerned with real problems and tried to satisfy important needs. The early residents who provided art exhibitions and musical concerts for people in the area were aware of a craving for beautiful things on the part of many who lived in those dreary surroundings. But they realized only gradually that this need could be better satisfied and utilized by letting the people themselves create things rather than by having them merely look and listen. A few settlements, therefore, began to hold exhibitions not of reproductions of great art, but of painting actually done by the neighborhood people, and they asked those skilled in painting or sculpture to teach others. Hull House, Greenwich House, and several other settlements supported successful amateur theaters which provided an artistic outlet for some and helped a great many immigrants learn English. "The number of those who like to read has been greatly over-estimated," Jane Addams decided, and the theater gave these knowledge of the language, and an education in the broadest sense.[18]

Miss Addams discovered that the plays of the ancient Greeks were very successful at Hull House, most obviously among the Greek newcomers in the neighborhood. Other settlement workers quickly learned to draw from the cultural heritage of immigrant groups in any educational experiment. Henry Street Settlement and Greenwich House in New York, and Elizabeth Peabody House in Boston were among those settlements which made use of pageants and festivals to dramatize the heritage of each immigrant group. In the process they helped launch the little-theater movement, and fostered the growth of neighborhood dramatic associations, including the Neighborhood Playhouse in New York.[19]

Many settlements also utilized and encouraged the musical talent of those in their neighborhood; a few offered musical instruction as well. The Hull House Music School was begun in 1893 under the direction of Eleanor Smith, and the following year Emilie Wagner began giving piano and violin lessons in College Settlement in New York. After 1899 the project was sponsored jointly by University and College settlements and in 1903 a separate organization, the Music School Settlement, was begun. There was no attempt to turn every student into a professional musician, but rather to allow those who loved music to find a way to express themselves through it. Some critics charged that by teaching the children of the poor to enjoy music and the finer things of life the settlement workers would only make them more unhappy and dissatisfied. Thomas Tapper, director of the New York Music School Settlement, admitted that this was occasionally true; he wished it would happen more often for he believed unhappiness was the first step on the road out of the slums.[20]

Most of the immigrants had to struggle desperately to survive and to learn something about their new country. Language was a difficult barrier, and the public schools did little to teach immigrants English: a few conducted evening classes in English or Civics, but these usually treated immigrant adults as American children just learning to read. Grown men read, "I am a yellow bird. I can sing. I can fly. I can sing to you," or "Oh Baby, dear baby, / Whatever you do, / You are the king of the home, / And we all bend to you." Philip Davis remarked that an English primer placed in the hands of the immigrant "should emphasize less the words 'cat,' 'rat,' and 'mat' and dwell more on the words 'city,' 'citizen,' and 'state.'" The settlements often tried to combine the teaching of English with the teaching of citizenship. Because they understood some of the immigrants' needs, settlement workers treated them like adults and tried to relate the problems of language and of government to their experiences.[21]

Kindergarten classes, classes in English for adults, in music, art, handicrafts, and homemaking—all these areas of education settlement workers experimented with before most public schools considered adding them to their curricula. They were important to the individual experiences and needs of the local population. In a sense they were practical courses, although few could earn a living in music or art.

The settlement workers, interested in relating education more closely to life, could not long ignore the pressing problems of training young men and women in their neighborhoods for worthwhile jobs. They knew that they could inspire the few with exceptional ability to go to college, but that the majority could never go. What would happen to them? Would they merely drift into unskilled jobs, or could the settlements do something to prepare them for a meaningful role in the industrial world?

Robert Woods of South End House was perhaps more concerned with this problem than any other settlement worker. He was especially troubled by the number of boys who dropped out of school at fourteen to become newsboys, bootblacks, and office boys—jobs that led nowhere and prepared them to do nothing. Woods pointed out that the courses then taught in the schools presupposed "the sort of life which existed at least a generation ago, when the shop, the farm and the home were all important and effective institutions for vocational training," and he argued that in an industrial age, some kind of vocational training was necessary. We have been "training too much the consumer citizen and too little the producer citizen," he remarked, "and concentrating too much on the two percent who get to college and the eight or ten percent who get to high school." Like Ellen Starr he was disturbed that industrialism had brought about a separation of cultural and vocational interests. The skilled workman, he believed, "must be helped to gain the position he had in the Middle Ages, when the artisans were poets and artists also." He advocated some manual training for everyone, so that even the lucky ones who went on to college would have an appreciation of the dignity and the difficulties of working with their hands or operating machines.[22]

Thus, Woods believed that vocational education would benefit all, but especially those who could not go to college. He cited as an example the way industrial education was being used in the South to aid the Negro in his slow rise toward equality, and advocated a similar system to help the immigrant in the North. If there was a suggestion of paternalism in Woods's plan to adopt Booker T. Washington's system to aid the immigrant, there was also an ingredient of realism. Woods desired every student to be "both vocational and cultural," and hoped that the schools would contribute to make this possible. "The School," he said at one point, "we want to make more and more a training ground and a council chamber for the actual affairs of life."[23]

Woods argued for state-supported vocational training in speeches before the National Education Association, and at a meeting of the Harvard Teachers' Association. As early as 1901 he spoke out in favor of public vocational education in an article in the *Boston Globe*. Woods in 1904 investigated the existing facilities for vocational training in Massachusetts, and in 1906 served for three months as temporary secretary of a state commission on industrial education which had the authority to set up industrial schools. There was opposition, of course. Labor leaders feared that trade schools would threaten their control of the skilled labor force, and educators were horrified by any attempt to change the curriculum of the public schools. However, other settlement workers joined Woods—Jane Addams, Ellen Starr, and Graham Taylor in Chicago, and Lillian Wald and Mary Flexner in New York—and they were especially insistent to point out the need for training hands as well as minds. When the National Society for the Promotion of Industrial Education was formed in 1906 Robert Woods and Jane Addams served on the board of managers. At the local and the national level settlement workers played a significant part in forcing public schools to take over the industrial and vocational training begun in the settlements.[24]

The settlement workers' interest went beyond vocational education to concern for the school drop-outs. Vocational training, they decided, meant little without vocational guidance, so almost every settlement worker at one time or another advised about jobs and training programs. Some settlements operated an informal employment bureau, but Civic Service House in Boston even went beyond that.

Mrs. Quincy Agassiz Shaw established Civic Service House in the North End of Boston in 1901 to promote civic and educational work among the immigrant population of that area, with Meyer Bloomfield, a young, brilliant, and energetic reformer then fresh out of Harvard, as the guiding force behind the venture. Bloomfield, who had grown up on New York's Lower East Side and had attended clubs and classes at University Settlement, felt he owed something to the recent immigrants still caught, as he had once been, in the slums. He explained his plans for a new settlement to Mrs. Shaw and she financed the experiment in reform.[25]

Bloomfield was soon joined by Philip Davis, another who had risen from the ghetto. They organized clubs and classes, helped immigrants learn English, and encouraged them to join trade unions. They also began to attract an impressive group of intellectuals and reformers. Students from Harvard and Boston University came in the evening to teach classes in American government, history, and English. Ralph Albertson, an itinerant reformer who had organized the ill-fated Christian Commonwealth in Georgia, drifted to Boston and Civic Service House. One of Albertson's closest friends was Frank Parsons, law professor, municipal expert, prolific scholar, and impassioned reformer. Through Albertson and Bloomfield (who had studied under him at Boston University Law School), Parsons became interested in the new settlement venture. He was especially impressed with Philip Davis's idea for beginning a workingmen's institute at Civic Service House. Having followed the work of Toynbee Hall's Workingmen's Institute in London for some time, Parsons devoted himself to the task of creating a similar institution at Civic Service House.[26]

The Breadwinner's College, as its founders named it, opened in 1905 with courses in history, civics, economics, psychology, and philosophy. Parsons and Albertson were the backbone of the faculty, aided by Philip Davis, Meyer Bloomfield, and Morris Cohen, a philosopher who had experience with a similar school in New York. There was also an occasional lecture by Josiah Royce and Lincoln Steffens, among others.

An ardent group of students from Harvard, Massachusetts Institute of Technology, and Boston University, including a young Harvard undergraduate named Walter Lippmann, aided the endeavor. Breadwinner's College offered a diploma at the end of two years, and a number of its graduates moved on to positions of prominence and responsibility. One became a judge, one an official of the Department of Labor, another an Assistant Attorney General. Although the students had great enthusiasm and the experiment was a success, Parsons and Bloomfield soon learned what Robert Woods and Jane Addams had realized earlier: that many of their students had problems that no course in philosophy or ancient history could solve.[27]

Some of the students at Breadwinner's College were out of work; others were unhappily toiling at jobs that held no interest, no meaning, and no future. When Parsons invited groups of high school boys to the settlement he discovered that most had no vocational plans or else had plans that were completely unrealistic. Since there was no organization to help them choose the right job, and none to help them utilize their latent and about-to-be wasted talent, Parsons created one. In 1908 he asked Mrs. Shaw for more money to support another experiment, a vocational bureau. The bureau began operation on April 23, 1908. Parsons talked with scores of young men eager for help in choosing a career. He emphasized the need for guidance by a counselor carefully trained and armed with industrial statistics and information about job openings. And he wrote down his ideas about an orderly and scientific way to guide young people in their choice of job or profession in his book *Choosing a Vocation,* published in 1909. But Parsons did not live to see the book; he had died from the strain of overwork in the fall of 1908.[28]

Frank Parsons was the founder of the modern vocational guidance movement which might never have been started if Bloomfield had not been ready to step in and take over as director. He expanded the activities, advertised in books like the *Vocational Guidance of Youth,* and *Youth, School and Vocation,* and in lectures at Harvard and elsewhere. Bloomfield helped "sell" the idea of vocational counseling to the school committee of Boston, which became the first city in the country to have such organized, systematic, job counseling. Bloomfield also called the first National Conference on Vocational Guidance, which met in Boston in 1910, and led to the organization of the National Vocational Guidance Association in 1913. The experiment begun by a few dedicated men in a Boston social settlement thus stimulated a national vocational guidance movement, with far-reaching and significant results.[29]

V

Vocational training and vocational guidance were later adopted by the public schools. This was somewhat unexpected because in the beginning, most settlement workers had no desire to alter or reform the public educational system; they saw their function only as supplementing schools. However, as soon as they became aware of the inadequacy of education, especially in the poorer districts of the great cities, the attempt to supplement became an attempt to change.

Some reforms were practical, such as the introduction of school nurses and school lunchrooms. Lillian Wald and her fellow workers at Henry Street Settlement simply demonstrated the need and proposed them as effective solutions to some chronic problems. Miss Wald had been troubled by the number of children she met who were kept out of school because of disease or sickness. Eczema or hookworm could prevent a child from receiving any education at all. Doctors had been inspecting school children since 1897, sending home those with diseases, but no one had made an attempt to treat these children. Ironically, the coming to power of Seth Low's reform administration in 1901 complicated rather than solved the problem, for the inspection of school children was made more efficient and more rigorous. Still, nothing was done in the way of treatment. At this point, Lillian Wald, well acquainted with the Health Commissioner and other officials of the Low administration, offered to show how school nurses could solve the problem by treating the diseases diagnosed by the doctors. First, however, she made the city officials promise that if the experiment proved successful they would use their influence to have the nurses put on a permanent basis with salaries paid out of public funds. The settlement nurses found that by making regular visits to the schools, working with the doctors, and in some cases visiting the families, all but the most seriously ill could be treated and kept in school. After only one month's trial, the Board of Estimate appropriated money to hire school nurses. Soon the experiment was being copied in other cities.[30]

Hot lunches for a penny began in much the same way. In 1905 a number of people in New York were aroused by a widely misquoted statement from Robert Hunter's book, *Poverty*, claiming that 70,000 school children went to school in the city without breakfast (he had said, underfed). Lillian Wald and other settle-

ment workers had tried to get the city to subsidize school lunches as
early as 1901. They continued to argue in favor of cheap or inexpensive lunches: "The needs of the body are as imperative as those
of the mind, and the successful training of the latter depends upon
the adequate nourishment of the former," Miss Wald announced.[31]
But for a time the settlement workers' suggestions were ignored.
Then the Salvation Army and several restaurants attempted to provide lunches for the children. However, the settlement workers
realized that private charity was not the answer; they sought to
have the school authorities take over the responsibility of serving
hot lunches. Eventually they were successful, and the "homemaking centers" inaugurated by the settlements demonstrated that the
idea was practical.

Another pioneer educational project at Henry Street Settlement
involved mentally retarded and handicapped children. Settlement
workers encouraged the work of Elizabeth Farrell, a neighborhood
teacher interested in helping the retarded, and they persuaded the
Board of Education to permit her to teach an ungraded class of
handicapped children. They furthermore got special equipment for
her and convinced the Board of the importance of her work. In
1908 the Board voted a separate department for teaching the retarded.

Settlement workers showed other special concern for the problems of immigrant children, and several residents, including Jane
Addams, Julia Lathrop, and Alzina Stevens, attempted to work with
and understand the juvenile delinquent. They were, in part, responsible for the law that provided for a special juvenile court in
Cook County, Chicago. It was no accident that the court, the de-
tention home, and the special school were located across the street
from Hull House; nor that Alzina Stevens was appointed the first
probation officer. Hull House reformers also inspired and supported the work of William Healy, a psychiatrist who believed that
social environment was the major cause of juvenile delinquency.
Altogether, the settlement workers did much to convince school
boards, teachers, and public officials that they should not reject the
diseased, the handicapped, or the troubled child.[32]

The settlement worker's interest in the public school and in education often led him to teach part time or to serve on school committees. Charles Stover, James K. Paulding, and James B. Reynolds of University Settlement all served as school trustees in their district, and Cornelia Bradford, founder of Whittier House, was a member of the Jersey City Board of Education. Raymond Robins and Jane Addams were members of the controversial school board that exposed graft in the school-book and coal contracts and fought for a number of school reforms.

A settlement worker's concern with local education often led him into broad reform movements, as the example of Florence Kelley illustrates. She taught at night in a nearby public school during her first year at Hull House. Although she had been concerned about child labor even before this, what she saw as a teacher played an important part in her decision to concentrate on winning better child labor laws. The frustration experienced by Jane Addams and others in trying to convince the City Council that the public school in the Hull House district needed enlarging led them to a futile attempt to unseat the local ward boss. They soon discovered that educational reform was closely related to economic and political reform.[33]

VI

While the settlement workers were most influenced by the concrete needs they saw about them, for improved school buildings, practical courses, and school nurses, they were concerned with educational theory, too, and with the implications of their experiments. Indeed, they made important contributions to the development of progressive education. They did not invent progressive education, but often borrowed from the advanced thinking of experts in many fields, frequently adopting the latest theories. They provided the practical testing ground for others' ideas. In their experiments with vocational training and their attempt to relate the work of the school to the reality of the world; through kindergartens, work with immigrants, and by their efforts to tailor the school to the needs of the student, the settlement workers tried to make the student the center of the school and the school the center of the community. Although they were never quite sure whether they sought to adjust the child and the immigrant to society, or whether they meant to transform society to meet the needs of their pupils, they used education as a method of social reform.[34]

The settlement movement and progressive education intertwined at many points, and both drew support from a broad area. The mutual influence of the two movements is most obvious with John Dewey. He was a member of the first board of trustees at Hull House, and a frequent visitor at the settlement. He lectured and on several occasions led the discussion at Julia Lathrop's Plato Club. He gave a formal address now and then and sometimes just dropped in to talk, to meet the interesting people who found their way to Hull House, to argue with the socialists, the anarchists, and the single-taxers, and to learn. When Dewey's eight-year-old son, Gordon, died, the memorial service was at Hull House and Jane Addams gave the address. Dewey's daughter, named after Miss Addams, remarked once that "Dewey's faith in democracy as a guiding force in education took on both a sharper and deeper meaning because of Hull House and Jane Addams." When he moved to New York and to Columbia University he became associated with Lillian Wald at Henry Street Settlement, and became chairman of the educational committee at Mary Simkhovitch's Greenwich House. When he went to Boston or another city he often sought out a settlement house.[35]

Dewey learned a great deal from his contacts with settlement workers. He sympathized with their attempts to broaden the scope of education and widen the impact of the school. Most of all, he learned from watching and participating in educational experiments and from taking part in the give-and-take of discussions.[36]

The settlement workers also learned from Dewey. Possibly his greatest contribution was making them see the meaning and the consequences or implications of their day-by-day educational experiments. "I have always thought that we were trying to live up to your philosophy," Lillian Wald wrote him on one occasion. Jane

Addams also saw the implications for social work of Dewey's ideas. "His insistence upon an atmosphere of freedom and confidence between the teacher and pupil . . . ," she wrote, "profoundly affected all similar relationships, certainly those between the social worker and his client." [37] Dewey's writings had a large impact on the settlement movement; in turn, the settlement movement had an important influence on him. In one of his books, *Schools of Tomorrow*, there is a chapter entitled "The School as a Social Settlement." [38] That sums up what Dewey and the settlement workers were trying to accomplish in the city. They were trying to make the schools more like social settlements, and to a large extent they succeeded.

4

Playgrounds, Housing,
and City Planning

The settlement workers' educational experiments and their commitment to neighborhood reconstruction led them into a series of closely related reform movements. If one accepted Friedrich Froebel's idea of creative play, or the belief of G. Stanley Hall that each child reenacted the history of the development of the race and must be provided an outlet for his animal energies, then it was a logical step from kindergartens to campaigns for public playgrounds. But the settlement worker did not need to read Froebel and Hall, or even to have a consistent philosophy of neighborhood regeneration; all he had to do was to look around him. "If we want decent adolescent boys we must give playgrounds to ten year olds," Jane Robbins announced. Lillian Wald agreed that the "young offender's presence in the courts may be traced to a play impulse for which there is no safe outlet." [1]

To many settlement workers, however, the best and most creative kind of play was rural play: many remembered their own childhood, vacations spent romping in the woods, swimming, riding, and fishing, and imagined that if other boys and girls could get out to the country in the summer, even for a short time, they would find strength of purpose and character. Many settlements established summer camps, a few maintained farms, and South End House regularly sent neighborhood boys as caddies to White Mountain summer resorts.[2]

The pioneer settlement workers themselves often closed up shop in the summer to escape to the country. Ellen Starr was constantly irritated by the dust and dirt at Hull House and loved to go to a clean New England village. Robert Woods maintained that the city was no place even for a settlement conference, and Lillian Wald said of New York, "this is an awful city to live in."[3] The city was an awful place to live for most of those in settlement neighborhoods, and if the residents sometimes became nostalgic it was understandable. After a few years of leaving in the summer months, however, they became realistically concerned with the misery of life in a hot tenement. Much of their energy they then devoted to fresh air excursions and summer camps with the thought of giving the youngsters a better place to play than the city streets, and of providing some relief for the mothers of small children. But they also felt that getting close to nature built character and independence. "The city girl benefits most from holidays in which she experiences nature in its more primitive aspects," Robert Woods and Albert Kennedy wrote.[4]

Some settlement workers had a tendency to romanticize "the green of the grass, the smell of the fields . . . the whir of the insects and the lowing of the cattle . . ." and a few of the early settlement residents spent time and energy collecting flowers to distribute to the tenement dwellers. John Gavit, editor of the *Commons,* even remarked on one occasion that this was one of the settlements' "most useful inventions."[5] Residents did not, however, spend all their time distributing flowers and exporting children to the country. Many set out to provide more and better play space in the city and pioneered in demonstrating to the public the need for planned recreation.

The residents of Hull House established the first public playground in Chicago in 1893. Florence Kelley, disturbed by the unsanitary and unsafe conditions of several tenements near Hull House, sat down one night and composed a letter to a Chicago newspaper describing the conditions of the property owned by "A. E. Kent and Son." The son, William Kent, who later became a prominent progressive politician, immediately went to Hull House, talked with Florence Kelley and Jane Addams, and offered to give the buildings to the settlement if they would be run as model tenements. The two women suggested tearing down the buildings instead and making a playground. Kent accepted.[6]

At about the same time, Lillian Wald turned the backyard of Henry Street Settlement into a playground. It served as a kindergarten in the morning, as a place for older children to play in the afternoon, and a dance and festival place for young adults in the evening. Only a short time later, East Side House opened a similar facility on the banks of the East River with sandboxes and play apparatus. Northwestern University Settlement organized a large playground in Chicago, and in Philadelphia, College Settlement and then Starr Center supervised a playground. One observer remarked about the play area near Greenwich House in New York: "If a tablet were to be erected to commemorate the service of Mary Simkhovitch and the settlement to this neighborhood, it might appropriately be placed in Hudson Park."[7]

Settlement workers did not originate the idea of neighborhood playgrounds; as with kindergartens, they adopted the idea before it had become widely accepted, demonstrated the need and usefulness, and then helped sell the idea to the city and eventually to the nation. They did not fight alone, of course. Robert Woods and Helena Dudley worked closely with Joseph Lee and the Massachusetts Civic League in the attempt to provide better playgrounds and public gymnasiums in Boston. In New York Jacob Riis, author of *How the Other Half Lives,* was one of the first to suggest the need for play areas near every public school and a leader in the campaign for small parks and playgrounds.[8]

Riis's ideas were in agreement with those of settlement workers: social reform had to begin by altering the environment of the neighborhood. He wanted to make parks not just places filled with trees and flowers to look at, but useful areas where old and young might come to relax and play. Like Riis, Charles Stover, one of the early residents at Neighborhood Guild, felt that "Keep Off The Grass" signs should be removed from the parks and replaced with play facilities. Stover led the battle in New York for neighborhood playgrounds, especially for Seward Park.

II

As early as 1887 a park act passed in New York City recognized the need not only for small parks, but more significantly for play apparatus in them. Yet the Park Department ignored this provision of the law. In 1890 Stover, influenced much more by what he saw on the Lower East Side than by what he read about the importance of play, enlisted the co-operation of ex-Mayor Abram S. Hewitt and organized the Society for Parks and Playgrounds in New York "to secure in public parks plots especially devoted to children's recreation." The Society ran a large playground for a time at Ninety-second Street and Second Avenue, but only a handful of settlement workers and the group of reformers associated with the New York Reform Club seemed interested. Finally, during Mayor Strong's administration in 1895, a committee headed by James B. Reynolds of University Settlement selected sites for two parks on the Lower East Side. The city purchased the property and tore down the tenements, but the parks were somehow never built. Seward Park was still a vacant lot filled with rubble, stagnant water, and exposed sewers—hardly a place for creative play.[9]

Stover, who had an unlimited supply of moral indignation as well as an ability to organize reform, interested Lillian Wald, James K. Paulding, Elizabeth Williams, Mary K. Simkhovitch, and a few other settlement workers and reformers, and in 1898 formed the Outdoor Recreation League. Felix Adler, Nicholas Murray Butler, president of Columbia University, Richard Watson Gilder, editor of *Century Magazine*, William Dean Howells, and Jacob Riis, were among the prominent citizens on the advisory board; Stover was the president, and J. G. Phelps Stokes, the treasurer (replacing Josephine Shaw Lowell, who served during the first few months). Settlement workers made up a majority of the executive committee, and the ORL headquarters was at Elizabeth Williams's College Settlement.[10]

Lillian Wald used her influence with the Commissioner of Health to get the city to level the land and erect a fence around the park. The League then went to work, raised the money, and installed a playground which opened June 3, 1899. Thousands of children poured in from the very first day, and the playground was a great success. The money for equipment, repairs, and supervision came from private donations; however, the Outdoor Recreation League made it clear that it was the city's responsibility to operate the playground in Seward Park and do the same elsewhere.

In February 1900 the ORL submitted to the Park Board suggestions for permanent improvements. They asked for sandboxes, shelters, basketball courts, and play equipment for both boys and girls. But the Park Board ignored their request. Instead it recommended a small park in the natural style covering as large an area as possible, "with a view to provide sufficient lawn, shrubberies, promenades and shade trees to make the park really useful and attractive for the hard-working people of the neighborhood." [11] The ORL protested vigorously, pointing out that a nearby park with shrubs and trees was nearly deserted while Seward Park with its playground was filled with children and its fence lined with adults watching the children play. They appealed to the council, the mayor, and the park commissioners. Finally, in April 1903, the city agreed to take over and run the playground.[12]

The innovators won the battle of Seward Park and gained national publicity. But their fight was merely one skirmish in a major campaign in many cities. Like so many other reforms, the play movement became organized on the national level in the first decade of the twentieth century. It is not surprising that the National Playground Association of America, formed in 1906, included Stover, Reynolds, and Jane Addams. J. G. Phelps Stokes was elected a member of its executive committee, and Miss Addams and Joseph Lee became vice presidents.[13] The settlement workers' contributions to the recreation movement were significant: as practical organizers, reformers, and initiators, they helped convince the nation that creative play was important to the development of better citizens. They showed, also, how small playgrounds could help reconstruct the urban social environment.

III

Settlement workers also took part in a long and frustrating attempt to improve the housing in tenement neighborhoods. The overcrowding and filth in the tenements was an oppressive and overpowering sight—the first reaction was simply shock. Many settlement workers described the "garbage-strewn streets," "pale, dirty, undersized children," and the dark, damp rooms where a whole family existed. One New York resident found eleven people living in two rooms, and another discovered a room on a hot summer day "crowded with scantily-clothed, dull-faced men and women sewing upon heavy woolen coats and trousers."

The settlement investigators were obsessed with the inadequate toilet and bathing facilities and the absence of light and ventilation, but they documented the incredibly bad housing conditions with precision and sympathy.[14] Joining a protest movement already under way, they made important contributions of their own to housing reform. They had, for example, intimate knowledge of the conditions in their neighborhoods, and often stressed the little amenities that the housing reformer overlooked, such as the need for a parlor or front room for respectability and status. From their point of view, the improvement of housing was not an end in itself, but only part of the larger movement to reconstruct neighborhoods and improve the total environment of the city.

Since the beginnings of cities, men have been critical of urban housing. The model tenement, inspired by John Ruskin and developed in England by Octavia Hill, was one popular solution in the late nineteenth century. Built by limited-dividend corporations, model tenements were designed to provide modest but attractive housing for workingmen and their families and to set a standard of excellence for other landlords to follow. Although many philanthropic citizens in New York, Boston, Philadelphia, and other cities, supported the movement, most settlement workers rejected this answer. They suggested that a more fundamental solution was needed for the housing problem.[15]

Starting with their own neighborhoods and moving outward, they began to document the need for better and more effective tenement house laws, then joined others in presenting their case to city councils and state legislatures. Robert Woods and several other residents of South End House co-operated with the Tenement House Committee of the Twentieth Century Club, while Harold Estabrook, a young resident of South End House, made a detailed study of a tenement district, and then worked to have some of the worst buildings torn down.[16]

Mary Sayles, a young Smith College graduate and fellow of the College Settlement Association, conducted the first systematic study of housing conditions in Jersey City in 1902. Living in the city at Whittier House, she had the enthusiastic co-operation of Cornelia Bradford. Twice she was arrested and many more times she was threatened or driven away by landlords. Yet when the results were published, Governor Franklin Murphy was so overwhelmed by the story of squalor and filth and dilapidated homes that he appointed a special tenement house commission which had its first meeting at Whittier House.[17]

Kingsley House in Pittsburgh, College Settlement in Los Angeles, Union Settlement in Providence, Kingsley House in New Orleans, and other settlements scattered around the country, played similar roles in their cities.[18] Northwestern Settlement and Chicago Commons held conferences and conducted housing investigations. But Jane Addams of Hull House and Mrs. Emmons Blaine, daughter of Cyrus McCormick and friend of the settlement workers in Chicago, really launched the housing movement in that city with the establishment of the City Homes Association in 1900. They persuaded Robert Hunter, wandering settlement worker, charity expert, and radical, to conduct a thorough investigation of housing conditions. Like most progressive reformers, they believed that "accurate knowledge of existing conditions must be the basis for future reform." Hunter's report shocked some loyal Chicago citizens who had always believed that because their city had plenty of room to expand, it would be saved from the evils of the New York tenements. "Chicago is both uninformed and unprepared for the future," Hunter concluded, and predicted that the evils he described could not possibly be prevented under existing laws.[19]

In large part because of the energetic leaders of the City Homes Association, Chicago got a better tenement house ordinance in 1902. The new law helped a little, but another investigation three years later disclosed that there was need for further change. Settlement workers and other reformers in the city continued to agitate and investigate, but over the years their success seemed meager compared to the energy spent. Yet housing reformers in Chicago attracted national attention with their investigations and reforms, and many cities sent experts to copy their methods.[20]

It was in New York that the most important work was done, and there that the outline of a national housing movement was drawn. The name Jacob Riis is almost synonymous with housing reform in New York. Born in Denmark in 1846, he came to America in 1870 and wandered from job to job before becoming a police reporter for the *New York Tribune*. He became the leading authority on life in the urban underworld, and recorded what he saw with notebook and camera. In 1890 he published *How the Other Half Lives: Studies Among the Tenements of New York*, a series of impressionistic sketches of the degradation and human pathos in the slums. It was a plea for sympathy and a demand for justice. There was a note of nostalgic agrarianism in his writing, but his ability to depict the human side of poverty came through stronger. More than any other single person he made Americans aware of the urban housing problem in the late nineteenth century. For Riis housing was only one aspect of a larger reform movement to regenerate the city.[21]

In many ways the settlement workers had much in common with Riis, but they were also realists interested in passing and enforcing legislation. They became directly involved in a more scientific and limited housing movement that also developed in New York, concerned primarily with restrictive legislation. The major credit for that movement belongs to the Tenement House Committee of the

Charity Organization Society, and especially to Lawrence Veiller.

After graduating from City College, Veiller had been a resident in the early 'nineties at University Settlement. His experience there, together with his work for the East Side Relief Work Committee during the depression of 1893, convinced him "that the improvement of the homes of the people was the starting point for everything." In 1898 Veiller talked Robert W. DeForest of the Charity Organization Society into forming a separate tenement house committee (though Veiller really wanted a separate organization); this committee became an important pressure group for tenement house reform in the city and the state and was primarily responsible for the appointment of a state tenement house commission in 1900.[22]

Veiller was principally a technician and scientific reformer who believed that the housing problem could be solved by passing restrictive legislation and housing codes. Settlement workers, many of whom had aided Richard Watson Gilder, the editor of *Century Magazine,* in his intensive investigation of housing conditions in 1894, joined Veiller. And he, like Gilder, found their energy and knowledge very useful. This was especially true in his educational campaign to show how poorly workingmen were housed. For this he organized an exhibition in the Sherry Building, at Thirty-eighth Street and Fifth Avenue in New York, that opened in February 1900. Exhibits demonstrated the incredible crowding in individual blocks, and photographs showed the "dark, unventilated airshafts" which provided the only air many tenements had. There were also display models of better designed buildings to show possible alternatives. Many New York settlements copied the idea in their neighborhoods and co-operated on a graphic study showing the actual income and expenditures of a large number of workingmen's families; other cities did the same thing. The Hull House group helped to prepare a similar display for Veiller's exhibition, and the residents of South End House worked on one sponsored by the Boston Twentieth Century Club. Over 10,000 people viewed the show in two weeks, and many more saw part of it when it was loaned to other cities.[23]

The exhibition aroused a number of influential people—including Governor Theodore Roosevelt—to the need for tenement house reform. The direct result was the passage of a bill, drafted by Veiller, providing for a New York Tenement House Commission. Veiller became the secretary of the commission and James B. Reynolds one of its members. The new agency made use of settlement workers in its investigations and public hearings. Thus armed with information, Veiller and his co-workers drafted a new housing code to eliminate some of the worst evils and provide ventilation and toilet facilities in each apartment. This new code was adopted in 1901. In order to enforce it, the housing reformers obtained a Tenement House Department in the city government. While the new arrangement did not solve the city's slum problem, it did put an end to some of the worst abuses.[24]

The New York movement, especially the exhibition and the new code, had an impact on nearly every large city in the country. When a man was needed to fill the position of chief sanitary inspector in Chicago to enforce its tenement house laws, Jane Addams and Mrs. Blaine looked to New York and persuaded the city to hire Charles Ball, one of Veiller's close associates and the chief sanitary inspector in the New York Tenement House Department.

The Chicago City Homes Association also borrowed the idea of the New York Tenement House Exhibition and established a permanent Municipal Museum in Chicago. This institution, also patterned after the Hull House Labor Museum, was "devoted to the collection and interpretation of materials illustrating the physical and social conditions and the administration of cities." More than just housing reform concerned its originators, however; they devoted space to vacation schools, parks, playgrounds, municipal art, and urban transportation. Jane Addams hoped thus to make the museum a place where historical and contemporary material about cities could be gathered and also a clearing house for urban reform.

Other cities also looked to New York for personnel and for ideas to solve their housing problems. It was natural, then, that the leader of the New York movement should become a key organizer of the National Housing Association in 1910. It is also significant

that at the Association's organizational meeting settlement workers
from Boston, Chicago, New Jersey, New Orleans, and Pittsburgh
played prominent roles.[25]

IV

Many reformers in 1910 optimistically believed that the end was in
sight, that investigation and legislation would eventually solve the
problem of urban housing. Many settlement workers agreed, but
more than most in the progressive era, they saw that housing was
part of a greater problem. Florence Kelley, who had spent two decades protesting child labor in New York and Chicago, was well
aware of the need for housing reform. But as she observed disease,
and death, and despair in the tenements, she was struck by an ele-
mentary idea: it was simply the congestion of people, the overcrowding itself, that created most other social problems in the city.
Housing reform, child labor reform, and a few scattered playgrounds would do no good unless some way was discovered to reduce the density of the population. "Instead of assenting to the
belief that people who are poor must be crowded, why did we not
see years ago that people who are crowded must remain poor?"

It was not an original idea, but to Florence Kelley an idea was of
little use unless it was put to work. She conveyed her analysis to
Lillian Wald, Mary Simkhovitch, Gaylord White of Union Settlement, and a few other settlement workers. Her explanation was
simple and straightforward, and soon her friends, especially Mrs.
Simkhovitch, began to catch some of her excitement. In 1907 they
formed a Committee on the Congestion of Population with Mrs.
Simkhovitch as chairman. Borrowing a page from the New York
tenement house movement, they planned an exhibit to show the
dangers and results of congestion.[26]

The committee hired Benjamin C. Marsh, a resident of Greenwich House, as secretary. He was a persuasive young man who,
before coming to New York, had been secretary of the Pennsylvania Society to Protect Children from Cruelty, and a graduate student in economics at Chicago and Pennsylvania universities.

Somewhere along the way he had been converted by the writings of Henry George, and had become interested in the relation of rents and taxes to congestion. In the summer of 1907 Marsh went to Europe to gather material on city planning and housing that might be useful for the congestion exhibit. When it looked as though the panic of 1907 might require a postponement of the project, Carola Woerishoffer, a wealthy and beautiful young graduate of Bryn Mawr College who had recently moved to Greenwich House, stepped forward with a check for $3000 to cover the expenses of the exhibit. George Ford, a young architect and a resident of Greenwich House, advised the committee on technical matters, and the settlement became the organizational center of the Congestion Committee's work. The group enlisted support from many organizations and arranged a "varied array of maps, diagrams, charts, statistics, models, photographs and pictures." They all carried one and the same message: there were too many people crowded into tenement rooms, too many people in the workingmen's districts, too many in the city, and the new tenement house law had barely touched the problem.[27]

The exhibit began on March 9, 1908, in the Museum of Natural History and ran for nearly three weeks. Governor Charles Evans Hughes opened it, and many important people saw it. Some of the exhibits were frankly anti-urban. The Children's Aid Society showed contrasting pictures of healthy, ruddy-faced, country children tending cattle, and anemic, sickly, urban slum children playing in the streets. Professor Liberty Hyde Bailey of Cornell and others suggested that the only answer to urban congestion was to move the city dwellers to the country. Benjamin Marsh saw the major problem as an economic one and found the remedy in the single tax. Florence Kelley, Lillian Wald, Mary Simkhovitch, and others, suggested that a migration to the farms was no solution; instead, the need was for more parks, playgrounds, and schools for the city, improved tenement house laws, better transportation, and above all, comprehensive city planning to limit the number of people that could live in a given area.[28]

The New York Congestion Exhibit received generous publicity

and then went on the road. It moved to Brooklyn first, then to Richmond for the meeting of the National Conference of Charities and Correction. The next year the Committee on Congestion, together with the Municipal Arts Society, organized another exhibit on city planning which traveled to Washington, D.C., Buffalo, Elmira, Rochester, and Boston. With each exhibit there were addresses and conferences on the problem of congestion and what could be done about it. The campaign paid off. Governor Hughes appointed a Commission on Distribution of Population, and a short time later Mayor William Gaynor of New York appointed a City Commission on Congestion. And the Committee on Congestion called the first national conference on city planning for May 21, 1909 in Washington, D.C. At this meeting the National Association of City Planning was born.[29]

Benjamin Marsh presided at the Washington conference, which was attended by such authorities in the field as Charles Robinson and Frederick Law Olmsted, as well as by Secretary of the Interior Richard A. Ballinger, Speaker of the House Joseph Cannon, and Senator Francis Newlands from Nevada. Among the many speakers were such settlement workers as George Hooker, George Ford, Benjamin Marsh, and Mary Simkhovitch.

Many of the reports were filled with unexciting details and statistics, but Mrs. Simkhovitch began her presentation by describing a little pageant of Robin Hood that had been put on by the children in the neighborhood of Greenwich House. She then described the overcrowded conditions that no pageant could erase. Though she used statistics, she also explained the consequences of congestion in terms of disease and death, the demoralizing effect of noise, and lack of privacy. Congestion had many causes, she said; among them were high rents, which forced many people to live in a small space, and industrial conditions, that made it necessary to live near work. But there were social as well as economic causes. The city had advantages and conveniences. Where else could one live so close to relatives and friends and near a wide variety of churches, stores and inexpensive theatres? she asked. "The reason the poor like to live in New York is because it is interesting, convenient, and meets their social needs. They live there for the reason that I do; I like it." With that one sentence Mrs. Simkhovitch cut through the assumption held by many people at the conference, that if given the chance the poor would move out of the city. She argued for reducing the density of urban population because she liked cities and wanted to make them more livable, not because she wanted to recapture the small town. She argued for better distribution of population, better transportation, restriction of the number of people who could live in a single area, and above all, city planning on a regional basis.[30]

Mrs. Simkhovitch and other settlement workers, and a few of the other social reformers who attended the first national conference on city planning, were primarily concerned with social and economic planning. When the conference met the next year, however, it was obvious that the architects and engineers—who were concerned most with the aesthetic aspects of planning—had taken over. George Ford, Benjamin Marsh, George Hooker, and a few others, nevertheless continued to urge comprehensive economic and social planning, but the National City Planning Conference came to be dominated by those who concentrated on making the city more beautiful rather than more livable. As a result, they were often more interested in planning for the benefit of the well-to-do than in making life bearable for the tenement dwellers.[31]

Most settlement workers rejected the City Beautiful Movement, even though they occasionally co-operated in grandiose plans to improve and beautify the city. J. G. Phelps Stokes and Charles Stover were for several years prominent members of the New York Municipal Arts Society, which sought to achieve urban beauty, order, and efficiency. In addition, Stokes was chairman of the Civic Center Committee, which tried to promote the effective grouping of public buildings. Graham Taylor served on the Chicago Plan Commission, and George Hooker, long a resident of Hull House, was an active and aggressive exponent of city planning in Chicago. The Boston settlement workers co-operated in the comprehensive and sometimes utopian "Boston 1915" movement, launched in 1909 by Edward Filene and Lincoln Steffens to make Boston a more beautiful and more livable city by 1915. Many settlement workers also played the role of admiring host to Patrick Geddes, the brilliant and eccentric Scotish planner and exponent of the Garden City Movement, which sought to bring some of the best of the country into the city.[32]

Settlement workers were not opposed to making the city more beautiful; sometimes they acted and talked as if they really wanted to bring the amenities of the country and the small town back into the city. Usually, however, they were more concerned with promoting playgrounds than elaborate, formal parks, and were more interested in clean streets and tenement house laws than in grand tree-lined boulevards or elaborate ceremonial buildings. The fact that they lived in a working-class neighborhood tempered their interest in elaborate, sweeping, "city beautiful" schemes, and made them seek "realistic" and "practical" programs.

V

The settlement workers were planners in a sense. Their planning activity often took the form of negative action to block a measure that they believed would make the city or neighborhood less livable. In 1903 and 1904 when Mayor McClellan and the tenement house department of New York sponsored a bill that would have allowed the erection of temporary school buildings in public parks, they were moved to protest. Well aware of the need of new schools, they also believed in the importance of the public parks and realized that temporary measures often became permanent. The Association of Neighborhood Workers and the Outdoor Recreation League, which had fought hard to win the parks and playgrounds, protested so vigorously and effectively that they were able to block the measure.[33]

In 1905 the New York settlement workers went into action again to oppose a projected elevated railroad loop to connect the Brooklyn and Williamsburg bridges. This might have improved transportation in the area, but the workers feared that the elevated loop along Delancey Street would cause needless blight and more congestion in the Lower East Side. Instead, they favored a subway and advocated widening Delancey Street into a boulevard. Lillian Wald and Lawrence Veiller led the campaign of protest that helped defeat the measure. Stover called the first meeting and enlisted the support of many organizations on the Lower East Side. They held mass meetings, sent out form letters, appealed to influential people, persuaded newspapermen to present their point of view, and bombarded the city council with letters and petitions. Henry Street, College, and University Settlements handled the clerical work, gathered most of the names on the petitions, and encouraged their members and supporters to protest the measure. The settlements had a great deal of help in the campaign, the source of which they never suspected; only after they had won did they learn that an unknown businessman, who opposed the elevated loop because he feared it would ruin his business, had spent $50,000 to defeat the measure.[34]

But their action was not always negative. Often they advocated another, unique kind of city planning—the revival of the neighborhood as a way of restoring the city. "Neighborhoods are the source of civic strength for progress," Graham Taylor announced at one point, in a phrase characteristic of the others.[35] Robert Woods and Mary Simkhovitch were the two who put the greatest emphasis on the neighborhood in city planning. "A settlement aims to get things done for a given neighborhood," Mrs. Simkhovitch wrote. "It proposes to be the guardian of that neighborhood's interest, and through identification of the interests of the settlement group with the local interests, it forms a steadying and permanent element in a community which is more or less wavering and in flux. To work out the methods by which a neighborhood may become a consciously effective group is . . . the difficult task of the settlement everywhere." [36]

Even more than Mary Simkhovitch, Robert Woods preached revival of the neighborhood, or as he sometimes phrased it, "the recovery of the parish." In an age when industrialism and immigration made the city expand at a fantastic rate, some unit smaller than the city but larger than the family seemed necessary to prevent the collapse of public morality, good government, and civic loyalty. "The neighborhood is large enough to include in essence all the problems of the city, the State, and the Nation . . . ," Woods wrote. "It is large enough to present these problems in a recognizable community form . . . It is large enough to make some provision for the whole variety of extra-family interests and attachments. . . . It is large enough so that the facts and forces of its public life, rightly considered, have significance and dramatic compulsion. . . ." Woods preached his idea of neighborhood revival so insistently that at one conference, Jane Addams, who argued that the settlement should appeal to the whole city, became annoyed and blurted out, "Mr. Woods, I do not believe in geographical salvation." Yet even Miss Addams on occasion talked about the need to restore loyalty to the neighborhood in the industrial city. Sometimes there was a tinge of nostalgia for the social unity of the small town in the settlement workers' argument for the need of city neighborhoods; but there was also a realistic appraisal of the dehumanizing forces at work in the city and recognition of the need, especially among the occupants of the dreary tenement districts, for pride and loyalty in something larger than themselves.[37]

VI

In the early days of the movement the settlement workers were opimistic about the neighborhood idea: they would change the whole complexion of the city by placing a settlement house in each district and making it the rallying point for reform and a means for restoring pride in the local community. Gradually, however, they realized the impossibility of this task. As they began to experiment with educational reform, they discovered that every city neighborhood had a ready-made neighborhood center—the public school—only waiting to be utilized and put to work.

By the end of the century reformers were advocating the extended use of public schools for recreational and social purposes, and by 1910 a nation-wide movement was in progress to make the school a social center. Professional educators and other reformers took over the movement, but the example of the settlement continued to be important. "I suppose whenever we are framing our ideas of the school as a social center what we think of is particularly the better class of social settlements," John Dewey remarked in an address before the National Education Association in 1902. "What we want is to see the school, every public school, doing something of the same sort of work that is now done by a settlement or two scattered at wide distances thru the city." [38] Not everyone who espoused the cause of the wider use of the public school would have agreed with Dewey, but in one way or another the settlement house was both the forerunner and the model of the new kind of school that would be the social center for the community.

This movement began in New York and was led by settlement workers. In 1897 Miss Winifred Buck and James K. Paulding of University Settlement obtained permission from the Board of Education to begin boys' club work in Public School Number 20. A few years before, Jacob Riis had suggested that each public school be required by law to have a playground attached and that it be kept open after school hours.[39] The idea of using schools as club houses and recreation centers soon caught on. In Greenwich Village a church group first obtained permission to use a public school building as a recreational center, then Greenwich House, which had for some time used the gymnasium of one school and the assembly hall of another, took over the idea and, with Mary Simkhovitch leading, created one center after another.[40]

Mrs. Simkhovitch argued that the school, along with the church, had been the community center, the rallying point, for the New England village. In rural communities work and play, training and recreation, were combined. A boy learned from his father how to plant a garden, harvest hay, and build a barn; he got his physical education and an intimate knowledge of nature from tramping through the woods, camping out overnight, and observing the changing seasons. The home, the school, and the church, along with the great outdoors, combined to give young people "mental power and depth, discipline and adaptability along with a sense of purpose and belonging." All of this was rapidly passing in the large industrial city, she noted; the school had, therefore, to accept responsibility for many aspects of education that the rural youth acquired naturally. The school might also become a center for the urban neighborhood, and perhaps help to replace the sense of belonging that had been lost in the transition from rural village to industrialized city. Indeed, the schools must become social centers, Mrs. Simkhovitch asserted, if opportunity and democracy were to be preserved in America.[41] But it would take more than a playground and movable seats in the class rooms (one of the favorite suggestions of those who supported the movement) to transform the school. Most settlement workers wanted to have resident social workers to make the school a kind of social settlement. This idea appealed to many educators, including John Dewey.

In 1902 Teachers College, Columbia University, used the gift of James Speyer, a benefactor of University Settlement, to create Speyer School Settlement and a school social center. Here, both teachers and social workers could live and learn practical educational methods. Many of those who planned and supervised the work of Speyer School were settlement workers, and they consciously tried to combine the school and the settlement as a school social center.[42] Julia Richman, district superintendent of public schools on the Lower East Side was closely identified with settlement work in the area. She launched an experiment in 1906, Teachers' House, a settlement for school teachers. She hoped that by living together in a settlement, the teachers could expand their influence, become natural social workers, and create a closer link between the school and the home.[43]

The Speyer School and Teachers' House are two examples of the impact of the settlement idea on public school education during the first decade of the twentieth century. But there were dangers in having too much influence. The school social center idea caught on so rapidly that for a time it seemed a threat to the settlement movement. In 1903 William Salter, leader of the Chicago Ethical Culture Society and a long-time friend of the settlement movement, published a provocative article that posed the question, "Shall the Settlements Merge into School Extension?" Two years later Elsie

Clews Parsons, a school teacher, in an article in *Charities,* suggested that the schools become neighborhood centers and take over most of the educational activities carried on by the settlements. She remarked, in passing, that settlements, in her opinion, were necessarily only makeshift and to some degree exotic and artificial institutions which did their best work as advance agents of social experimentation but which had little permanent value.[44]

Settlement workers rose to defend their institutions and methods. Mary Simkhovitch, Graham Taylor, and James Hamilton, of University Settlement admitted that one of the settlements' important functions was to conduct social and educational experiments. It followed that they must be prepared to give up successful activities when these could be taken over by the city or by other groups. They maintained, however, that there would always be a need for further experiments, and that there were some functions that could never be taken over by the school social centers. For example, the settlement was concerned with politics and all areas of social welfare. Could a school center conduct a social survey or lobby for a bill, or be a clearing house for reform? Many settlement workers thought not; moreover, without residents, the school center could not hope to become a vital influence in the neighborhood. Yet the questions raised by Salter and Parsons were troublesome, and the speed and animosity with which the settlement workers replied revealed that they were apprehensive about the future of the settlement.[45]

The school center movement did not absorb the settlements, however; it soon became a national movement quite independent of settlement organization. In Boston, Mary Follett, a young Radcliffe graduate and later a staunch advocate of social planning, led the movement. As early as 1900, taking a clue from her club work at Roxbury Neighborhood House, she suggested that the schools be kept open after hours. Working largely through the Women's Municipal League, Miss Follett was successful in establishing several school centers for recreation and club activity in Boston. With Edward Ward, however, the school social center movement reached national significance. He had been a football and track star at Ham-

ilton College and spent his college vacations as a playground super-
visor in Buffalo. After graduation he became a Presbyterian minister, but gave up this career after a few years to go to Rochester,
New York, as director of the school center movement in that city.[46]
A number of civic organizations that had been interested in ex-
panding the use of the public school in the city had formed a
"School Extension Committee," and had established several centers.
Edward Ward crystallized the movement and made the Rochester
social centers nationally famous.

Ward, who was not a settlement worker, borrowed something
from the settlements. Before going to Rochester he studied the
school centers in New York and talked over his plans with Jane Addams in Chicago. Then, determined, he set out to make the schools
in Rochester meeting places and rallying points for their neighborhoods. He began experimentally with one school in a middle-class
neighborhood and expanded the program to include sixteen the
following year. These schools became recreation centers for all
ages: they were used as libraries, municipal baths, as people's
theatres, and assembly halls. Their overriding purpose, however,
was to revive "the neighborly spirit, the democracy that we knew
before we came to the city." The school social center was Ward's
answer to urban social disorganization and political apathy; sometimes he eagerly talked of it as the answer to all the country's
problems. He hoped, for example, that the school would replace
the saloon as a gathering place and suggested that the schoolhouse
be used at election time as a voting place.[47]

The Rochester centers received national publicity and seemed for
a time to be a great success, but some political leaders saw them as
a threat to their power and blocked the appropriations for the experiment in 1910. By that time Ward had gone to the University of
Wisconsin to organize school centers throughout the state, and to
work with the extension division of the University. He founded the
Wisconsin Bureau of Civic and Social Center Development, and in
October 1911 he called the first national conference on social centers. There was such enthusiasm that the next year the National

Community Center Association was founded. The social center idea spread, and in the 1912 campaign all three major party candidates endorsed it as a worthwhile reform.[48]

Closely associated with the school center movement was the attempt to create recreation centers in the parks. While New York pioneered in developing the school social center, Chicago led in creating recreation centers. In 1905 the South Park Commission opened ten new parks in Chicago, each equipped with a field house that had club rooms, assembly halls, as well as a gymnasium. Henry G. Forum, the president of the park commissioners, borrowed from the settlements in trying to create a recreation center to foster community loyalty. He had been a frequent observer of the various activities at the settlements, especially at Hull House and the Commons, and many of the young men and women he hired to supervise the field houses had been settlement residents. The directors of the recreation centers held folk festivals, installed branch libraries, and tried everything they could to make them into neighborhood centers. It was not easy. Flocks of people came to watch the festivals and use the field houses, but no one knew them. There was no resident group as there was in a settlement, and the recreation centers served very large areas. Yet one study showed that the recreation centers reduced juvenile delinquency in the areas.[49] There were other difficulties in transferring the settlement idea to city-owned field houses, but the movement spread. Los Angeles in particular picked up the idea of creating recreation centers out of parks and playgrounds. One of the leaders in the movement in that city was Bessie D. Stoddart, the secretary of the playground commission and a resident of the Los Angeles College Settlement.[50]

Schools and parks were not the only places in the city neighborhood that offered opportunity for development as social and community centers. In several cities settlement workers agitated for wider use of the public libraries for lectures, concerts, and social evenings.[51] Some crowded neighborhoods, however, did not have enough public buildings or social settlements for community functions even if the existing buildings were utilized to capacity. This was the situation in the area around Henry Street Settlement on the Lower East Side where one writer estimated that of 100,000 people only 1000 were served by the settlements in the area. Lillian Wald was especially worried about the effect of the cheap dance halls which attracted young people and the meeting rooms over saloons that appealed to the labor and political organizations in the area. With the aid of Jacob Riis and some other prominent citizens she was able to collect $100,000 and organize 'The Social Halls Association," which built Clinton Hall in 1904, a building containing restaurants, bowling alleys, billiard rooms, a dance hall, and assembly rooms. More than twenty labor unions used the building as their headquarters; and though the building did not prove self-supporting, in part because no liquor was served in the main building (there was a bar in the basement), it provided a badly needed social center for meetings and recreation in the area.[52]

Most settlement workers were aware that the saloon provided a natural social center in their neighborhoods. Many (though by no means all) were opposed to consumption of alcohol. Every day they observed the effects of over-indulgence on some of the men and their families. They saw the saloon as a refuge for the derelict, the street gang, the prostitute and pimp, and also as the source of much political corruption. Most of all, they saw the saloon as leading to the downfall of the young, who were first attracted by its gay and gregarious atmosphere, then trapped by its temptations. Many settlement workers for this reason came to support prohibition as a method of social reform even though they realized that there were social and economic circumstances that often drove a man to drink —poverty, living in an overcrowded room, working at a meaningless job. Yet in 1904 the New York Association of Neighborhood Workers came out officially against closing the bars on Sunday; they recognized that the saloon served as a social center, and that was more important in this instance than the dangers that lurked there.[53]

Thus, at least part of the settlement worker's motivation in campaigns to make social centers out of schools, parks, and libraries, came from the attempt to find a social substitute for the saloon. And though they never found a really adequate substitute, in their efforts to revive the neighborhood and improve the environment of the city they made important contributions to the progressive movements for social centers, housing, playgrounds, and city planning.

5

Immigrants and Negroes

Settlement workers in America discovered that, with very few exceptions, to live in a settlement was to be surrounded by immigrants and sometimes Negroes. And when they came to their work with the idea of building or restoring the neighborhood in the city, they often discovered that each immigrant or Negro group had already established a community of its own, and that such groups were themselves alienated and cut off from the rest of American society. Not all settlement workers were free of the prejudice, bigotry, and racist ideas that were so widespread in the progressive era, but being one of the few groups that had direct contact with the immigrant and the urban Negro, they learned to have a greater sympathy for the lot of the Negro or the immigrant and a better understanding of the needs of those groups than most of their generation.

The residents of Hull House began observing a bewildering number of immigrants who lived crowded together in tenements within a short distance of the settlement. "Between Halsted Street and the river live about ten thousand Italians; Neapolitans, Sicilians and Calabrians, with an occasional Lombard or Venetian," Jane Addams wrote. "To the south of Twelfth Street are many Germans, and the side streets are given over almost entirely to Polish and Russian Jews. Still farther south, these Jewish colonies merge into a huge Bohemian colony, so vast that Chicago ranks as the third Bohemian city in the world." The settlement workers were not just guessing. They laboriously identified the origins of every family in the area around Hull House. In about a third of a square mile they found people of eighteen different nationalities. They carefully transferred their data to maps, and described what they found in articles. In 1895 they published the results as *Hull-House Maps and Papers*. The book was patterned in part after Charles Booth's monumental *Life and Labour of the People of London*, and was the first systematic and detailed attempt to describe the immigrant communities of an American city. Charles Zeublin, sociologist and founder of Northwestern University Settlement, struck the tone of the book in his article on "The Chicago Ghetto" with his remark "opportunity is what the foreigner in our city needs." [1]

This indeed was the essence of the settlement approach to the problem of the immigrant; first to understand the peculiar customs and traditions of each group, and then to seek as much opportunity for them as possible. This was the settlement workers' ideal but not all were able to avoid the extremes of bigotry and hatred on the one hand, and sentimentality and condescension on the other.

Frederick A. Bushée, a young resident at Robert Woods's South End House, combined both pity and contempt for the immigrants he studied in Boston in the social investigations that later became part of book-length studies. "While the newly arrived immigrant manifests a certain degree of energy," he wrote in *The City Wilderness*, "the chief ambition in a district like this is merely to keep from falling in the social scale; and the exertion put forth is often all too small to accomplish it." His characterization of the various ethnic groups was based more on popular stereotypes than on careful observation: thus the Jew is close with his money and mainly interested in his job; the Italian is dirty and "somewhat of a liar withal"; the German is industrious; the Syrians are deceitful and "next to the Chinese, who can never be in any real sense Americans, they are the most foreign of all foreigners." Bushée continued his study of Boston's population after he left the settlement, and his "Ethnic Factors in the Population of Boston," together with his articles in *City Wilderness* and *Americans in Process* provide a great mass of statistical data on Boston's population and its problems. Occasionally Robert Woods or another settlement worker would betray the same attitude, but Bushée was not a typical settlement investigator.[2]

Most workers came to their task with sympathy and compassion. At University Settlement in New York, residents like Walter Weyl, Ernest Poole, Kellogg Durland, and William English Walling, and contributors from other settlements, like Lillian Betts and Lillian Wald, made a study of the immigrant on the Lower East Side and their articles were published in *University Settlement Studies*.[3] Another resident, John Bernheimer, edited an important study of the *Russian Jew in the United States*, to which many other settlement workers contributed.[4] Emily Greene Balch, a resident of Denison House in Boston, made herself an expert on the Slavs in America; Frances Kellor and Edith and Grace Abbott became national authorities on immigration and the immigrant; and Philip Davis developed into an important authority on Americanization and became editor of a major anthology, *Immigration and Americanization*.[5] Almost every settlement worker at one time or another wrote articles about the immigrant community in his neighborhood, or gave a speech at the women's club or the local church. A few, like Jane Addams and Lillian Wald, wrote popular accounts of their experiences with immigrant neighbors. As a group they probably erred on the side of sentimentality rather than of bigotry, but more important than the statistics they gathered was the sympathy they mustered, which allowed them to picture the immigrants as fellow human beings with joys as well as problems.

II

It was one thing to have compassion, to gather statistics and write articles, and something else again to overcome the distrust with which most immigrants regarded the settlement workers. Despite everything they did in the neighborhood, the settlement workers remained outsiders. "No one but a member of our own race can really understand us," one immigrant remarked. "No outside agency can undertake to tell my people what to do," an editor of a foreign language newspaper told John Daniels.[6] The settlement workers, most of them unmarried, had their own life, their own fellowship within the settlement. This meant that they were only artificially a part of the neighborhood. Few residents spoke any language except English, (though Mary Simkhovitch and Ernest Poole learned Yiddish and Vida Scudder knew Italian), and this further cut them off from the immigrant community.

John Gavit, a young writer who lived with his wife and family at Chicago Commons, knew first-hand the division that existed between the settlement residents and their neighbors. His wife and a woman across the street had given birth on the same day. The two mothers became well acquainted; they exchanged visits and shared problems. But within a few months, the other baby was not nearly as clean or healthy, and Mrs. Gavit constantly reminded herself how the mother across the street had to struggle to make ends meet. Gavit recalled: "Then it was difficult to get good milk in their neighborhood; even with a refrigerator and other conveniences the milk spoiled, and when the mother across the way asked how they fed their baby, and they replied that they used ——, she said, with a sigh, 'yes, but that costs too much.' It did cost. . . . Here at one blow was cut away all common ground between them. How could they advise, how could they confer, how could they pretend to help the family across the way when the conditions under which they were living were so different, when they were not on the same economic basis at all." Gavit was torn by the experience. He was tortured by the thought that his presence in the neighborhood was a mere sham until something could be done to improve the economic conditions. He decided that if each settlement could establish some co-operative scheme in its neighborhood and "put itself in part at least, on a common economic basis, that it [would] have an industrial foothold instead of being nothing but a high-flown 'ambassador' among these suffering swarms. . . ." [7]

Most immigrants found it difficult to understand the settlement workers' interest in reform and their concern for developing cooperative schemes. Instead, the political boss, who was considered corrupt by settlement workers, appeared to be a leader to the immigrants. Many immigrants found the investigations, committee meetings, and all the settlement workers' elaborate paraphernalia of reform annoying or at best meaningless. Perhaps the most serious limitation of all was that the settlements failed to attract the men in the neighborhood; the women and children came, but the men, who were the dominant force in most immigrant families, stayed away. "The social settlement here meant nothing to us men," one immigrant remembered, "we went there for an occasional shower, that was all." Yet despite limitations, many settlements became important instruments for interpreting America to the immigrants as well as interpreting the immigrants to America.[8]

The settlements especially played a part in developing leaders; they influenced only a small number but sometimes the few could be crucial. They helped inspire many young men and women to get an education or to break the dreary pattern of their lives. A young Russian Jew named Manual Levine stumbled on Hiram House in Cleveland one night a few months after his arrival in America; George Bellamy, the head resident there, helped him to revive some of the hopes and dreams that had been shattered by his initial experiences in America. Levine joined a social reform club, learned English, and worked his way through night school by teaching classes in German at the settlement. With Bellamy's aid he was admitted to Western Reserve Law School, and in 1903 Newton Baker appointed him assistant police prosecutor.[9] Philip Davis, another Russian immigrant, found encouragement and inspiration at Hull House. There he found people with whom to discuss socialism, trade unions, and democracy; there, also, were books to read. Jane Addams encouraged him to study and found money for him to attend the University of Chicago and later Harvard. His experiences prompted Davis to conclude that Hull House was "the University of good will, good English, good citizenship, in brief everything good that America stands for." Francis Hackett, another immigrant who was confused, dismayed, and discouraged with what he found in America until he discovered Hull House, said simply, "Life began for me at a social settlement." [10]

It was easier for the settlement worker to understand and inspire the young people who had intellectual interests and ambitions than to encourage the majority who, with sullen stubbornness, endured the strange and hostile environment. Vida Scudder quickly gave up the idea of reaching the Italian peasant; instead she organized an Italian Club at Denison House which appealed primarily to the intellectuals and the professional class. The club, which became an important force for promoting better understanding between Italians and Americans in the area, conducted its meetings in Italian and held lectures and debates. One of the debates turned into a riot between the socialists and anarchists. This taught the settlement workers something about the Italian's vital concern with politics, and at the same time, Italians learned something about the American's penchant for compromise.[11]

Other settlements had successful clubs for recent immigrants and most developed classes to teach English and American history. The settlement became the outpost of the English language in the middle of a foreign neighborhood. Many, like David Levinsky in Abraham Cahan's novel, must have sought out the settlement simply because it was one of the few places one could hear English spoken.[12] But the settlement's greatest contribution lay not in its teaching history or English but in its insisting that immigrants preserve the customs and traditions of the old country, assuring immigrants that it was not necessary to reject the past to become an American. Settlement workers appreciated the fact that for many immigrants the process of Americanization was harsh and often meant ripping out beliefs of a lifetime. They also witnessed the alienation of immigrant parents and their children—something the settlements tried to attenuate by teaching the children in clubs and classes. To ease the process of assimilation and to help the immigrants preserve some of their customs, and with that some of their

self-respect and feeling of identity, settlements began in the 1890's
to encourage festivals, pageants, and folk art, and to emphasize that
each group had something to contribute to American culture.[13]

III

Labor museums, handicrafts exhibits, and folk festivals did serve a
useful purpose, but of course they did not solve all the problems.
Yet the settlement's way of showing what each group could bring
to American culture made many Americans see the newcomers in a
different light, and in the twentieth century the emphasis on the
immigrant's contributions became an argument against the nativists
and those who favored restriction of immigration. Those who
defended the immigrant and his contributions to American life,
however, were not necessarily of one mind toward restriction. As
the debate over the problem reached a crescendo in the first part
of the twentieth century, settlement workers realized that the
problem could not be solved at the neighborhood level, so they
became members of national organizations and persuasive advocates for national legislation. But they could not agree on immigration policy. Walter Weyl, for several years a resident of University Settlement in New York, supplied a key to understanding the
attitude of one group of settlement workers and social reformers
who supported restrictions. "It is significant today," Weyl wrote
in the *New Democracy* in 1912, "that many of the people who are
opposed to a practically unregulated immigration are the very ones
who are seeking to promote the welfare of those immigrants who
are already in." Pointing up the settlement worker's dilemma was
Lillian Wald's argument which said almost the exact opposite. "In
discussions throughout the country of the problems of immigration," she wrote in *The House on Henry Street* in 1915, "it is significant that few, if any, of the men and women who have had
extended opportunity for social contact with the foreigner favor
a further restriction of immigration." [14]
Despite Miss Wald, Walter Weyl and other settlement workers

did come to favor some kind of regulation, usually because for them the problem of the immigrant was closely allied with the industrial situation and the problem of organized labor. They knew there was some truth in the argument used by labor leaders that unrestricted immigration would keep wages low and the labor force unorganized. In an article published in *University Settlement Studies* in 1905, Weyl supported the case of organized labor against unrestricted immigration. "The immigrant must enter American life through a job," Weyl maintained; "it is not his ability to work, but his ability to secure work that gives him a foothold." [15]

Paul Kellogg, editor of the *Survey*, a former resident of Greenwich House, and a lifetime friend of the settlement movement, argued in a similar vein before the 1911 Conference of Charities and Correction. "We suffer not because the immigrant comes with a cultural deficit," he maintained, "but because he brings to America a potential economic surplus above his wants, which is exploited." He went on to suggest a plan of regulation, applying the principle of child labor legislation: for five years after an immigrant arrived he would not be permitted to work for less than a living wage. This, according to Kellogg, would provide a breathing spell to allow the reformers to conquer the housing and congestion problems, find seats for the school children, and help eliminate crime and misery. A Slavic priest on one occasion told Emily Greene Balch, "my people are not in America, but underneath it." Kellogg's plea was, "Let us start the immigrant on the ground floor of our civilization or not at all." [16]

Robert Woods not only agreed with Kellogg and Weyl but went beyond them. He idealistically looked at his settlement as an "outpost" where all people regardless of class, sect, or ethnic group could discover what they owed to one other; but he began early to recognize that the problem of the immigrant was closely connected to political and industrial conditions in the neighborhood and the city. He appreciated the wisdom as well as the underlying motives that prompted the ward boss to find a job for the recently arrived, and decided in 1900 that the most important way to help the newcomer was to raise his economic standard "to the American level."

Woods favored the isolation or segregation of the unfit—"the
tramp, the drunkard, the pauper, the imbecile"—in order to concentrate on those who might be helped. He came eventually to the
conclusion that some immigrants were unfit, and supported "reasonable limitation of immigration in the interests of all
concerned." [17]

Although Jane Addams never came to advocate immigration restriction, she did point out the connection between immigration
and the industrial situation. In a convocation address at the University of Chicago in 1904 she challenged scholars to study the immigrants with sympathy and imagination, but also to remember that
theirs was a complex problem, more industrial than political. Despite the natural fear that organized labor had of the waves of foreigners, labor unions provided "the first real lesson of self government to many immigrants . . . for the union alone has appealed to
their necessities." Miss Addams however, did not move from an
understanding of the problem faced by organized labor to an acceptance of their solution. Later she remarked, "Until industrial
conditions in America are faced, the immigrant will continue to be
blamed for conditions for which the community is responsible." [18]

Grace Abbott, Hull House resident and immigration expert, illus-
trated the absurdity of blaming urban difficulties on the immigrants. She cited a paper done by a sanitary engineer showing that
most typhoid epidemics started in the foreign colonies and spread
to other sections. But the engineer also concluded that germ-
filled American water, not the foreigners, was ultimately to blame.
Why not demand pure water rather than the exclusion of the immigrant? [19]

IV

Settlement workers could not agree on immigration restriction, but
most of them avoided the argument of nativist propaganda which
warned that the newcomers would cause the decline of the Anglo-
Saxon race and endanger the American way of life. Most were opposed to a literacy restriction because, as Lillian Wald put it, "the

ability to read and write is what we can most easily give the immigrants when they arrive." Grace Abbott testified against this test before a Congressional Committee in January 1912. The bill passed Congress, but President Taft vetoed it. He later told Julius Rosenwald that it was Grace Abbott's statement that persuaded him to veto the bill.[20]

Most settlement workers were also quick to reject any scheme for the migration of immigrants to the farms as a solution to the problem. Many did urge, however, that immigrants be informed of the job opportunities in various sections of the country.[21] The problem of Americanizing the immigrant and the debate over restriction reached a peak as World War I forced the hasty re-examination of the immigrants' role in American culture. Even before this, however, a few settlement workers like James B. Reynolds and Robert Woods had joined the racial purists and the nativists in the formation of immigration restriction leagues.[22]

More typical of the settlement response to the "immigrant problem," however, was the action of the Hull House residents who organized the Immigrant Protective League in Chicago in 1908. More concerned for the immigrants themselves than with debates over assimilation and deterioration of Anglo-Saxon stock, this organization, under the direction of Grace Abbott, sought to ease the adjustment of the newcomer. It established waiting rooms at the railroad stations where men and women who could speak several languages could talk to recent arrivals, arrange for lodging and transportation, or help them find their relatives. Members of the League tried to take some of the heartache out of the process of moving to a new country and a new city and to prevent the very common occurrence of an immigrant's leaving one city to meet relatives in another and never finding them. The League made investigations of employment agencies, immigrant banks, and evening schools to determine how reception and adjustment could be improved and fraud prevented. While others argued for or against restriction, Grace Abbott, a tireless organizer with a quick sense of humor, worked through the Immigrant Protective League, testified before Congressional Committees, and even traveled to Europe to understand better the problems of the immigrant by seeing his homeland. Moreover, she sought to ease the social and industrial adjustment of the immigrant, a problem that she maintained was much more vital than the discussion over which groups should be excluded. She also urged that local and national governments take over the tasks begun by private organizations like the Immigrant Protective League.[23]

The same year that the Chicago workers organized the Immigrant Protective League, Lillian Wald and the residents of Henry Street Settlement, convinced that the foreigner was being exploited and that the state ought to give him protection and aid, invited Governor Charles Evans Hughes to dinner at the settlement and bombarded him there with maps, statistics, and documentary evidence. A few months later he appointed the New York Commission on Immigration to examine "the condition, welfare and industrial opportunities of aliens in the State of New York." Among the nine members were Frances Kellor and Lillian Wald. The Commission's investigation and report led to the establishment of a permanent state bureau of Industries and Immigrants with Miss Kellor as director. But state action was not enough. By 1912 most settlement workers were thinking in terms of national legislation, and they were in large part responsible for the inclusion in the Progressive party platform of a plank urging federal action to promote the assimilation, education, and advancement of immigrants.[24] Reform at the neighborhood level led almost inevitably to activity for reform in the nation.

V

Efforts to aid the urban Negro were closely related to attempts to help immigrants. Settlement workers were not free of prejudices, of course, but many were exceptions in an era that usually thought of the progressive movement as progress for whites only.

A few settlements welcomed Negroes along with Italians, Slavs, and Russian Jews, but many of the settlement workers decided that special segregated facilities would best serve the interest of Negroes.

This attitude was based partly on the idea that each neighborhood should have its own social center and partly on the fear that the presence of Negroes would drive others away. As one Boston spokesman explained, "white people would keep away from any place except a church where it was known that colored people resorted." Or as another in a Philadelphia Negro settlement put it: "Our settlement has its unique problem for it deals not with a race that is intellectually hungry, but with a race at the sensation stage of its evolution and the treatment demanded is different." [25]

By 1910 there were ten settlements scattered across the country designed especially for Negroes and several more which claimed, at least, that they had mixed clientele. In almost every case the initiative for the settlement came from interested whites rather than Negroes. In many cases larger settlements established special branches in a colored district with the dual purpose of serving the Negro population and keeping them away from the main settlement. Lillian Wald's Henry Street Settlement welcomed Negroes but also had a special colored branch. College Settlement of Philadelphia supported a separate branch for a time before it was reorganized as Starr Center. Wendell Phillips Settlement in Chicago was begun with the help of a group of Hull House residents; it was one of the few that consciously tried to provide services for both races, and that had both Negro and white residents. Cambridge Neighborhood House had, in 1914, a Negro enrollment of about 10 per cent in its classes primarily because its benefactor, Mrs. Quincy Agassiz Shaw, insisted that there be no racial discrimination. Robert Gould Shaw House in Boston was founded in 1908 as the result of work among Negroes started in 1900 by residents of South End House; it sought to lessen prejudice and secure better opportunities for the Negroes. Another important Negro settlement was Frederick Douglass Center in Chicago, founded in 1904 by Celia Parker Wooley, who championed the Negro's cause and spoke out in favor of equal opportunity.[26]

Other settlement workers more clearly mirrored the dominant attitude of the progressive era. A committee in Boston decided in 1910 that Boston was not a "healthy or suitable home for the Negro race." Hence, it was argued, settlements should not try to tempt more Negroes from the farms in the South where they naturally belonged. Yet the committee decided it did have a responsibility to aid those foolish enough to remain in the North. Frederick Bushée characterized the typical Negro in Boston as "low and coarse, revealing much more of the animal qualities than the spiritual." [27] There were probably some who agreed with Bushée; many more supported Booker T. Washington's idea of docile acceptance of an inferior status and gradual progress through manual training. But a significant number of the most important and the most vocal settlement workers felt otherwise. They opposed the dominant thought of their time and sought to aid the Negro by helping him achieve equality.[28]

For settlement workers, investigation always preceded action. Sometimes they overemphasized the gathering of statistics, but in a day when little reliable information on social problems was available, research was often a necessary prerequisite to reform. The first and most important study of the northern, urban Negro was the investigation carried out by William E. B. Du Bois, called *The Philadelphia Negro: A Social Study*, published in 1899. This study was initiated by Susan Wharton, a member of the executive committee of Philadelphia College Settlement. Impressed by the extent of the Negro problem in the city, she called a conference of interested people in her home in 1895 and arranged for the co-operation of the University of Pennsylvania in a study. The university appointed Du Bois, a young Negro intellectual then teaching at Wilberforce College in Ohio, to conduct the major portion of the study. College Settlement selected Isabel Eaton, a Smith graduate and former resident of Hull House and New York College Settlement, to investigate the nature of Negro domestic service, and her report was appended to Du Bois's study. Throughout the investigation, College Settlement and its Negro branch worked closely with Du Bois and Miss Eaton.[29]

On a more modest scale, Mary White Ovington, the daughter of a former abolitionist, undertook for New York what Du Bois had done in Philadelphia. Her interest in the plight of the Negro came primarily not from her ancestry (though that may have helped), but from her settlement experience at Greenpoint Settlement in Brooklyn, and her membership in the New York Social Reform Club. She was inspired by what she saw as a settlement worker and what she heard from the amazing circle of reformers in New York to do something for the "most neglected element" in that city. At first she planned to organize a settlement in a good Negro district to attract the intelligent Negro and the white men and women interested in the Negro. The settlement, she felt, would provide a social center where both groups could sit down together to work out a solution to the problem, but she decided to investigate first. With the help of a Greenwich House fellowship arranged by Mary Simkhovitch, she launched a study of the New York Negro that was eventually published as *Half A Man*. Her investigation reinforced her concern with the difficulties faced by the Negro, and made her revise her plan of reform. The difficulties, she decided, were too massive for any local solution; what was needed was a national movement. Mary White Ovington devoted the rest of her life to the task of fighting for equal opportunity, and became one of the major organizers of the National Association for the Advancement of Colored People.[30]

Frances Kellor, social investigator and friend of the immigrant, was another New York social worker concerned with problems faced by the urban Negro. A fellow of the College Settlement Association, she plunged into an investigation of employment agencies that was published in 1904 as *Out of Work*. She also wrote a series of articles on criminality among Negroes. One by-product of her larger study was the discovery of a network of slick agents who lured Negro girls to the cities with the promise of good wages and easy work. The Negro girls thought they were going "where the streets will be paved with gold, all will be music and flowers." They could hardly have been worse prepared. At best they were exploited; at worst they were forced to become prostitutes. Out of Miss Kellor's investigations came the National League for the Protection of Negro Women, one of the three organizations that in 1911 formed the National League on Urban Conditions among Negroes.[31]

John Daniels, a Harvard graduate from Iowa who became a resident at South End House in Boston in 1904, made another survey of the status of the Negro as a result of his settlement experience. It was Robert Woods who encouraged Daniels to undertake the study, which was finally published ten years later as *In Freedom's Birthplace*.[32]

These studies and others, together with a special issue of *Charities*, published in October 1905 and devoted entirely to the problem of the urban Negro, provided the first reliable information about the actual status of the Negro in the Northern cities.[33] They showed beyond a doubt that there were large numbers of northern Negroes living under incredibly bad conditions. They demonstrated further that the problems present in any large urban center were magnified for the Negro: in most cases he was unskilled, often unable to join a labor union, and was the first to feel the effects of unemployment; for him the problem of housing and child labor was increased, and the whole situation was complicated by unreasoning prejudice on the part of the white population, as well as by a lack of initiative and leadership among his fellow Negroes. Most of the investigators, including Du Bois and Ovington, rejected the thesis that the Negro's position and slow progress could in any way be blamed on innate racial defect or inferiority. Daniels, however, wavered over this issue and decided that in the final analysis the Negro was "found wanting in . . . fundamental moral stamina." He was inferior, Daniels concluded, but his inferiority could be reduced, if not completely abolished.[34]

The overwhelming effect of settlement investigations was to show that the position of the Negro could be improved through organization and social reform. It is not surprising that many men and women who first confronted the problem in their settlement experience took part in the organization of the National Association for the Advancement of Colored People.

VI

William English Walling, more than any other single person, was responsible for the organization of the NAACP. A Kentuckian by birth, Walling came from a wealthy family but early developed an intense sympathy for the underdog. After graduating from the University of Chicago, he spent a year at Harvard Law School, and then took a job as a factory inspector in Chicago. Living in a tenement district there, he saw the conditions of life and labor in a big city, and became concerned for the first time with the problem of the urban Negro. In Chicago he met labor leaders and radicals; he also met Jane Addams, Mary McDowell, Graham Taylor, and the rest of the remarkable group of Chicago settlement workers. He was so impressed with what he saw and heard at Hull House and other Chicago settlements that when he moved to New York in 1902 he became a resident at University Settlement on the Lower East Side. Here he joined Ernest Poole, Arthur Bullard, Walter Weyl, J. G. Phelps Stokes, Kellogg Durland, Robert Hunter, Isaac Friedman, and Howard Brubaker in what must have been one of the most remarkable collections of young reformers and writers ever assembled.

Walling was stirred to wrath by the things he saw in New York. His sister-in-law later remarked, "He felt every injustice and wrong as a personal injury." But unlike some reformers, Walling never stopped at wrath or sympathy. He had the capacity to arouse other people's interest in the problems that disturbed him. He had a genius for organization, for collecting a group of people to discuss a problem, and for looking beyond the discussion to some practical method of getting the reform started. He organized a group to publish the findings of the Industrial Commission (1893–96) in one volume—a project that finally collapsed because of lack of funds. He helped organize the New York Child Labor Committee in 1902, and was one of the small group responsible for establishing the National Women's Trade Union League in 1903. He also wrote a great many articles for the *Outlook,* the *Independent,* and other magazines, exposing conditions in a large city and suggesting reforms.

In 1905 Walling went to Russia to cover the abortive Russian Revolution that seemed so promising to many American reformers when it began. In 1907 he returned from Europe with his new wife Anna Strunsky, and took an apartment in New York which quickly became a gathering place for many of the young radicals and social workers in the city. By 1907 Walling was a socialist, though he did not join the party officially until later. Like most of the New York socialist intellectuals, however, he never rejected social reform, and he continued to have much in common with the social workers and progressives who wished to alter the American system through reform rather than overthrow it by revolution.[35]

Although the Wallings spent most of their time writing articles and giving lectures on the Russian Revolution, they remained concerned with American social problems. When they were in Chicago late in 1908, a race riot broke out in Springfield, and their decision to observe the racial tension and unrest there led, ultimately, to the organization of the NAACP.

They stayed a week in Springfield and were horrified by what they saw. Before returning to New York, Mrs. Walling described the riot for a Boston Negro newspaper, and Walling wrote an article for the *Independent* entitled "The Race War in the North." He discussed the Springfield riot and the larger aspects of the Negro problem, and urged national action to promote Negro equality. "Either the spirit of the abolitionists, of Lincoln and of Lovejoy, must be revived and we must come to treat the Negro on a plane of absolute political and social equality," Walling announced, "or Vardaman and Tillman will soon have transferred the race war to the North." The Wallings continued their lecture tour on the Russian Revolution, but the problem of the American Negro was not far from their minds. They found themselves talking more and more about the condition of the Negro in the United States and less and less about the condition of the peasant in Russia.

After their lecture at Cooper Union in December 1908, Mary

White Ovington, who had read the *Independent* article, introduced herself to the Wallings and asked if a movement to aid the Negro had been organized. Mary Ovington was then living in a Negro tenement, completing her research for *Half A Man*. She agreed with the Wallings that "The spirit of the abolitionists must be revived." The Wallings and Miss Ovington adjourned to a nearby restaurant to discuss the practical organization of a movement to help the Negro achieve equality. They agreed to meet a few days later at the Wallings's New York apartment and invited Charles Edward Russell and Henry Moskowitz to join them. Russell, like Walling, was a socialist and writer; Moskowitz, a Rumanian Jew, was then head resident of Madison House, a social settlement on the Lower East Side. As it turned out, Russell was not able to come to the first meeting, so Walling, Moskowitz, and Miss Ovington drew up the initial plans for the organization of the NAACP, conceived the idea of a major call for action to be issued on Lincoln's birthday 1909, and called for a conference on the status of the Negro in the United States. It has been noted that the three who organized the NAACP were a Southerner, a daughter of an abolitionist, and a Jew; it seems even more significant that all three were settlement workers.[36]

Walling, Moskowitz, and Miss Ovington invited settlement workers Florence Kelley and Lillian Wald to join them. Miss Ovington also asked some of her Negro friends to come to the early planning sessions, and Charles Edward Russell joined the small group that met frequently in January 1909 at the Wallings's apartment at 21 West Thirty-eighth Street. The early meetings were mostly concerned with publicity, organization, fund-raising, and membership, and the settlement workers with their wide variety of experience proved invaluable.[37] They knew influential people, and for them fund-raising and publicity were almost daily tasks. Most importantly, they had helped to organize, among other things, the Immigrant Protective League, the National Women's Trade Union League, a national investigation of women and children in industry, and a campaign for a federal children's bureau. Thus, the NAACP was not organized in a vacuum; it was part of a broad movement for social justice and reform, part of the progressive movement.[38]

The few who began the NAACP were very much concerned that their organization might appear too radical, and it was primarily for this reason that they asked Oswald Garrison Villard, the respectable and influential editor of the *New York Evening Post* and the *Nation* to join them to help with the publicity and perhaps counteract the impression that the Association was made up of crackpots and radicals. Villard drafted a call for a national conference on the status of the Negro that was issued on Lincoln's birthday 1909. More than a third of those who signed the document were settlement workers. They played an important part in organizing the conference that opened on May 30 with a reception at Henry Street Settlement, one of the few places in the city that would accept a mixed group. William E. B. Du Bois and several other members of the Niagara Movement, a militant Negro organization formed in 1905, attended the conference.

The delegates, both Negroes and whites, adopted a platform of fundamental rights that included the abolition of all forced segregation, equal educational advantages for colored and white, enfranchisement of the Negro, and enforcement of the Fourteenth and Fifteenth Amendments. They also elected a permanent committee "to organize a complete plan of defense for the legitimate rights of the Negro race in this country." From this grew the National Association for the Advancement of Colored People, incorporated in 1910. Of the thirty-five members of that first committee, eight were settlement workers. One was Jane Addams, elected even though she was not present because, in the words of Mrs. Walling, she was one of "the few whom we felt we can lean upon." [39]

It was not just coincidence that settlement workers played an important part in the organization of the NAACP. Just as they were leaders in the struggle to Americanize the immigrant, so were they in the vanguard of the fight for Negro equality. They fought for equal rights for all in an era often dominated by racist hysteria.

6

The Settlements and
the Labor Movement

Settlement workers soon discovered that to create parks and playgrounds, to attempt to improve the lot of the immigrant, indeed merely to observe the struggle for existence going on in the industrial city, was to become convinced that there were economic roots to most problems. And this conclusion made them sympathetic toward and sometimes allied with organized labor. "Settlement workers soon learn that economic conditions control the social structure," Mrs. Alzina Stevens decided in 1897, "and if they fail to see this they do not make very valuable settlement workers."

Mrs. Stevens, had been forced to go to work in a textile mill when only thirteen, and had a finger missing on one hand to remind her of the experience. She had been an important leader in the Knights of Labor before going to Hull House. It is not surprising that she was an ardent champion of labor, but many settlement workers with more genteel backgrounds also learned to defend labor's right to organize and bargain collectively.[1] "At Hull House one got into the labor movement as a matter of course, without realizing how or when," Alice Hamilton remarked. What was true of Hull House was true of many other settlements. Labor unions met regularly at Denison House and South End House in Boston, at University Settlement and Henry Street Settlement in New York, at Chicago Commons and the University of Chicago Settlement, and there at least, workingmen and women could usually find support for their point of view.[2]

At first many of the workingmen distrusted the motives of the settlement workers; some even feared that they were spies sent by the employers to detect secret labor organizations. Others refused to have anything to do with a settlement because they thought it was connected with charity or the church. As one trade union member who belonged to a club at University Settlement in New York commented, "It is not a charity in any sense of the word, yet many people in this vicinity will not attend on that account."[3] Labor leaders often charged that settlement workers were ready to give up the cause of a strike in the name of arbitration or mediation, more eager to investigate than to act, and more concerned with gathering statistics than with improving the lot of the workingman. "The workers are not bugs to be examined under the lenses of a microscope, by intellectuals on a sociological slumming tour," Samuel Gompers announced petulantly at one point.[4]

There was some justification for the labor leader's suspicion and resentment of settlement workers. There were always a few residents like the pallid young man in Isaac Friedman's novel *By Bread Alone,* who had come to a settlement "with the avowed purpose of regenerating the laboring men in a month at the outermost, within a week provided he struck the right material." There were even a few who opposed raising wages because they believed that workingmen would simply use the extra money to indulge their "vulgar passions."[5] Even the majority of settlement workers who were sympathetic to the cause of organized labor could not always avoid paternalism. And nearly all abhorred violence. "If the labor union could become more of a school," Graham Taylor decided, "its usefulness would be vastly increased." "It is only occasionally that I get a glimpse of the chivalry of labor," Jane Addams admitted to Henry Demarest Lloyd, "so much of the time it seems so sordid."[6]

Of course some of organized labor was sordid, and settlement workers constantly worried both about the corruption and violence practised by a few labor leaders, and the racial prejudice and narrow exclusiveness promoted by others. Mrs. Stevens was equally critical of those who were sentimental in their support of labor and those who opposed labor's right to organize. When one young resident of Hull House defended a notoriously corrupt labor leader, Mrs. Stevens informed her sharply that it was the worst kind of snobbishness "to assume that you must not have the same standards of honor for working people as you have for the well to do." [7] Despite difficulties and misunderstandings, however, settlement workers did support organized labor with both words and actions, and sometimes the two groups co-operated in promoting reform.[8] They investigated and publicized working conditions in several industries, and fought for social welfare legislation to aid workingmen. Moreover, some of them, notably Alice Hamilton, made important contributions toward public health and combatting industrial diseases.[9]

Not least among the settlement workers' contributions, however, was their ardent defense of labor unions at a time when they had few defenders. "The organization of labor is, for the future, one of the safeguards of democracy and of social progress," the editor of a settlement periodical announced in 1897. "The great improvement in all the conditions of labor that has been wrought during recent years, is without all possible question, the result of working class organization," Robert Woods wrote. "If the trade unions of this city were better understood . . . they would generally be regarded . . . as the most practical bond of brotherhood next to the Christian Church," Graham Taylor decided.[10] No one defended organized labor more vigorously or consistently than Jane Addams, even though some aspects of labor's struggle did seem sordid to her. She made thousands of speeches supporting the worker's right to organize, and even during such tense situations as the Pullman Strike in 1894 and the strike of the Chicago Building Trades Council in 1900 when anti-labor feeling was rampant, she publicly defended the worker's right to strike and to bargain collectively. To make her point, she was not afraid to attack people as prominent as the president of Harvard and the president of the Pullman Company.[11]

II

Settlement workers, however, did more than talk. Jane Addams made it a policy to hire only union members for work at Hull House. But on one occasion she employed a Negro cook who was not permitted to join a union in Chicago. She protested, to no avail. Finally Grace Abbott arranged for the cook to join a Negro local in St. Louis, and Jane Addams, always the pragmatist, accepted the compromise and continued to work for the rights of Negroes and of organized labor.[12]

In 1896 Hull House reformers came to the aid of a group of striking textile workers who lived nearby. They held mass meetings to protest against wages and working conditions, and collected money to help feed the workers; and when the strike proved unsuccessful they raised more money to send the black-listed leaders out of the city. When Eugene Debs was arrested during the Pullman Strike, Alzina Stevens and Florence Kelley organized a mass protest meeting, and Mrs. Stevens arranged a hiding-place where Debs could drown his discouragement in drink away from the prying eyes of newspapermen.[13]

Not every settlement worker in Chicago wanted his name associated with Debs, and not every settlement worker volunteered to join the picket lines during a strike. Jane Addams rarely picketed because she thought she could be more useful in other ways. Alice Hamilton admitted that she would picket only in the evening, when she was least likely to be arrested. Yet Ellen Starr, gentle and introspective, often put aside her other projects and fearlessly joined the strikers; she also collected money, made speeches, and wrote articles in defense of workingmen. Once, when she joined the striking employees of a Chicago restaurant in their protest of long hours and low wages, she was arrested for interfering with the police. At other times, in 1910 and 1915, she supported the textile workers in their strikes for better wages and working conditions and for recognition of their union. Explaining why the textile workers went on strike against hopeless odds, she wrote: "if one must starve, there are compensations in starving in a fight for freedom that are not found in starving for employers' profits." Statements of this kind and her active and aggressive support of labor won Ellen Starr the co-operation and gratitude of such labor leaders as Sidney Hillman and Jacob Potofsky.[14]

Raymond Robins was another Chicago settlement worker who was respected and praised by labor leaders in the city. "Organized labor has no truer friend or abler advocate," John Fitzpatrick, the president of the Chicago Federation of Labor, asserted in 1908. Robins won this praise by defending labor in speeches around the country and by working closely with labor leaders while he was a settlement worker at Chicago Commons and Northwestern University Settlement. He was especially effective in protesting against the 1907 Supreme Court decision in the Danbury Hatters' case. Like Mrs. Stevens, he had been a member of a labor union; he had led a strike in a Tennessee coal mine and joined a union in a Colorado silver mine before he was twenty. Robins defended labor's right to use the strike and the secondary boycott to win a fair wage and decent working conditions.[15]

Not every settlement worker was free of paternalism or sentimentality, but there was a considerable amount of co-operation between settlement workers and labor leaders, especially in the twentieth century. John F. O'Sullivan, a seaman turned streetcar operator and labor organizer, served for many years on the Council of Robert Woods's South End House. Woods also had the friendly co-operation of Henry Abrahams, the secretary of the Boston Central Labor Union, whom he once helped elect to the school board. Sidney Hillman, a labor leader and pioneer industrial unionist, was strongly influenced as a young man by Jane Addams and the Hull House group. When he moved to New York in 1914 to become chief representative of the International Ladies Garment Workers Union before the Board of Conciliation, Hillman went to live at Lillian Wald's Henry Street Settlement. The settlement represented one of the few places where the cause of organized labor could get sympathetic support.[16]

The settlement workers' active and vocal support of organized labor, although pleasing to young labor leaders like Hillman, sometimes got them into difficulty with the people who served on their boards and those who contributed money to the settlement. "Denison House threw itself into one or two strikes," Vida Scudder remembered. "We welcomed strike meetings at the house, we picketed a little, we incurred horrified criticism from our patrons uptown." A prospective doner refused to give money to the University of Chicago Settlement when he learned that the settlements sympathized with labor; he was convinced that the unions in Chicago were "nothing but a band of lawless sluggers who seek to attain their ends by intimidation and violence." Hull House also lost contributions and support from some who thought that it had become "thoroughly unionized." Several donors withdrew their financial gifts from Elizabeth Peabody House in Boston when Eva White, the head resident, insisted that the new settlement building be constructed by union labor. Yet Mrs. Quincy Agassiz Shaw, the principal benefactor of Civic Service House, was in complete agreement with Philip Davis's and Meyer Bloomfield's support of organized labor. And in Chicago, though Julius Rosenwald disagreed with the Hull House ladies, he had his personal chauffeur deliver Grace Abbott to a meeting of garment workers where she joined them in picketing his factory.[17]

III

While most of the important settlements were pro-labor in their attitudes and actions, they also felt it was their responsibility, as Jane Addams expressed it, to "take a larger and steadier view than is always possible for the workingman . . . or the capitalist . . . ," and they believed that they had a special responsibility to promote conciliation and industrial peace by re-establishing communication between labor and management. Lillian Wald and Henry Moskowitz represented the public on the board of sanitary control that enforced standards of health and safety in New York's textile factories. James Mullenbach of Chicago Commons served for many years as chairman of the Joint Arbitration Board of the garment workers and the clothing firm of Hart, Schaffner, and Marx.

Graham Taylor was also an arbitrator of industrial disputes. His position as head resident of a well-known settlement and his reputation for moderate fairness often made him one of the few men acceptable to both sides. Taylor learned, however, that a mediator risked losing the support of one or both parties in a bitter conflict. In 1900, for example, while the Chicago Commons Association was building a new settlement house, the workmen went on strike against the contractor. The walkout was city-wide in scope, but Taylor believed that he had "an insight into the real differences which divided them," and he eventually succeeded in getting a temporary solution because he had "the confidence of the more conservative men on both sides." But there were many workers and labor leaders who disapproved of the concessions; and Taylor admitted that his part in the arbitration hurt the Chicago Commons for a time. Though he maintained that it was his public duty "to stand between and try to make peace on the basis of justice," he discovered, as others had, that the role of labor champion and the role of industrial conciliator often led to conflict and uneasiness.[18]

In addition to arbitrating strikes many settlement workers made conscious, if often artificial, attempts to bring labor union members and employers together at the settlement houses for discussions and lectures. Probably the most successful of these groups was the "Free Floor Discussion" at Chicago Commons, where once a week for seven years professor and anarchist, labor leader and employer, argued over their differences, but with a three-minute limit for each speaker. A resident of the Commons described the "Free Floor Discussion" as "one of the few cases of self-conscious democracy in the wilderness of social confusion and industrial chaos. . . ." This appraisal was overly optimistic; but at least the weekly meetings allowed a variety of people to express their opinions harmlessly.[19]

Many settlements organized elaborate conferences on social and economic problems. With men like Henry Demarest Lloyd, Richard T. Ely, and Clarence Darrow giving addresses, the settlement workers hoped to attract employers as well as laboring men and professors. In addition, radicals from Europe stopped at the settlements. Sidney and Beatrice Webb, H. G. Wells, Peter Kropotkin, the Russian anarchist, and Catherine Breshkovsky, "the grandmother of the Russian Revolution," were among those visiting the settlements. Usually they spoke without limitations, although on one occasion Emma Goldman was not allowed to talk at Chicago Commons. English radicals often startled the settlement workers by supporting socialism but opposing universal education, and by talking about the nobility of labor while snubbing American workingmen and socialists.[20] These foreign and American visitors helped make some settlements exciting places to live, but the conferences and discussions never fulfilled the settlement workers' broader hopes. Differences remained between laboring men and employers, and among socialists, anarchists, and professors, that no amount of talking could erase. Nor could the settlement workers prevent those differences occasionally from flaring into strikes and violence.

The settlement workers did run the risk of being charged with supporting and harboring radicals when they allowed anarchists and socialists to use their facilities and when they supported organized labor. On several occasions Chicago newspapers (especially the *Inter-Ocean* and the *Chronicle*) attacked the settlements in the city as "nests of anarchy." In 1901, shortly after the assassination of President McKinley, a police dragnet arrested hundreds of suspected radicals. One of those picked up was Abraham Isaaks, a philosophical anarchist and editor of a little publication, *Free Society*, who had been a frequent visitor at both Hull House and Chicago Commons, and an ardent participant in many discussions. As soon as Raymond Robins and Jane Addams heard of Isaaks's arrest, they rushed to his defense, feeling that free discussion at the settlements was at stake. They tried to get the prisoners released on bail, and when that failed, they went directly to the mayor to protest his use of police power. Because of the settlement workers' intervention, the mayor soon released the prisoners; but those who disapproved of this sympathy for radicals broke windows at both Hull House and Chicago Commons.[21]

In 1908 the Chicago settlements joined other groups in challenging the threatened deportation of an obscure Russian carpenter. He was finally granted political asylum in the United States, but the *Inter-Ocean* attacked the defenders of the immigrant as identical with those "always expressing 'sympathy' for the murderers and would-be murderers who call themselves 'anarchists.' " The *Chronicle* charged that

> the Social Settlements in this city have been made identical with opposition to the Constitution of the United States and hostile to the laws of Illinois. . . . It is a cruel fate which guides the ignorant immigrant into the socialist precincts of Hull House and Chicago Commons. It is a sad misuse of Chicago money which maintains these alluring pitfalls for the trustful and helpless.

The same year the settlements protested the gunning down of a feeble-minded youth named Jeremiah Averbuck, who called himself an anarchist. The *Inter-Ocean* pointed out that he had learned his radicalism at the settlement houses, "schools expressly established . . . for teaching anarchy." Actually, the settlement workers successfully prevented a demonstration at the burial of the slain boy, and although some papers referred to them as anarchists and disturbers of the peace, to many socialists in the city, they were "cowards and bourgeoisie." This, in itself, was a fitting tribute to the success of the settlement workers' middle-of-the-road policy of conciliation.[22]

It is ironical that settlement workers like Jane Addams, Graham Taylor, and Robert Woods should have been criticized for defending radicals, for like most progressives, they advocated no drastic change in the economic system. Most opposed such organizations as the Industrial Workers of the World. Instead, they aligned themselves with the conservative labor movement to prevent the more radical elements from gaining control and to preserve the American system of free enterprise.

During the first decade of the twentieth century, however, a few settlement workers, including J. G. Phelps Stokes, Robert Hunter, William English Walling, and Ernest Poole, decided that trade unions and social settlements would never solve the increasing problems they saw in America. They joined the Socialist party, though they did not cease to work for social reform. Florence Kelley and Vida Scudder, on the other hand, had been avowed socialists for many years and impatient with the lack of class consciousness among the workingmen in America. Increasing labor conflict in the twentieth century only convinced them more that the American economic system could not be saved through organized labor. "Can anything short of the socialistic reorganization of industry do anything more than use rose water for the plague?" Florence Kelley asked in 1907.[23] Most workers felt that organized labor was more useful than rose water; and they believed strong unions were necessary to the survival of American democracy. But they were often caught by the dilemma of wanting to help labor and to prevent violence and promote industrial peace at the same time. Despite difficulties, they did help. Their dilemma and their contributions can be seen most clearly in the Chicago stockyards strike of 1904.

IV

At 11:30 on the morning of July 12, 1904, "knockers" on the killing floors of the six largest packing plants in Chicago stopped stunning cattle, and two thousand men went on strike. An aura of suspense settled down over the stockyards, for many of the workers and their families remembered the violence and bloodshed of the strikes of 1886 and 1894. Mary McDowell, who came to be called by some "the angel of the stockyards," remembered the 1894 strike. She had come to live at the University of Chicago Settlement only a few weeks after the strike had been settled, and she had found her neighbors "more hopeless than bitter, more conservative than radical, without courage and self confidence." To everyone's surprise, however, the strike of 1904 began in an orderly fashion. There was no violence, no confusion, no disorder. The men simply walked out. In the ten years since 1894 things had changed in the "district back of the yards." [24]

The two people primarily responsible for the changed situation in the stockyards district were Mary McDowell and Michael Donnelly. Mary McDowell, the daughter of a prosperous Chicago businessman, became a settlement worker primarily because of her interest in children. She taught a kindergarten at Hull House for a few months in 1890. In 1894, a faculty committee at the University of Chicago, on the advice of Jane Addams, selected her as head resident of their settlement, which was to serve in part as a laboratory for the departments of economics and sociology. "Here was something I had been looking for all my life," she later recalled, "a chance to work with the least skilled workers in our greatest industry; not *for* them as a missionary, but *with* them as a neighbor and seeker after truth. . . ." This "immigrant from Evanston," as she described herself, quickly discovered that the people "back of the yards" needed more than kindergartens and social surveys. The neighborhood near the stockyards was virtually isolated from the rest of Chicago; it was an area of drab houses, dirty streets, and smoke-filled air. Open sewers, uncollected garbage, and the rotting refuse from the stockyards provided a combination of odors that was unbearable and inescapable. Nearby, the stagnant backwater of the Chicago River added its own stench, and waste carbonic acid gas gave it the descriptive name of "Bubbly Creek." Packing plants dominated the area, and jobs there drew Slavs, Poles, and Lithuanians to the district. Employment was at best uncertain, and a surplus of nearly five thousand served to keep wages low, hours long, and working conditions incredibly bad. In 1894 the only labor organizations in the district were a few small unions which met secretly. During her first year at the settlement Mary McDowell stumbled upon one of these organizations and invited them to hear Jane Addams, but the workmen thought the settlement workers were spies sent by the packers.[25]

Mary McDowell and the other residents at the University of Chicago Settlement set out to change conditions in the neighborhood. They organized civic clubs which worked to improve the garbage collection, they protested to City Hall and the Health Department, they lectured and pleaded and preached, but they managed to improve conditions of living and labor very little. Gradually, however, the settlement workers began to break down the suspicions of the people in the neighborhood. By 1900 the men no longer feared that they were packer spies; they admired Mary McDowell and thought of her as a friend and ally.[26]

In 1900 Michael Donnelly, a tall Irish sheep-butcher with piercing eyes and a handle-bar mustache, came into the stockyards district and began to organize the men into labor unions. One of the first persons Donnelly sought out was Mary McDowell, and he quickly won her support and encouragement. Donnelly was a labor leader of the Samuel Gompers type; he sought higher wages and better working conditions through organization, and opposed strikes, at least until the union was strong enough to have a chance of victory. To organize the workers in the stockyards district of Chicago was no easy task, but by the summer of 1904 Donnelly had started twenty-seven unions, all affiliated with the Amalgamated Meat Cutters and Butcher Workmen of North America, and the American Federation of Labor. Settlement residents co-operated with him in organizing the men in the neighborhood, and took the initiative in enlisting the women. "The unions are leaving a loophole for their own undoing by not organizing the women," Mary McDowell announced in an address reported by the press, "and the women are lowering their own position in the industrial world by not following the example of the men and forming their own unions." [27]

Some of the women in the neighborhood who worked at the stockyards had organized the Maud Gonne Club (after the Irish patriot), and had even tried to protest against their low wages by staging a demonstration. When they heard that Mary McDowell favored women's trade unions, they asked her to help them turn their club into a union. She in turn approached Donnelly, called a meeting in the settlement gymnasium, and the Maud Gonne Club became the nucleus for "Local Number 183, Amalgamated Meat Cutters and Butcher Workmen of North America." "With you so kind, we ought to grow in the right direction and have patience to make everything successful," one of the members of the union wrote to Mary McDowell. The girls made her a member in full standing, and for a time she served as vice president of Local 183, which met regularly at the settlement.[28]

Organization increased the morale of the workmen, but it did little to improve the pay scale or the working conditions in the packing plants. Unskilled wages were raised from sixteen cents an hour to eighteen and a half cents an hour, however, and the extra two and a half cents sometimes enabled a family to stay above the poverty line. Donnelly and the trade unions joined the settlement workers in agitating for a child labor law, and their combined efforts helped to win the passage of a law that prohibited children under sixteen from working more than eight hours in the packing plants. The surplus labor force, however, increased every day by immigrant Slavs and Lithuanians, gave the packers a weapon that effectively kept wages low.[29]

Early in May, 1904, the National Convention of the Amalgamated Meat Cutters and Butcher Workmen of North America, meeting in Cincinnati, agreed on a demand of twenty-five cents an hour for unskilled workers. In the face of this demand, the Chicago packers on May 28 reduced the unskilled wage rate to sixteen cents an hour. Pleading and talking accomplished nothing, and on July 12 the workers went on strike. Though the issue was unskilled wages, skilled workers struck in sympathy.[30]

With more than twenty thousand men and women on strike and Negro scabs being imported by the carload, the danger of violence and bloodshed was great. These had been present at every other major strike in the stockyards district, but this time settlement workers and labor leaders co-operated to keep the violence at a minimum. They kept the gymnasium at the settlement open all day long for meetings, receptions, and teas. Indeed, one of the men in the neighborhood later labeled the upheaval of 1904 "the pink tea strike." [31]

A number of Chicago settlement workers, many of them members of the newly formed Women's Trade Union League (which Donnelly also had a part in founding), spoke to groups of men and women in the gymnasium of University Settlement during the course of the strike. In previous strikes, the women had been the most hysterical, but in 1904, aided by the settlement workers, they co-operated with Donnelly in setting up a warning system to prevent violence and unnecessary incidents. They printed placards and handbills in several languages, urging men to stay off the streets and away from the saloons, and distributed them throughout the district. The settlement workers and the labor leaders were primarily responsible for the success of the campaigns. There were fewer arrests in July and August 1904 than there had been the previous summer.[32]

Despite precautions, however, incidents did occur, and the headlines of the newspapers screamed: "Two Men Shot in Riot," "Strikers Wage Bitter Fight," "Mobs Lynch Non-Union Man." Mary McDowell felt that the press, by blowing up small incidents, was unfair to the strikers. In order to counteract the sensational publicity, she wrote articles for newspapers and magazines. She contrasted the contest of 1904 with that of 1894. In 1894 the strikers could not tell Mr. Armour why they had walked out; they did not know. In 1904 the strike order was not issued until after a favorable referendum. Mary McDowell credited the labor unions with improving conditions in the district, but she also demonstrated, by describing the conditions of life and labor in the stockyards district, that there was much yet to be done.[33]

Miss McDowell was not alone in defending the workers in the strike. The University of Chicago Settlement, located next door to the labor union and strike headquarters, became a convenient base for muckrakers, newspapermen, economists, and others who came to report the strike or help the workers. One of these, Ernest Poole, a young resident of University Settlement in New York who had written muckraking articles on child labor and "the lung block," came back to his hometown to cover the strike for several magazines, and stayed to become the press agent for the labor unions. Because he was a settlement worker himself and knew Mary McDowell, it was natural that Poole stayed at the University of Chicago Settlement while he reported the strike. Poole wrote several articles, including one for the *Independent* in which he told the story of a young Lithuanian stockyards worker who was given hope and self-respect through a trade union.[34]

Poole collaborated on a piece for the *Outlook* with William Hard, a "brilliant, witty, dark, little man" who had been head worker at Northwestern Settlement and a resident at Hull House while employed as a reporter and editorial writer for the *Chicago Tribune.* Hard was one of the group who often gathered at the University of Chicago Settlement for dinner or for an informal discussion during the strike.[35] Upton Sinclair also ate his meals at the settlement and lived in a room nearby when he collected material for his novel *The Jungle.* Sinclair loved to argue about socialism and the labor movement, and he enjoyed baiting the more moderate settlement workers like Jane Addams, Alice Hamilton, and Mary McDowell; but he welcomed their advice when it came to sources and color for his novel. John Commons, a young economist from the University of Wisconsin, was another frequent visitor during the strike. Here was a chance to study the labor movement at first hand, and Commons made the most of his primary source. Along with Poole, he evaded the pickets one night and explored the inside of one of the packing plants.[36]

From the dedicated band that gathered each evening for dinner came a flow of articles, editorials, novels, and speeches that told the social and human implications of the strike. "Eighteen cents an hour, ten hours a day, four days a week, seven in a family—this is the economic problem that Packingtown is trying to solve," wrote Mary McDowell. "Shall men be treated as mere expense items?" This was the immediate question of the strike, Ernest Poole asserted. Graham Taylor and his son, writing in the *Daily News* and the *Commons,* pleaded for arbitration and conciliation. Ernest Poole and William Hard, however, told in the *Outlook* how the strikers were making their own contribution to the science of arbitration by holding out for a living wage against the law of supply and demand, the packers' only criterion in setting a wage scale.[37]

On July 22, 1904, the strike appeared to be settled. The labor leaders recommended that the unions accept the packers' offer to arbitrate the issue of wages after the strikers returned to work, but when the men started back there was obvious discrimination against the leaders of the strike. When the packers refused to guarantee that all the union members would be rehired, Donnelly called a second strike. What should a settlement worker do in the face of the labor leader's decision to reject the packers' offer of arbitration? This was the dilemma that Mary McDowell faced after Donnelly called the second strike. Like most settlement workers, she had always preached arbitration as the only reasonable answer to a strike. Graham Taylor criticized the strikers for refusing to accept the packers' offer, but Mary McDowell decided that the labor unions in the stockyards were more important than the principle of arbitration. If the packers did not take back the leaders, there could be no real arbitration. She therefore stuck by Donnelly and the unions.[38]

The newspapers, which in the beginning had been sympathetic to the strikers, now became hostile, and the danger of violence increased. Union members had been kept under control by the combined efforts of the settlement workers and Michael Donnelly, but, as the second strike dragged on through August and funds dwindled, some of the men demanded more positive action. Ernest Poole, who spent much of his time circulating among the strikers, one Saturday night overhead a group of discontented union men planning to emphasize their grievances by lynching one or two of the Negro scabs. The next day he went to see Jane Addams, explained the situation, and asked for help in collecting money for the strike fund. Miss Addams spent all day Sunday calling on her "sympathetic rich friends," and by nightfall she had collected five thousand dollars. With the money in hand, Poole was able to dissuade the angry strikers from carrying out their plans, and no Negroes were lynched.[39]

Mary McDowell was also busy collecting money to enable the workers to remain on strike, but at the same time she was growing more and more concerned over the hungry children who came every day to the settlement. Here was the settlement workers' problem in human terms, and it also was faced by the labor leaders— how hungry did the children have to become before one gave up fighting for principle, or even for a living wage, and chose conciliation? In the end, the hunger of the children won out. September came, and labor leaders realized that they could not hold out much longer. Fearing that a radical element might take charge, one of the leaders invited Mary McDowell to a meeting of the strikers because he knew that if anyone could quiet the men it was she. She reluctantly urged the workers to try to reopen negotiations, knowing full well that the packers would not give an inch and that the reopening of negotiations would mean the loss of the strike. Yet she feared that the unions themselves would be destroyed if the strike continued much longer. Donnelly and the other leaders agreed with her that negotiations had to be reopened, but the labor leaders did not stand a chance of even getting inside the packers' office. Miss McDowell, therefore contacted her friend Cornelia DeBey, a young doctor, who had sympathized with the union but had taken no active part in the strike. Dr. DeBey went to see J. Ogden Armour and opened the way for negotiations. A short time later Miss McDowell, accompanied by Jane Addams, placed the strikers' position before Armour. He agreed to negotiate with Donnelly and a committee from the labor unions.[40]

The packers refused to give the unskilled workers the two and a half cents they had demanded. The strikers surrendered, there was no doubt about that; but it was an honorable surrender. The packers negotiated with a committee from the labor unions and agreed to reinstate the leaders. One labor journal, while admitting defeat, still considered the fact that the packers had negotiated with the leaders, "a triumph of union labor," and a demonstration to the world that union labor was far superior to non-union labor. A butcher told Mary McDowell as he went back to work that the strike had been worthwhile, because the world had learned that "Michael Donnelly represents quite as important an interest as does Mr. Armour."[41] The world had not really learned that lesson in 1904, but the butcher had salvaged some self-respect out of the strike, and that was important, too.

V

Yet more than salvaging a workman's self-respect was accomplished by the stockyards strike. The settlement workers played an important part in winning some positive gains from the bitter struggle of the summer of 1904. The strike received nation-wide publicity, and for that the settlement workers were in part responsible. Even before the strike was over, two items, one an article by Mary McDowell, the other, an editorial by William Hard, caused President Roosevelt to act. Both settlement workers described conditions in the stockyards and emphasized the role labor unions had played in Americanizing the immigrants and decreasing violence during the strike. Roosevelt sent the article and the editorial to Carroll D. Wright of the Department of Commerce and Labor and asked him to investigate conditions in the stockyards. Ethelbert Stewart stayed at the University of Chicago Settlement while conducting the inquiry, and his findings were printed in a Bulletin of the Department of Commerce and Labor in January 1905. The report did not mention working conditions in the stockyards, and made no attempt to justify or condemn the wage scale. It substantiated the settlement workers' claims that through activity in a labor union the immigrants were inspired to learn English, and because of the unions the European peasant learned to be dissatisfied with the Old World standard of living.[42]

The Bulletin of the Department of Commerce and Labor caused little excitement, but when Upton Sinclair's novel *The Jungle* was published late in 1905 thousands of Americans suddenly became concerned about the quality of American meat, if not about the working and living conditions in the stockyards. The settlement workers' accounts of conditions in the stockyards were corroborated by Sinclair's more dramatic story. Again Roosevelt ordered an investigation; this time he chose James B. Reynolds and Charles Neill for the job. Reynolds had gone from University Settlement in New York to serve as Mayor Seth Low's private secretary and troubleshooter. He had known Roosevelt for many years and in 1906 had just completed an investigation of housing in Washington, D.C., for the President. Neill, ex-professor of political economy at Catholic University, and former resident of the University of Chicago Settlement, became Commissioner of Labor in February 1906. He was chosen by Roosevelt for the investigation with the support and approval of Jane Addams.[43]

Before the investigators began their work, Roosevelt called Mary McDowell to Washington to ask how much of *The Jungle* was based on actual conditions in the stockyards. She admitted that Sinclair had exaggerated some aspects of the actual story, but assured Roosevelt that there was a large element of truth in the novel. Her testimony was supported by the report that Reynolds and Neill submitted to Roosevelt in May 1906.[44]

Roosevelt did not reveal the contents of the report (though some of it was learned by Upton Sinclair); instead, he used it to bargain with the packers. Knowing that if the report were published it would hurt the meat-packing industry, he promised to keep it secret if the packers would not oppose a bill (introduced by Albert Beveridge in the Senate) calling for federal inspection of meat-packing plants. The Beveridge bill passed the Senate easily, but it languished in the House. During the hearings, several of the members of the House Committee were given a royal tour through the Chicago packing plants, and they found little to criticize about the conditions of the plants. A representative of the packers maintained before the House Committee that no changes had been made since the Neill-Reynolds investigation. Mary McDowell, however, had observed the packers desperately making improvements in preparation for the visit of the congressional delegation. She mentioned this in a letter to Reynolds, and he passed it on to President Roosevelt. This proof of the packers' duplicity, plus their attempt to obstruct the inspection bill in the House Committee, so angered Roosevelt that he released the Neill-Reynolds report on June 4, 1906.[45]

The Neill-Reynolds report helped to arouse public opinion in favor of the Beveridge meat-inspection bill, and James B. Reynolds, who was carefully watching the progress of the bill in committee, realized the effect of public indignation on elected officials. He wrote to Jane Addams asking her to secure "a strong expression of public sentiment in Chicago favoring passage of the Beveridge amendment." Reynolds used the statements of settlement workers and excerpts from his own report to influence the members of his committee, and was partly responsible for the final passage of the bill.[46]

Government inspection of meat-packing plants did not solve the problems of the workingmen in America, but the stockyards strike is one illustration of the way some settlement workers operated at various levels to support the cause of organized labor. Their efforts led them from their neighborhoods to the nation's capital. Though occasionally they were patronizing or sentimental in their relations with labor leaders and workingmen, and though they were sometimes caught in the position of supporting labor and arguing for arbitration and conciliation, as a group they offered important and genuine support to organized labor at a time when labor had few friends.

7

Working Women and Children

Settlement workers were often important defenders of organized labor in the progressive era, but despite their efforts they succeeded in altering industrial relations very little. Much more important in the long run were their attempts to aid working women and children, who were usually more desperately in need of help and more willing to accept aid than were the men. The settlement workers often co-operated with organized labor, but reformers, rather than labor leaders, led the fight to abolish child labor and to regulate and improve the conditions of work for women. Settlement workers helped to organize the National Child Labor Committee and the National Women's Trade Union League. They conducted investigations, lobbied for bills, and organized committees.

The fact of child labor was difficult for the settlement worker to overlook. When Hull House residents offered candy to neighborhood children at Christmas time and the children refused to accept it, the settlement workers were perplexed, until they learned that the children worked six days a week in a candy factory. They could not stand the sight of candy. Other children worked in more dangerous places where they could be crippled or killed in accidents. A common sight was that of a stunted child with sallow complexion and weary eyes, with not enough energy to stay awake at a club or class because he worked all day in a factory or tenement loft. It was "perhaps inevitable," Jane Addams remarked, "that efforts to secure a child labor law should be our first venture into the field of state legislation." [1]

Soon after she and Ellen Starr established Hull House, the residents began to speak and write about the evils of child labor, which they observed all around them. General impressions of the conditions and extent of child labor were adequate for talks to church groups and women's clubs, but general impressions were not enough when dealing with legislatures or politicians. They needed statistics on the industrial situation in Chicago that were not available in 1891. The one person most responsible for gathering the information to make a case against child labor was Florence Kelley. Educated at Cornell and at the University of Zurich, translator of Engels, wife of a young Russian socialist doctor, and a socialist herself, Florence Kelley had been an expert social investigator before she became a resident of Hull House. In 1889 she had delivered a paper on the evils of child labor. She visited the new College Settlement in New York and saw much that was impractical and sentimental about the new movement. She also saw that a settlement could become an effective base for social reform. In 1891 she got a divorce and moved to Hull House with her three children. [2]

Florence Kelley was a big woman with dark, braided hair. She was often carelessly dressed "always in black; no stays," but she was driven by a concern for others. "No other man or woman whom I have ever heard so blended knowledge of facts, wit, satire, burning indignation, prophetic denunciation—all poured out at white heat in a voice varying from flute-like tones to deep organ tones," Josephine Goldmark, her friend and colleague, remembered.

Mrs. Kelley knew something of the evils of child labor before she came to Hull House, but it was the experience of teaching in night school during her winter in Chicago, seeing children drafted from their classes to wrap candy at Christmas time and watching the brightest girls drop out of school because of overwork, that impelled her to devote a lifetime to the cause. At Hull House she met a number of other women concerned with the problem, including Julia Lathrop and Alzina Stevens. She also met Mary Kenny, organizer of the first bookbinders' union for women in Chicago, and Henry Demarest Lloyd. Lloyd, who was working on *Wealth Against Commonwealth* in 1891 when Jane Addams took Mrs. Kelley out to Winnetka to meet him, was a close friend of the Hull House group and a partner in their fight against child labor.[3]

The fight began informally, with Florence Kelley and Alzina Stevens writing down the evidence of what they saw every day, that thousands of children were employed under deplorable conditions in the tenement houses and factories near Hull House. The investigation became official when Governor John P. Altgeld appointed Florence Kelley as a special investigator for the Illinois State Bureau of Labor, assigned to study child labor in the sweat shops of Chicago. For the settlement workers, however, investigation was merely the prelude to reform. After presenting their statistics to the Illinois legislature, they conferred with a committee sent to Chicago to check on conditions, helped draft a bill to be introduced at Springfield, and then lobbied for its passage. Their statistics and energy played a major role in the passage of the Illinois Factory Act of 1893, which provided for factory inspection and prohibited the employment of children under fourteen at night, or for longer than eight hours during the day.[4]

Governor Altgeld offered the new position of factory inspector to Henry Demarest Lloyd. When he refused, Altgeld appointed Mrs. Kelley; he also made Mrs. Stevens an assistant factory inspector, and Mary Kenny a deputy. Together the settlement workers launched an attack on those manufacturing firms employing children. "I have engaged counsel and am getting testimony and hope to begin a series of court cases this week," Florence Kelley wrote to Lloyd in the fall of 1893. "The Board of Health and Education, the medical profession, and the *Herald, Inter-Ocean* and *Record* are all cooperating. . . ."[5]

The cooperation and enthusiasm of the first few months died, however, leaving Mrs. Kelley and the others with the job of trying to enforce a law that had many loopholes. Despite persistent attempts to enlist the churches in the fight, they were unco-operative. Many lawyers refused to touch the cases against the employers, and the Board of Education turned a deaf ear to the settlement workers' pleas that the only way to enforce the child labor law was through compulsory school attendance. The labor unions did co-operate with the settlement workers, but their small interest in social legislation and their lack of class consciousness sometimes exasperated Florence Kelley. "I think it will take a quarter century to make our working class as clear to itself, its needs and the way to meet them, as the German working class is today," she remarked.[6]

It was the courts, however, that provided the real difficulty. In March, 1895, the Illinois Supreme Court found the eight-hour provision of the Factory Act unconstitutional. The settlement workers had to cancel two evening classes in literature because the girls no longer finished work at six but had to continue until nine. Although much disappointed, they fought back. Even before the court had handed down its final decision, the Hull House group introduced two bills in the legislature at Springfield. One called for the further regulation of the employment of minors; the other concerned public health and safety. Florence Kelley explained their tactics to Lloyd: "We are not publishing the bills yet because we want to get them out of committee before the editorial column raises its voice in defense of the infant newsboys and the toddling 'cash,' who will both come under its provisions." The settlement workers were learning a great deal about the reality of politics and social reform: when to use pressure, and when to use publicity.[7]

This attempt in 1895 to improve the child labor law failed. Two years later they tried again. Florence Kelley drew up the amendments, and one of the Chicago representatives introduced them. Jane Addams led a contingent of social workers, labor union representatives, and employers to Springfield to testify before the Senate Committee on Labor. Mrs. Stevens got a number of workingmen in Chicago to contact members of the Senate Committee on Labor in support of the child labor amendments. She also asked Henry Demarest Lloyd to attend the Executive Board Meeting of the Chicago Federation of Labor to get their endorsement. "You are the one man of whom no workingman thinks evil," she wrote. George Hooker, a Hull House resident who was an ordained Congregational minister as well as a lawyer, visited the meetings of Protestant ministers in Chicago in an attempt to obtain their support of the child labor amendments. William Kent, an alderman from the thirty-second ward and donor of a playground to Hull House, also joined the fight for a better child labor law. After the bills were reported out of committee the settlement workers prepared pamphlets and collections of clippings to show that ministers, labor leaders, employers, and social workers supported the amendments, and sent them to all members of the Illinois Legislature. The amendments passed, but the victory was short-lived. Governor Altgeld's successor did not reappoint Florence Kelley, and the new factory inspector had no interest in enforcing the existing laws or in trying to get better ones passed.[8]

Promoting social legislation meant fighting the same battle over and over again. Despite setbacks, however, the settlement workers kept up their battle to outlaw child labor in Illinois. In 1903, with the support of the Illinois Federation of Women's Clubs and the Illinois Federation of Labor, they introduced another bill in the legislature. Mary McDowell enlisted the support of Michael Donnelly and the labor unions in the stockyards district, and one of the best state child labor bills was passed on July 1, 1903. The next year Jane Addams and Harriet Van Der Vaart of Neighborhood House in Chicago managed to obtain the co-operation of the Catholic archbishop and the superintendent of schools in Chicago in enforcing the compulsory school attendance law and in establishing a state child labor office. The *Chicago Tribune* remarked: "Miss Addams' talent for getting things done in the habitations of men is continually establishing a greater and greater difference between her and the reformers whose talent . . . consists just at present in producing vocal disturbances in the wilderness."[9]

II

Those interested in child labor legislation in other states often sought advice from the Hull House reformers. The Wisconsin Commissioner of Labor, for example, asked Jane Addams to send him the statistics and an outline of her arguments before the Illinois legislature, for use in obtaining a better law in Wisconsin. Settlement workers in other cities followed the Hull House example by agitating for better legislation. In New Jersey, Cornelia Bradford, head resident of Jersey City's Whittier House, led a number of organizations in a campaign that won a better child labor law in 1903. She held meetings on the bill at the settlement, began an investigation of the bottle-blowing industry and helped found the Children's Protective League. The South Park Settlement in San Francisco conducted an investigation of child labor which helped in the campaign for a better California law, passed in 1905. The head resident, Lucile Eaves, became a special agent of the State Labor Bureau and appeared before hearings at Sacramento in behalf of the bill. In Massachusetts, which had adequate child labor laws already on the books, the Boston settlements, through the Boston Social Union, co-operated with the Massachusetts Child Labor Committee in strengthening the laws. In Pennsylvania, Kellogg Durland, a young Harvard graduate, head resident of a Boston settlement, and later assistant head resident of University Settlement in New York, made an investigation of child labor abuses in the coal mines. He testified before committee hearings at Harrisburg and, with the support of the United Mine Workers, helped raise the minimum age for mine work from fourteen to sixteen.[10]

Settlement workers in several cities publicized the exploitation of children in the street trades. Meyer Bloomfield and Philip Davis of Civic Service House in Boston helped to win a better child labor law in Massachusetts. A committee from the Federation of Chicago Settlements made an investigation showing that many newsboys under twelve were on the streets until midnight. In New York a committee from University Settlement spent months studying the newsboys; then, with statistics to show the need for reform, they drew up a bill that was later passed by the legislature.[11]

The New York settlements did more than investigate newsboys. In April 1902, the Association of Neighborhood Workers, at the suggestion of Felix Adler, appointed a committee on child labor. The immediate impetus came from a rash of criticism in the North about the horrors of child labor in the South, and the conviction that the public needed to learn that conditions were just as bad in New York. But the formation of the committee was also the natural culmination of the settlement workers' ten-year struggle against child labor in the city. Florence Kelley, who had been living at Henry Street Settlement since 1899 and working for child labor reform through the Consumers' League, responded to Adler's suggestion, as did many other settlement workers. They made Robert Hunter, head resident of University Settlement, the chairman of the new committee.[12]

Robert Hunter was born in Terre Haute, Indiana (the town that produced Eugene Debs and Theodore Dreiser). He graduated from Indiana University, served as organizing secretary of the Chicago Bureau of Charities, and was a resident of Hull House and Northwestern University Settlement. He was the author of a study of Chicago's housing problem, and in 1902 was at work on another book that he planned to call simply *Poverty*. Impetuous and outspoken, Hunter had little patience with the dilettante reformers, but he had tremendous energy and an amazing ability to organize reform.[13]

Hunter's committee quickly went into action; it collected enough money to hire Helen Marot, a young Philadelphia socialist and labor reformer, as a full-time investigator, and many settlement workers spent part of their time gathering statistics on child labor. One of the first men whom Hunter enlisted in the crusade was J. G. Phelps Stokes, a tall, serious resident of University Settlement. Stokes worked in his father's office uptown on Madison Avenue, and used the office staff to get out leaflets and circular letters for the Child Labor Committee.[14]

The original goal of the New York Child Labor Committee was

to carry the investigation far enough so that the state would appoint a child labor commission. The settlement workers soon realized, however, that immediate legislation was desperately needed, and joined in setting up a Committee with prominent local citizens.[15]

A special subcommittee on legislation prepared three model bills to strengthen the existing laws in New York. They submitted these bills to the State Labor Bureau, the Superintendent of the Board of Public Health, and the Governor before any public announcement was made to the press. Florence Kelley, Josephine Goldmark, and Helen Marot prepared the statistics on child labor for presentation, while Robert Hunter, J. G. Phelps Stokes, and others made frequent trips to Albany to testify and lobby for the bills. The New York Child Labor Committee was primarily responsible for the passage in 1903 of a law that became a model for other states to follow.[16]

Just as important as the settlement workers' direct influence on legislation was their more subtle work in arousing public opinion against child labor abuses. Through speeches, articles, and books, they brought public opinion to the point where legislation was possible. They became expert at making the point that something was wrong with a country that sacrificed its children to the drive for profit. "Children are deformed, maimed, weakened, and made diseased for life in many of the trades flourishing in every industrial community," William English Walling declared. "The bodies of children are maimed and their minds dwarfed solely that we may have cheap labor, increased profits on our capital, and a slightly reduced cost of commodities," Robert Hunter wrote. "Children are put into industry very much as we put in raw material, and the product we look for is not better men and women, but better manufactured goods," Jane Addams announced at a meeting of the National Conference of Charities and Correction. Over and over again the settlement workers made their point; they cited statistics and related personal experiences, and gradually the nation woke up to the fact that something needed to be done about the evils of child labor.[17]

State laws were passed, but these were easily side-stepped by unco-operative officials, or invalidated by the courts. Gradually the settlement workers began to realize that national legislation and organization were necessary if child labor was to be permanently regulated. The first concrete suggestion for national organization for child labor reform came, however, not from a settlement worker but from an Alabama clergyman and publicist, Edgar Gardner Murphy. He had been aroused to spirited opposition to child labor by an investigation of Alabama textile mills conducted by the American Federation of Labor. At the annual meeting of the National Conference of Charities and Correction held in Atlanta, Georgia, in May 1903, Murphy read a paper on "Child Labor as a National Problem." Florence Kelley and Jane Addams also gave papers at the same session on the general problems of "Destitute Children." The two settlement workers and the Alabama clergyman talked in general terms about a national child labor organization. A few weeks later the New York Child Labor Committee appointed a special committee of William Baldwin, Florence Kelley, and Felix Adler to confer with Murphy. Out of this conference came the organization of the National Child Labor Committee in April 1904.[18]

Thirty individuals who had been active in campaigns against child labor were invited to become charter members of the National Committee. Florence Kelley, Lillian Wald, and Jane Addams specifically represented the settlement movememt on the committee; other prominent people who had for many years worked closely with the settlement workers were also included. The National Child Labor Committee established its headquarters in the same building in New York that housed the Charity Organization Society, the Association for Improving the Conditions of the Poor, and the Consumers' League. The reformers drew up a model child labor law and encouraged state campaigns, but reform moved slowly.[19]

The National Child Labor Committee did much to wipe out the most blatant evils of child labor, but progress was uneven and the same battles had to be fought again and again. Many of the settlement workers came to the conclusion that a federal law was the only workable solution to the problem. When Albert Beveridge introduced legislation in Congress in December 1906 "to prevent the employment of children in factories and mines," they rallied to support the bill. But the concept of federal regulation of child labor was too advanced for Congress or for most of the members of the National Child Labor Committee to accept in 1907, and the bill went down to defeat.[20]

The settlement workers, however, were more successful in their fight for a federal children's bureau. As early as 1900, Florence Kelley had pointed out the desperate need for a central agency to correlate the information on child labor gathered by private and government agencies. In 1903 Lillian Wald made the first specific suggestion for a children's bureau. Her suggestion was picked up by Mrs. Kelley and Edward T. Devine and forwarded to President Roosevelt who invited Miss Wald to Washington. She later recalled that the morning she arrived "the Secretary of Agriculture was departing . . . to the South, to find out what danger to the community lurked in the boll weevil. That brought home, with a very strong emphasis, the fact that nothing that could have happened to the children would have called forth such official action on the part of the Government." [21] Despite the efforts of the settlement workers and the National Child Labor Committee little was accomplished until January 1909, when President Roosevelt called a White House Conference on the Care of Dependent Children. Lillian Wald arranged the conference, and hearings were finally opened on the bill.[22]

Miss Wald testified before a Senate Committee and compared the treatment of children with the treatment of pigs (to the concern of some of the members of the committee). Jane Addams helped to draft a form letter sent out by the National Committee urging interested groups to write their congressmen. Settlement workers had a great deal of assistance from leading progressives. The bill drafted by Florence Kelley and Lillian Wald finally passed Congress and received President Taft's signature in April 1912. Taft appointed Julia Lathrop of Hull House as the first director of the Children's Bureau. She was, in the words of Lillain Wald, "irrespective of sex, the best qualified person in the country . . . for the job." It was no accident that the settlements, which were in the vanguard of the slow and frustrating movement to abolish child labor in the progressive era, should have produced the person best qualified to direct the Children's Bureau.[23]

III

The settlement workers' attempt to regulate the hours and conditions of work for women was a natural corollary to their attempts to abolish child labor. "I do not know why it is that women and children are invariably classed together," Mary Simkhovitch remarked; "I suppose it came from two reasons: one because of the maternal relation; and second from their common political disabilities." There was also another reason for lumping the working woman and child together, for the child labor reformers thought it inconsistent and inhuman to protect a girl until she was sixteen and then give her the "right to work from 8 A.M. to 10 P.M., thirteen hours a day, seventy-eight hours a week for $6." [24]

Only a year after the organization of the National Child Labor Committee, three settlement workers intimately aware of the problems faced by both women and children in the industrial world met for dinner in Chicago. Mary McDowell, Edith Abbott, and Sophonisba Breckinridge talked about many things, but they kept coming back to the difficulties faced by working women. They remarked that there was no concrete information about the extent or conditions of female labor. They agreed that a federal investigation was needed to publish the exact nature of existing conditions throughout the entire country, to dramatize the problem, and to quiet the critics who said it did a woman no harm to work in a factory. It was just a casual conversation, but the next morning the three began to act.[25]

They enlisted the support of Jane Addams, who agreed to write President Roosevelt. They got the co-operation of the newly formed Women's Trade Union League and the National Federation of Women's Clubs. Other settlement workers in Chicago and New York joined the campaign; Anna Nichols, a young resident of

Neighborhood House in Chicago, helped to draft a letter that was sent to all congressmen and many women's organizations, urging a national investigation of the problems and consequences of "the influx of women into the industrial fields." Mary McDowell, in part because of her stand during the stockyards strike, was able to get a hearing before the convention of the American Federation of Labor convention and, consequently, their endorsement for the investigation. Altogether, the small group of settlement workers used their experience, their reputations, and their wide acquaintances to arouse the public to the need for an investigation of women in industry.[26]

More than the support of public opinion, however, was needed to make the idea work. Jane Addams presented the idea to Roosevelt, who approved but requested more information. So, with the help of Mary McDowell and Lillian Wald, she drew up a tentative plan. The three settlement workers conferred with the President in March 1905. He was persuaded to include a recommendation for the study in his annual message to Congress in December; but before legislation could be prepared, another bill was introduced in the House calling for an investigation of child labor. The settlement workers decided to try to broaden this bill to include women. It required several trips to Washington, but they won the support of Commissioner of Labor Charles Neill, the officials of the Bureau of the Census, and the members of the Committee on Labor, which reported favorably on a bill calling for a joint investigation of the problems of women and children in industry.[27]

The legislation was introduced in both the Senate and the House in March and April 1906. Settlement workers marshalled their forces for a fight. They enlisted the support of the National Child Labor Committee, and drafted a letter to be sent to businessmen, social workers, and congressmen. They argued for a federal—not a state or a private—investigation of the problems of women and children in industry. "Only by having the entire inquiry planned and executed under the direction of a single head will the material be in uniform shape in the different states, and permit comparative study of conditions and results of any economic or social value," the settlement workers pointed out. "There are hundreds of thousands of helpless, untrained, unorganized women, without the power of legislating for themselves, who are forced by stress of circumstances to earn their livelihood," Mary McDowell announced in an article in *Charities and the Commons,* "and it is of vital importance that they be given the chance to be decently self-supporting under conditions which shall not unfit them for wifehood and motherhood, and the care of the home." The settlement workers played a major part in the passage of the bill authorizing the investigation, which President Roosevelt finally signed on January 31, 1907.[28]

The passage and the signing of the bill for the investigation did not end the problem, however. For a time it appeared that Congress was not going to appropriate any money for the investigation. Mary McDowell, who had gone to Washington three times in support of the original bill, wrote letters to Mrs. Emmons Blaine and to other prominent people, urging them to get letters from "conservative employers who have good conditions and are willing to have this significant subject of women in industry freed from confusion." [29]

The settlement workers' vigilance and realistic approach to the task of getting a bill through Congress was at least partly responsible for the passage of the appropriations bill. The Department of Commerce and Labor conducted the investigation and published the results in nineteen volumes between 1910 and 1913. For many years these volumes remained the chief source of information on women and children in industry, and proved a valuable aid to the reformer as he continued the frustrating fight for the protection of working women and children.[30]

IV

One part of the *Report on the Conditions of Women and Child Wage Earners in the United States* was devoted to the connections between low wages and lax moral conditions among young women in various industries. Settlement workers had long been aware of the underworld of red-light districts and prostitution rings. In the early twentieth century many settlement workers played important roles on vice commissions and in the massive attempt to wipe out the "social evil" and the white slave trade. The crusade against prostitution was part of the progressive campaign to preserve and improve human resources and prevent the exploitation of women and children.[31]

Prostitution was practised openly in many settlement neighborhoods. "On sunshiny days the whores sat on chairs along the sidewalks," the novelist Michael Gold recalled. "They sprawled indolently, their legs taking up half the pavements. People stumbled over a gauntlet of whores' meaty legs. The girls gossiped and chirped like a jungle of parrots." [32] Lillian Wald confirmed the deplorable conditions on the lower East Side. While walking near the settlement one night she noticed that in every house there were "bedecked, unfortunate creatures, who tried by a peculiar hissing noise to draw the attention of the men." Nearby, children imitated the actions of the women, and little babies on the stoops played with the "business cards of the houses." [33]

Settlement workers were understandably disturbed by these conditions, and sought to close the houses, but it was obvious that prostitution was a city-wide problem. In New York, Henry Moskowitz and James Reynolds played a part in organizing the Committee of Fifteen in 1900 to investigate and assist the Tenement House Commission in controlling the problem. This committee was the prototype of vice commissions appointed in every major American city within the next years. Graham Taylor served as a member of the important commission in Chicago, and settlement workers in other cities helped in various attempts to investigate and control prostitution. The investigations moved to the national level in 1909, and the work of the United States Immigration Commission resulted the next year in the passage of the Mann Act, which prohibited interstate transportation of women for immoral purposes. Jane Addams contributed to the growing literature of exposé. She used the records and case histories collected by the Chicago Juvenile Protective Association to write a series of articles on the "social evil" for *McClure's* in 1911, and the next year she published them in book form as *A New Conscience and an Ancient Evil*.[34]

The settlement workers, like the other vice reformers, were especially concerned by what seemed like a well-organized network of pimps and procurers who lured innocent girls into lives of debauchery. The problem became obvious to Graham Taylor in 1900 when a seventeen-year-old girl, who lived near the Commons and taught Sunday School at a local church, applied for a position caring for an elderly woman. The girl was captured and held by the "elderly woman," who turned out to be part of a prostitution ring that recruited in this way.[35]

Miss Addams described various techniques used to lure immigrant girls into prostitution. Marie, the daughter of a Breton stone mason, thought she was joining a theatrical troupe, and a young Polish girl, looking for her mother, was induced by two men to leave the New York train at South Chicago. "It is obvious," Miss Addams wrote, "that a foreign girl who speaks no English, who has not the remotest idea in what part of the city her fellow countrymen live, who does not know the police station or any agency to which she may apply, is almost as valuable to a white slave trafficker as a girl imported directly for the trade." [36]

To Jane Addams, the "social evil" was closely connected with the need for better protection for the immigrant. It was also intimately involved with the problem of low pay, long hours, and depressed working conditions for women. She demonstrated that economic conditions often drove young women to become prostitutes. " 'I was too tired to care,' 'I was too tired to know what I was doing' . . . 'I was dog tired and just went with him,' are phrases taken from the lips of reckless girls endeavoring to explain the situation in which they find themselves." "Is it any wonder," asked the Chicago Vice Commission, "that a tempted girl who receives only six dollars per week working with her hands sells her body for twenty-five dollars per week when she learns there is a demand for it and men are willing to pay the price?" Waitresses and other girls who served the public were in an especially vulnerable position. Miss Addams described the case of a young girl from northern Michigan who worked in a Chicago restaurant. When she heard that her sister was dying she agreed to accompany one of the patrons on an overnight boat trip if he would pay her round-trip fare. "She reached home twelve hours before her sister died, but when she returned to Chicago a week later burdened with the debt of an undertaker's bill, she realized that she had discovered a means of payment." [37]

For the settlement worker prostitution was also closely related to the saloon and the disreputable dance hall, and their campaigns for adequate play spaces, for social centers, and for prohibition were in part connected with their fear of the "social evil." Prostitution, the reformers believed, not only destroyed many unfortunate women, but through the spread of venereal disease it killed or crippled thousands of innocent women and children. "This slaughter of the innocents, this infliction of suffering upon the new-born, is so gratuitous and so unfair, that it is only a question of time until an outraged sense of justice shall be aroused on behalf of these children," Jane Addams announced. She went on to point out that a generation which had found new meaning in the phrase "children's rights" ought at least to "insist upon a child's right to be well born and to start in life with its tiny body free from disease." [38]

Like other vice reformers, the settlement workers denied the time-honored defense of the prostitute—that it was necessary for the unmarried male to "sow his wild oats"—but they did play an important part in the sex and social hygiene movement, for they understood that ignorance and old wives' tales contributed to the problem.[39] Most of all, they saw their crusade against prostitution as part of their larger campaign to limit the exploitation of women and children.

V

The settlement workers also helped women organize into labor unions. Several settlements encouraged women's unions to meet in their buildings, and early in the twentieth century they helped to organize the National Women's Trade Union League. They co-operated with labor leaders in the formation of the League, but the idea and the impetus came from the settlement workers.

A great many people had a hand in the organization of the National Women's Trade Union League, but the two people most directly responsible were Mary Kenny O'Sullivan and William English Walling. Mary Kenny O'Sullivan, "a noble young woman on fire for her cause," was a bookbinder by trade, but an agitator and organizer by temperament. The daughter of Irish immigrant parents, she had been forced to go to work at an early age in a bookbindery. Unlike many of her fellow workers, however, she rebelled against the long hours and incredibly bad working conditions that were commonplace in Chicago in the 1880's. Almost singlehandedly, she organized the first bookbinders' union for women in Chicago, but fighting alone she accomplished little.[40]

Mary Kenny lived and worked on the West Side of Chicago not far from the big house that a group of well-educated, upper-class ladies turned into the first social settlement in Chicago in 1889. It was natural that Jane Addams and Ellen Gates Starr should meet the Irish working girl and agitator, and that Mary Kenny should be suspicious of the upper-class ladies who called themselves settlement workers. Gradually, however, she became convinced that Jane Addams and the others were serious when they said they wanted to work with the working girls, to help them organize and win better pay and working conditions. "It was that word 'with' from Jane Addams that took the bitterness out of my life," she later remembered. "For if she wanted to work with me and I could work with her, it gave my life new meaning and hope." [41]

Through Jane Addams, Mary Kenny met Henry Demarest Lloyd, and with his support, plus the encouragement and aid of the Hull House ladies, she was able to expand her activities and influence. She began organizing the shirtwaist workers into unions, and helped enlist support for the passage of the Illinois Factory Act, which provided for the protection of women and children wage earners. She even started a co-operative factory on Halsted Street with capital supplied by Jane Addams, Henry Demarest Lloyd, and Clarence Darrow. In 1892, at the age of twenty-eight, Mary Kenny

became the first woman organizer for the American Federation of
Labor and a delegate to their national convention in Philadelphia.
A short time later, Samuel Gompers sent her to New York and then
to Boston to continue her organizing activities. She was officially
employed by the AFL for only five months, but unofficially she
remained a labor organizer all her life.[42]

During her last year in Chicago, Mary Kenny lived at Hull
House and helped Florence Kelley, Alzina Stevens, and the others
in the fight against child labor. When she moved to New York for a
few months, quite naturally she stayed at a social settlement; and
when she transferred her activities to Boston she carried a letter of
introduction from Jane Addams to Helena Dudley, the gentle radical who was head resident of Denison House.[43]

Even before Mary Kenny became a resident, Denison House had
been active in the labor movement. The Federal Labor Union organized by John F. O'Sullivan and affiliated with the AFL met regularly at the settlement, and a number of settlement workers were
members of the union. Jack O'Sullivan was a friend of Samuel
Gompers, and served for many years on the council of Robert
Woods's South End House. He met Mary Kenny one night after a
labor union meeting at Denison House and quickly fell in love. It
was "our romance," Vida Scudder later recalled. After they were
married, the O'Sullivans lived at the settlement, and Mary continued her fight to organize women workers in Boston.[44]

William English Walling came from a very different background,
but as a factory inspector in Chicago and a settlement worker in
New York he became convinced that Amerian wage earners needed
to organize into trade unions. Along with J. G. Phelps Stokes, he
attended the weekly meetings of the New York Central Federation
of Labor that were held at University Settlement. Then he would
often talk far into the night with labor leaders, socialists, and anarchists at a nearby bar. The things he saw and heard as a settlement
worker eventually made him a socialist, but before that he served
on the New York Child Labor Committee, wrote frequent articles
on labor problems, and became especially concerned about the lot
of the working woman.[45]

Books on socialism, economic theory, and trade unionism were stacked high in Walling's settlement room. He read accounts of the British Women's Trade Union League, which had been organized in 1874 and had had considerable success. Lillian Wald and Florence Kelley, whom he often saw at lunch at Henry Street Settlement, urged him to find out more about the British organization, and during the summer of 1903 he traveled to England. He talked to many leaders of the British Labor Movement including Mary McCarthur, secretary of the British Women's Trade Union League, and returned to America convinced that a similar national organization would help American working women organize to win shorter hours and better working conditions.[46]

In November 1903 Walling took a train from New York to Boston, timing his arrival to coincide with the annual meeting of the American Federation of Labor. Through his settlement friends Walling met Mary Kenny O'Sullivan. He explained his idea for an American Women's Trade Union League to her over lunch in the dining-room of the Revere House in downtown Boston. She approved his plan, and offered her support. Thus did the grandson of a Kentucky millionaire and the daughter of an Irish peasant, one a labor leader, one a reformer, both settlement residents, both influenced by Jane Addams, join forces to translate their sympathy for the working women into a national reform organization.[47]

At the meetings of the American Federation of Labor in Faneuil Hall, Walling and Mrs. O'Sullivan spent most of their time circulating among the labor leaders and the friends of labor, outlining their tentative plans for a National Women's Trade Union League. Philip Davis, assistant head resident of Civic Service House in Boston, was one of those excited by their idea. He invited Walling and Mrs. O'Sullivan to continue their discussion at his settlement. Other settlement workers and several delegates to the American Federation of Labor convention joined them in what turned out to be the preliminary meeting of the Women's Trade Union League. This group, meeting late into the night at Civic Service House, agreed on the basic structure of the League and arranged for further organizational meetings. Walling was the driving force behind the plan. He maintained that the League must be a genuine co-operative effort between labor leaders, working women, and those sympathetic to organized labor; and he insisted that the League must have the support of the American Federation of Labor.[48] The next morning Walling and Mrs. O'Sullivan conferred with Samuel Gompers. "When they submitted to me a proposal, I gave it most hearty approval and participated in the necessary conferences," Gompers recalled in his autobiography. He sent Max Morris, a member of the Executive Council of the AFL, to the early meetings and allowed Mrs. O'Sullivan to announce the meetings from the podium of the AFL Convention, but his support was largely passive. The settlement workers took the initiative, and they had the enthusiastic support of a sizable number of labor leaders, especially from the garment industry.[49]

Harry White, president of the United Garment Workers, Michael Donnelly, president of the Amalgamated Meat Cutters and Butcher Workmen, and John O'Brien, president of the Clerks' International Protective Union, together with many lesser labor delegates, joined settlement workers Robert Woods, Vida Scudder, and Helena Dudley, along with Mrs. O'Sullivan, Walling, and Davis, in further organizational meetings on November 14, 17, and 19. They elected a slate of officers and an Executive Board, and approved a constitution. They made Mary Morton Kehew, a long-time friend of the labor movement in Boston, the first president, Jane Addams the vice president, Mary Kenny O'Sullivan the secretary, and Mary Donovan (secretary of the Lynn, Massachusetts, Central Labor Union) the treasurer. Lillian Wald and Mary McDowell were among those elected to the Executive Board, and in a gesture suggestive of the co-operative nature of the organization, their names were submitted by labor leaders Harry White and Michael Donnelly.[50]

The organizers of a National Women's Trade Union League announced simply in their constitution that the object was "to assist in the organization of women wage workers into trade unions," and a short time later they added, "and thereby to help secure conditions necessary for healthful and efficient work and to obtain a just return for such work." There was no word about promoting legislation, no hint of paternalism; the object was organization. Anyone could join the League who was sympathetic to its purpose, but Mary O'Sullivan and William English Walling, who were primarily responsible for drawing up the constitution, made it clear that no one should attempt to organize any group of women workers until they had checked with the national and local secretary of the union in the industry involved.[51]

It was one thing, of course, to draft a constitution and elect a slate of officers and another thing again to begin the task of forming unions. The British Women's Trade Union League had concentrated much of its effort on getting women admitted into men's unions, and after 1889 had become virtually a federation of trade unions. The founders of the American League decided to concentrate on organizing women's unions, and they began by opening branches of the Women's Trade Union League in Boston, Chicago, and New York. Again, settlement workers began the work. It was not coincidental that the first branches were opened in the three cities where the settlement movement was most strongly established: the Boston League was born at Denison House, the Chicago League at Hull House, and the New York League at University Settlement. In each case the settlement workers tried to enlist the support of labor leaders. The organization of the New York League was typical. Walling called a meeting in late November 1903 at University Settlement and invited Lillian Wald, Mary Simkhovitch, Florence Kelley, Elizabeth Williams, Jane Robbins, and Leonora O'Reilly as well as a large group of trade union members of both sexes. In order to attract as many workingmen and women as possible, he scheduled the meeting on a Sunday night directly following the meeting of the Central Labor Union at the settlement. "It was a great evening full of enthusiasm and determination," Mary Simkhovitch later remembered.[52]

The feature attraction and the main speaker at the New York meeting was Leonora O'Reilly, a member of the Executive Board of the National Women's Trade Union League. She was well qualified to talk about organizing women's trade unions, for like Mary

O'Sullivan and Philip Davis, she had become a settlement worker only after years of experience in the labor movement. Leonora O'Reilly was an indispensable member of the Women's Trade Union League during the crucial first years and helped win the co-operation of some of the labor leaders in New York. It was not an easy task. Many New York labor leaders remained suspicious of the new organization which included so many well-to-do women among its members. Leonora O'Reilly became very upset herself on one occasion in 1905 and resigned from the League, charging that the organization had become a tool of the employers. But she thought better of her action a few weeks later. The position of the New York League was strengthened by its active support of the garment workers, especially during the major strikes of 1909 and 1910. Miss O'Reilly and a significant group of labor leaders in the city were reassured by this that the League sincerely sought to help the cause of labor.[53]

The Boston and Chicago branches of the League received a more friendly reception from the ranks of organized labor than did the New York League, but even there animosity and suspicion remained. Walling and Mrs. O'Sullivan decided that if the League was to be of any use it must reassert its affinity with the American Federation of Labor and increase its membership. To accomplish both these goals they decided to hold the first national conference of the League in New York in the spring of 1905 and to invite Samuel Gompers to address the convention. He gave a rousing speech, promising the Women's Trade Union League the support and co-operation of the American Federation of Labor, "not as a mere compliment, not from a mere desire to please, but . . . as a matter of right and fraternity. . . ." The League "has broadened the work of the unions," he decided, "because it has had the coop-eration of the other women and other men who sympathize with them." He continued, "It is not a work of charity. It is not a work of endowing someone with a gratuity. It is instituted so that the girls and the women may be placed in a position where they may be helped to help themselves. What the workingmen want," Gompers concluded, "is less charity and more rights." [54]

Gompers's support helped the Women's Trade Union League, but occasionally the president of the American Federation of Labor and the leaders of the new organization found it difficult to agree. Gompers was willing to allow the League to hold its national conference at the same time as the AFL convention, but he made it clear that the representatives of the League should not consider themselves delegates to the convention. This attitude annoyed the leaders of the Women's Trade Union League; but when they decided to hold their meetings in the fall of 1905 in New York rather than Pittsburgh (where the AFL was meeting), it was Gompers's turn to be angry, for he had already announced the League meeting in the program. Despite disagreement and lingering suspicion, however, the American Federation of Labor accepted non-voting delegates from the Women's Trade Union League to their convention each year, and made a small annual donation to help the work of the League.[55]

Walling, Mrs. O'Sullivan, Leonora O'Reilly, and the other leaders of the Women's Trade Union League welcomed the support of the American Federation of Labor and the encouragement they got from other labor leaders, for they realized that they might seem like a dilettante reform movement. But if the organizers of the League had relied on Gompers and the AFL to carry the organization once it was started it would have collapsed in short order. The reformers had to enlist support not only from the ranks of organized labor and from working women, but also from leisure-class sympathizers who had the time, money, and influence to make the League work. During the first years the reformers were very careful to restrict the number of sympathizers they allowed to join, but early in 1904 when Walling and Leonora O'Reilly won the support of Mary and Margaret Dreier, two daughters of a wealthy and socially prominent New York family, they went a long way toward assuring the success of the League.[56]

Mary Dreier remained an important member of the New York League. She was not afraid to speak out even in time of crisis, and on one occasion made headlines when she was arrested for picketing during a strike. She was also quick to defend the original purpose of the League against those who argued that legislation rather than organization was more important. "While we make laws, let us not forget the more important work of organization," she announced, "for we know that the greatest power to enforce labor laws is trade unions, and a strong trade union can demand better conditions and shorter hours than the law will allow, and then, too, we get education and power through organization, which we do not get through law." [57]

Margaret Dreier married settlement worker Raymond Robins in 1905 and transferred her activities to Chicago. Even though they were both independently wealthy, the Robins chose to live in a fourth floor, cold-water flat, midway between two settlements on Chicago's West Side. For more than twenty years this modest apartment was the center from which they launched their crusades for democracy, peace, and social justice. They spent a great part of their energy supporting and aiding the cause of organized labor. They defended the workingman's right to bargain collectively, to use the strike, the picket line, and the secondary boycott. They fought for social welfare legislation, but always maintained that labor organization was more important. They were examples *par excellence* of progressives who ardently and consistently supported organized labor.[58]

In 1907 Margaret Dreier Robins was elected president of the National Women's Trade Union League, a job she held until 1921. More than any other single person she was responsible for making the League an effective and efficient force for the organization and protection of women wage earners. She radiated a religious sincerity and a contagious enthusiasm that served to challenge the working women and social workers who continued to make up the membership of the Women's Trade Union League. She possessed an ability to smooth over the differences that continued to arise among the members and supporters of the League. Yet she could become very angry when she saw workingmen and women and labor leaders exploited. Under her leadership, the League established branches in several cities, lobbied for a federal investigation of the problems of women in industry, supported striking workers, agitated for protective legislation for working women, and most important, perhaps, trained a large number of working women to become leaders in the struggle for the organization and protection of women in industry.[59]

Labor leaders played a part in the diverse movements that sought to help working women and children, but a group of idealistic settlement workers who gathered statistics, made speeches, wrote articles, lobbied for legislation, and organized committees had more initial importance. They were often frustrated by the large gulf between their expectations and their accomplishments, but they usually demonstrated a realistic understanding of the process of organizing reform.

8

The Settlement Worker
Versus the Ward Boss

Most of the early settlement workers had little interest in politics when they first opened their outposts in the slums. They learned, however, that they had invaded a political world. They talked about re-creating the neighborhood in the industrial city, but they discovered that the ward and the precinct already provided a semblance of neighborhood organization and spirit. The settlement workers came to realize that for the workingman, politics was intimately connected with a job, and that any attempt to improve working and living conditions involved them in politics. In fact, they found that educational reform, labor reform, and even attempts to create parks and playgrounds became political matters. They learned also that to promote reform in the neighborhood often meant to clash with the ward boss.

Many settlement workers refused to take sides in the political struggle they observed in their neighborhood, and only a small percentage of settlements ever took part in ward politics. Mary Simkhovitch and Robert Woods especially, insisted that the residents had little to gain and much to lose by taking a stand in local politics. "In nearly all cases it is idle for the settlement to attempt to win away the following of local politicians," Woods decided. "To make such an attempt is to leave out of account the loyalties of class, race and religion which bind the people of the crowded wards to their political leaders." Instead of attempting to defeat the ward boss, Woods believed the settlement workers should try to co-operate with him in promoting a program of playgrounds and public baths for the ward. Through a gradual process of education the settlement workers could teach the voters to demand more from their elected representatives and force the ward boss to become an enlightened local leader.[1]

Through co-operation rather than opposition Woods and the other residents at the South End House in Boston were able to accomplish a great deal, but the situation in Boston's ninth ward was not exactly typical. Like most of the downtown wards, the ninth was controlled by the Democratic party, but the political leader in the ward was James Donovan, an affable and reasonable Irish boss whom Woods called "Honorable Jim." Unlike many local politicians, Donovan seemed to be more concerned with the welfare of the people than with his own pocketbook, and he joined the settlement workers in many projects, including the erection of a public bathhouse. His help was not based entirely on altruism, however. In the fight for political control in Boston, he had lost out to the combined forces of Martin Lomasney and John Fitzgerald. "Honorable Jim" badly needed an ally to protect his position in the ninth ward. By aligning himself with the sedate settlement worker, Donovan was assured of the support of the "better element" in the ward. Woods occasionally supported a candidate for alderman, but never tried to challenge the Democratic party or the political rule of Jim Donovan. In return, Donovan co-operated in the settlement's struggle to improve working and living conditions in the South End. It was a profitable partnership for both the settlement workers and the ward boss.[2]

The residents of South End House were careful observers of the political struggle going on around them, even if they were not participants. Their studies of the political forces at work beneath the surface in the struggle for power helped reveal the sources of political corruption and the reasons for boss rule in city politics. William

Clark, a young Harvard graduate who was a resident of South End House and later head resident of Lincoln House in the same ward, wrote on the "Roots of Political Power" in *City Wilderness*. He discovered that the strength of the ward boss rested on an elaborate structure of boys' gangs that duplicated, in miniature, the political organization in the district. The shrewd politician recruited his "healers" and "lieutenants" from these gangs. And the ward boss himself rose to power, first as the leader of a boys' gang, then as the boss of young men's clubs. From the club to politics was a natural step, and the ward boss stayed in power through a combination of Machiavellian shrewdness and a spirit of genuine neighborliness.[3]

"Ordinary public standards of intellectual fitness count for little or nothing in these parts of the city," Woods remarked in *Americans in Process*. "Fair play," he said, was a hundred times more important than honesty for local voters in the typical crowded city ward. Woods went on to describe two powerful political bosses in the North End with such accuracy and color that one threatened to sue. William Clark who, unlike Woods, had political ambitions, discovered first-hand that there were risks involved in studying the political structure of a ward. Clark tried twice and without success to win nominations, once for City Council and once for the legislature. The second time some of the local politicians used his statements about the district to defeat him. Woods believed that Clark's political activities diminished the effectiveness of his work at Lincoln House; for that reason, Woods argued, a settlement worker should not take an active role in local politics.[4]

Yet if South End House had been located in the eighth ward, the domain of Martin Lomasney, Woods might have been provoked into opposing the political boss. Elizabeth Peabody House was the only settlement in the eighth ward. Eva Whiting White, the head resident, found that she could learn a great deal from Lomasney, but co-operation was only on his terms. In another section of the city a young settlement worker named Kellogg Durland discovered that a rising young politician named James Michael Curley had little sympathy for Tech House. Curley's unwillingness to co-operate helped persuade Durland that it was better to give up and move his settlement activities to New York.[5] Tech House was too recently established to oppose a ward boss, and Elizabeth Peabody House had too few men residents to be an effective force in local politics.

Settlement workers in Cleveland, Detroit, San Francisco, and Philadelphia only rarely became involved in ward politics. Anna Davies—by all odds the most important settlement worker in Philadelphia—noted in 1905 that the settlements there were "noticeably weak in their relation to municipal and state politics." The next year College Settlement, with Miss Davies leading the way, played an active role in a reform campaign, but all it accomplished was the election of two women residents to the school committee. Charles Bernheimer, a young settlement worker, was confident in 1906 that, if only a larger group of men residents could be attracted, the settlements could lead a civic renaissance. But the renaissance never came, and the Philadelphia settlements, like those in most cities, remained more concerned with kindergartens, clubs, and classes than with municipal reform.[6] In New York the men's clubs at University and Henry Street settlements, and Madison House were organized specifically to counter the influence of the gang and the boss in local politics, and occasionally settlement workers like Henry Moskowitz entered politics at the ward level.[7]

II

It was in Chicago that settlement workers played the most significant role in local politics. There, two-party rivalry was part of the political pattern in most wards, making reform campaigns more feasible than in Boston or New York. The presence of an aggressive group of young reformers was equally important in making the settlements a strong influence in Chicago ward politics.

Jane Addams had, typically, little political concern in the beginning; but she came to believe that politics was the most vital interest of the area "and to keep aloof from it must be to lose one opportunity of sharing the life of the neighborhood." A settlement, she decided finally, had no right to get involved in all other parts of community life and ignore politics. In the 1890's the nineteenth ward, where Hull House was located, contained about 50,000 people of twenty different nationalities, all crowded into a few square miles of flimsy, depressing tenement houses. It was a shifting, restless mass of people; the Irish and the Germans still predominated and held much of the political power, but in the last decade of the nineteenth century these two groups were being replaced by Italians, Bohemians, Poles, and Russian Jews. The newer residents had little experience with American customs or American politics, and as one reporter commented, "they are capable of being herded and driven by anyone . . . strong enough to wield the rod." [8]

In the 1890's Johnny Powers did most of the herding and driving in the nineteenth ward. A short, stocky little Irishman with a smooth-shaven face and gray hair, Powers was fifty years old in 1896. He had been the nineteenth ward's alderman since 1888, but he was no ordinary politician—he was one of the most powerful men in Chicago. In 1898 he was chairman of the Finance Committee of the Chicago City Council and boss of the caucus that distributed the chairmanships of the other committees. He controlled the Cook County Democratic Committee, also, and had been personally responsible for giving away millions of dollars in street railway franchises to Charles Yerkes and his associates. In partnership with his political henchman, William J. O'Brien, Powers owned several saloons, one conveniently located near City Hall. Although he drew a salary of three dollars a week for his services as alderman, he lived comfortably in one of the largest houses in the ward and was reportedly worth $400,000 in 1896. "He is coolheaded, cunning and wholly unscrupulous," one reporter decided. "He is the feudal lord who governs his retainers with open-handed liberality or crushes them to poverty as it suits his nearest purpose." [9]

It did not take the Hull House ladies long to realize who controlled the nineteenth ward. They noticed that a large portion of the men in the neighborhood were streetcar employees and many of the girls were telephone operators; it soon became apparent that Johnny Powers was responsible for their employment. And as the settlement workers tried to improve living and working conditions in the ward, they found their plans checkmated at almost every move. Powers acquiesced in the Hull House schemes for a park and a public bath, but when it came to a new public school, he was not so co-operative.[10]

The settlement workers maintained a kindergarten and an elaborate system of clubs and classes that did much to supplement the overcrowded school in the nineteenth ward. They also conducted an investigation that revealed that there were three thousand more pupils in the ward than seats in the school. With these statistics and a petition signed by many residents in the ward, they put their case for a new school before the Chicago School Board. The Board approved, but Powers wanted a new parochial school for the ward. His henchman O'Brien, who was chairman of the City Council Committee on Education, saw to it that the settlement workers' plan was quietly pigeonholed.[11]

Dirty streets disturbed the settlement workers even more than inadequate schools, and the streets of the nineteenth ward were filthy enough to concern anyone who could smell. Slaughterhouses, bakeries, fish peddlers, and livery stables, as well as ordinary citizens, dumped their refuse into streets and alleys that were already clogged with dirt. The Hull House reformers thought at first that a lack of understanding about the spread of disease and a lack of pride in the neighborhood caused the deplorable conditions, so they launched a campaign of education. They held meetings with the mothers in the neighborhood, set up incinerators and boxes, and organized teams to inspect the alleys. It soon became apparent, however, that other factors were responsible for conditions in the nineteenth ward. The workers reported hundreds of violations to the Health Department, but nothing was done about them. They made protests at City Hall, but the filth remained, and the death rate in the nineteenth ward continued to be one of the highest in the city. Jane Addams assigned Edward Burchard to investigate the collection system in the ward, and he discovered that Alderman Powers had used the position of garbage inspector as a political plum, handing it out to a local henchman who was more interested in collecting the money than the garbage.[12]

In the spring of 1895 Jane Addams took direct action to improve the situation. Surprising even her closest friends, she submitted a bid for the collection of garbage in the nineteenth ward. Her bid was finally thrown out on a technicality, but the publicity it received caused the Mayor to appoint her inspector for the nineteenth ward. Miss Addams took her job seriously. She appointed Amanda Johnson, a young graduate of the University of Wisconsin, as her deputy, and together they launched an attack on the filth and the garbage in the ward. They were up at six in the morning to follow the garbage wagons to the dump, and they spent much time keeping charts and maps, complaining to City Hall, arresting landlords, and arguing with the contractor. "The ward is really cleaner," Jane Addams could declare in August 1895, but the campaign against filth convinced the settlement workers that if the ward was to be kept permanently clean, they had to defeat Johnny Powers.[13]

The fight against Powers began with the Hull House Men's Club, which had been organized in 1893. The club met regularly at the settlement and was composed largely of young men from the neighborhood and a few residents. Although they held lectures and discussions on a variety of topics, most of the members were primarily interested in politics. With Jane Addams's encouragement the group nominated one of its members, Frank Lawler, as an independent candidate for alderman in the spring of 1895. Powers was more amused than concerned by the reformers' "Sunday School" attempt to enter ward politics, but with the help of the settlement workers Lawler won. The Hull House victory was short-lived, however, for the successful candidate was unable to resist the attractive inducements put before him by his colleague from the nineteenth ward. Within a matter of months, Frank Lawler, the Hull House reform alderman, was Johnny Powers's most loyal supporter.[14]

Encouraged nevertheless by "victory" in the 1895 campaign, Jane Addams decided to attack Powers himself when he came up for reelection in 1896. In opening the campaign she was thinking beyond the situation in the nineteenth ward. "I really believe," she wrote to Henry Demarest Lloyd, "that if we could get an investigation in the

19th ward against our corporation alderman it might extend to the whole city." [15]

It was not easy to find a candidate willing to oppose Powers, but after a long search the Hull House reformers settled upon William Gleeson, a forty-two-year-old Irish immigrant who was a member of the settlement Men's Club and a former president of the Chicago Bricklayers' Union. Jane Addams persuaded Hazen Pingree, the reform mayor of Detroit, to come to Chicago to open the campaign, despite the fact that Pingree was skeptical about the wisdom of trying to unseat a man like Powers. His feeling was that municipal reform had to start first in the "good" wards, the respectable areas of the city, and then spread gradually to sections like the nineteenth. Jane Addams, however, argued that in Chicago, at least, it was difficult to separate the good wards from the bad, and that, in any case, Powers's influence was city-wide.[16]

As the campaign progressed, the settlement workers attacked Powers as a tool of the trusts and the street railway magnates. They charged that he had robbed the people of the nineteenth ward by depriving them of clean streets and adequate schools while he amassed a personal fortune. They saturated the ward with posters and placards denouncing, "Yerkes and Powers, the Briber and the Bribed." They bombarded the citizens with handbills listing the grievances suffered by residents of Powers's ward. "Incomparably filthy, ill-paved, and snow-laden streets, high rates, low services, double fares . . . scant public school accommodations, lack of small parks and playgrounds, rapidly increasing tenements . . . taxation that favors the corrupt and oppresses the honest"—these were some of the things that Powers's rule had brought to the nineteenth ward. The reformers promised relief from corruption and advocated municipal ownership of the streetcar lines.[17] Jane Addams used her wide contacts throughout the city to bring outside speakers to the ward. George Cole, chairman of the Committee of One Hundred of the newly organized Municipal Voters' League, spoke to a rally in Hull House gymnasium and assured the crowd that they had the support of the League. Judge Murray F. Tuley addressed a large mass meeting at Central Music Hall and chastised the citizens of the nineteenth ward for not having enough civic pride "to overthrow this prince of the boodlers." The settlement workers, however, received little except sympathy and good wishes from the "better element" in Chicago, and their reform movement went down to defeat. Yet Gleeson did reduce Powers's usual majority. More importantly, the campaign provided the settlement workers with an education in the realities of neighborhood politics.[18]

The Hull House reformers learned, for example, that their crusade for better streets had antagonized the property owners in the ward, since the streets could not be repaved without a special tax assessment. They also learned that it had been unwise to attempt to appeal to the ordinary workingmen in the ward by nominating a workingman to run against Powers. One of the campaign posters showed Gleeson in working clothes eating from a dinner pail while Powers was shown in a dinner jacket drinking champagne. "To the chagrin of the reformers," Jane Addams later noted, ". . . it was gradually discovered that in the popular mind a man who laid bricks and wore overalls was not nearly so desirable for an alderman as the man who drank champagne and wore a diamond in his shirt front. The district wished its representative to stand up to the best of them." By the same token, the rumor that circulated widely during the campaign to the effect that Powers had received the sum of $50,000 from Charles Yerkes for campaign expenses seemed to help Powers more than it hurt him. Yerkes had recently given a large sum to an educational institution, and in the eyes of the average voter in the nineteenth ward he was a good, upright, and philanthropic citizen. In contrast, the professors and reformers who came into the ward from other sections of the city and talked about corruption seemed like cranks to the average voter.[19]

Jane Addams and the other settlement workers also got a lesson in how a successful ward boss operated to win votes. Since Powers considered the Hull House reform movement more of a joke than a threat, he resorted to nothing unusual in 1896. For him, winning votes was a year-round job: he was always on hand. When a death occurred in the neighborhood, Powers provided a stylish burial; he had a standing account at the undertaker's. When a man lost his job, Powers provided him with work; he boasted that 2600 of the residents of the nineteenth ward were on the city's payroll. When a resident of the ward got into trouble, Powers would bail him out of jail and fix matters with the judge. If a citizen of the ward needed to travel out of the city, Powers got him a free pass on the railroad. At Christmas time the loyal voter could expect a turkey from the benevolent alderman, and when Powers made gifts it was with none of the restrictions of the charity organization society. Soon after the election of 1896, the reformers discovered that many of the people in the ward who had supported the Hull House candidate expected the settlement to continue to act like a ward boss. The settlement workers were besieged with requests for aid, for help in bailing a son out of jail or getting a husband a job. Hull House could challenge Johnny Powers at election time, but the settlement could not begin to compete with the benevolent ward boss when it came to passing out favors.[20]

Despite attempts by the settlement workers to attack Powers as a corrupt man who robbed the city treasury, took bribes from the street railway magnates, and lined his own coffers while giving the nineteenth ward little in return, they could not change the image in the mind of the average voter—the image of Powers as a good friend and neighbor, who could be depended on in time of trouble. Even before the election, Jane Addams hit upon the secret of Johnny Powers's success as a ward politician. "He isn't elected because he is dishonest," she decided. "He is elected because he is a friendly visitor." [21]

Only after the campaign of 1896, however, did she begin to realize how persuasive and skillful Powers was. In the two years following the election, Powers offered a job to nearly every man who had been prominent in the campaign against him. Most of these men were members of the Hull House Men's Club. He appointed a printer who had played an important role in the reform campaign to a clerkship at City Hall. He gave a driver a new job and a large salary at the police barns, and offered William Gleeson, his opposing candidate, a lucrative position in the city construction department.[22]

Jane Addams and the other settlement workers were still not convinced that Powers was unbeatable. They pondered their mistakes, added up the lessons they had learned, and vowed they would defeat Powers in 1898. They were encouraged by the large vote piled up in 1897 by John Maynard Harlan, a reform candidate for mayor, and pleased by the passage of a new civil service law and by the election of a reform alderman in the seventeenth ward. Reform seemed to be in the air in Chicago in the last years of the nineteenth century, and reform was surely needed in the nineteenth ward.[23]

Powers himself provided fresh incentive for the reform movement in 1898. Although he continued to give away streetcar franchises and was constantly in the news because of illegal gambling in his saloons, his attack on the settlement worker who was deputy garbage inspector aroused anew the wrath of the Hull House residents. In 1896, when the position of garbage inspector became a civil service job, Amanda Johnson took the examination and passed at the top of the list. It looked as though Powers had permanently lost a job for one of his heelers. Early in January 1898, however, he demanded that the Civil Service Commission discharge Miss Johnson from her post because she had been actively campaigning against him and finding fault with his record as alderman. The newspapers as well as the Commission found Miss Johnson innocent, but Powers, as chairman of the Finance Committee of the City Council, decided that it was necessary to cut expenses. By merging the Bureau of Street and Alley Cleaning with the Department of Streets, he deprived Miss Johnson of her job.[24]

Over four hundred people meeting in Hull House gymnasium "sizzled and boiled" with indignation over Powers's attack on Miss Johnson; one of the speakers called him a disgrace to Ireland and the Catholic religion. A few days later the reformers held another meeting at Hull House and elected Professor William Hill of the University of Chicago chairman of a campaign committee that prepared once again to do battle with Johnny Powers. Hill had earlier moved to Hull House in order to vote in the ward.[25]

Jane Addams officially opened the campaign against Powers with a remarkable address to the Chicago Ethical Culture Society on Sunday, January 23, 1898. The speech, which received nation-wide publicity, was at once an attack on Johnny Powers and his methods (although his name was never mentioned) and a shrewd analysis of the forces and motives involved in city politics at the ward level. It was one of the first attempts to analyze the methods and motives of a city boss. "There has been no more important contribution to the literature of municipal government, and the study of its problems . . . ," John Gavit, editor of the *Commons* decided, and Robert Woods wrote Miss Addams, "I think it is the best thing you have ever done with the pen." [26]

Miss Addams based her address on the experience of two campaigns and eight years of observation in the nineteenth ward. "The successful candidate must be a good man according to the standards of his constituents," she emphasized. "He must not attempt to hold up a morality beyond them, nor must he attempt to reform or change the standard. His safety lies in doing, on a large scale, the good deeds which his constituents are able to do only on a small scale." She gave concrete illustrations from her experience of how a boss was able to remain in power, and she blamed the reformers for not learning from the boss. When compared with a colorful figure like Johnny Powers, most reformers seemed drab indeed. "The reformers give themselves over largely to criticism of the present state of affairs, to writing and talking of what the future must be," she decided, "but their goodness is not dramatic; it is not even concrete and human." [27]

Even though Jane Addams could understand why a man like Powers was re-elected time after time, she did not condone his actions. She attacked him for assigning city jobs in violation of the civil service law, and for saving men from prison and "fixing things" with the judge. His actions had a "blighting effect on public morals," she charged. "The positive evils of corrupt government

are bound to fall heaviest upon the poorest and least capable," she
decided. Powers gave away street railway franchises, and the people in the nineteenth ward had to pay an increased fare. He gave
them turkeys at Christmas time, but he refused to give them clean
streets and more public schools.[28]

Powers meanwhile had grown annoyed with the publicity he was
getting because of the settlement workers. "The trouble with Miss
Addams," he told a reporter, "is that she is just jealous of my charitable work in the ward." But he was in no mood to risk defeat in
1898; there was too much money at stake. Charles Yerkes was
planning to ask the Council for an ordinance extending the street
railway franchise for fifty years. By making sure the Council co-
operated, Powers stood to share the gain, but he first had to be re-
elected, and Jane Addams was all that stood in his way. "Hull
House will be driven from the ward, and its leaders will be forced
to shut up shop," Powers angrily predicted as he opened his attack
on the settlement workers.[29]

Powers was not the only one to criticize Jane Addams and Hull
House. The *Chicago Chronicle,* a newspaper with a vested interest
in the street railway franchises, issued attack after attack on the
reformers. Some of the Catholic priests in the nineteenth ward, out
of jealousy and because their churches received a large amount of
money from Powers, campaigned actively against Hull House,
charging that the settlement was anti-Catholic and anti-immigrant.
Posters and placards appeared denouncing "petticoat government,"
and Jane Addams received letters—some of them obscene—prais-
ing "that good, noble, and charitable man, Johnny Powers," and
pointing out that by living in the slums and entering politics she
had "long since forgot the pride and dignity so much admired in a
beautiful woman. . . ."[30]

The settlement workers fought back. They finally found an appealing candidate who would not sell out to Powers—Simeon Armstrong. Armstrong had lived in the ward for thirty years, and was,
like Powers, Irish and Catholic and a member of the Democratic
party. The reformers persuaded the Republican organization in
the ward to nominate Armstrong so that the opposition to Powers

would be concentrated on one candidate. The Hull House Men's Club, which had been reorganized after the election of 1896, formed a Nineteenth Ward Improvement Committee which established an organization in every precinct in the ward.[31]

The Hull House reformers printed and distributed posters, made speeches, followed up rumors of fraud, and helped to co-ordinate the precinct organizations, but they were forced to devote much of their time to raising money. Florence Kelley, Ellen Gates Starr, and Alzina Stevens worked hard in the campaign, and George Hooker, director of the Chicago City Club, supplied the campaign speakers with statistics proving Powers's corruption. Mary Kenny O'Sullivan came back to Hull House from Boston for the campaign. Well known in the nineteenth ward, she proved a valuable aid in quieting some of the Catholic opposition. One of the Italian newspapers in Chicago, *La Tribuna Italiana,* opposed Powers, and John Harlan, "the tiger of the twenty-second ward," came into the nineteenth to answer some of Powers's charges against Hull House. "There are signs that the nineteenth ward is beginning to get ashamed of Powers," he announced to a packed auditorium. "The Women of Hull House have headed the revolt against him. They have no votes, but they have influence. They have helped more people than Powers, and those whom they have aided know that it has not been done for selfish motives." [32]

Despite flowery speeches, outside support, and a vigorous campaign, the Hull House reformers were defeated again. The final results were: Powers, 5450; Armstrong, 2249. Powers had not only won; he had also wiped out the gains the reformers had made two years previously and restored his usual margin of victory.[33]

Ray Stannard Baker, the muckraking journalist who spent a few weeks at Hull House during the campaign, saw indications that Powers would be re-elected even before the results were in. Some of the small businessmen who had supported Armstrong early in the campaign began to drop away. Powers dropped a hint to a landlord here or a coal dealer there, and the men decided that they could not afford to rebel. A threat or rumor that a peddler would lose his license or a city employee his job was enough to prevent

many from supporting Hull House and Simeon Armstrong. The settlement workers made elaborate efforts to limit the number of
frauds in the registration and voting, but as Jane Addams remarked
on the day before the election, with nearly everybody corrupt, it
was "hard to prove anything." [34]

In gloating over his victory, Johnny Powers paraphrased the
words Jane Addams had used at the beginning of the campaign. "I
may not be the sort of man the reformers like," he announced, "but
I am what my people like, and neither Hull House nor all the reformers in town can turn them against me." Yet shortly after the
election, a measure to enlarge one of the public schools in the ward
was approved by the Board of Education and passed by City
Council. Johnny Powers and the Catholic priests, who had opposed such an enlargement for seven years, were strangely silent.
Perhaps the settlement workers' efforts had not been entirely in
vain.[35]

After the campaign excitement died, the inevitable question had
to be answered—should the settlement workers continue to oppose
the ward boss? Florence Kelley, one of the most able of the group,
believed that the fight should be continued. To admit defeat, to
withdraw from politics, she argued, would be to accept the conventional ethics of too many organizations that preached reform in
theory but failed to practise it in fact. "True to its avowed purpose
'to provide a centre for a higher civic and social life,' Hull House
entered the campaigns of 1896 and 1898 to make its protest on
behalf of municipal honesty," Florence Kelley maintained, "and
from that task it cannot turn back." [36]

Jane Addams could not agree. She had no intention of revising
the original purpose of Hull House, but she was more pragmatic
than Mrs. Kelley and believed that little more could be accomplished by trying again to defeat Powers. She had learned a great
deal about the realities of ward politics and more about the limitations of reform movements. She had also learned that it was impossible to accomplish much in one ward, that it was necessary to
move to the city and beyond.[37]

III

Only a short distance from Hull House, in the seventeenth ward, Chicago Commons continued to play an important role in ward politics long after Jane Addams had given up the task of unseating Powers. The seventeenth ward was as crowded and as dirty as the nineteenth, but with one major difference; the seventeenth ward did not have a Johnny Powers. There were political bosses, of course, but one man had never been able to consolidate his control and build an empire in the seventeenth ward as Powers had done. The absence of one powerful boss and the presence of an aggressive group of young reformers allowed Chicago Commons to build a ward organization that controlled the political balance of power for nearly two decades.

Not many months after Graham Taylor founded Chicago Commons in 1894, some of the men in the neighborhood, with the aid and encouragement of the settlement workers, organized a club similar to Hull House Men's Club. They called it the Seventeenth Ward Civic Federation, and they formed committees on education and political action and another to investigate the "moral evils" of the ward. The Seventeenth Ward Civic Federation met regularly at the Commons to hear lecturers like Edward Bemis or Clarence Darrow discuss municipal ownership of public utilities and other topics relating to the problems of the modern city; but the members of the Civic Federation were primarily interested in politics.[38]

They began by studying the structure of politics in the ward. Herman Hegner, a student of Taylor's at Chicago Theological School and one of the first residents of the Commons, led an investigating team that uncovered a great many irregularities in the ward's voting record. They discovered corruption in unsuspected places; thirty-nine votes, for example, had been cast in the previous election from a small house where a respected judge lived alone. They traced most of the irregularities to the leader of the Republican organization in the ward, James H. Burke. The political action committee from the Federation, accompanied by Graham Taylor, visited Burke and demanded two things: that he nominate reasonable men for alderman, and that the ballots be counted as they were cast. Burke laughed at the reformers and boasted that he controlled the elections because four hundred residents of the ward were employed by the city and voted as he directed, or lost their jobs.[39]

The leading Democrat in the ward was no more co-operative, so the settlement club decided to enter the election for alderman in 1895. With some misgivings, they supported an independent candidate, Thomas Johnson. The Seventeenth Ward Civic Federation held five large mass meetings and provided two inspectors at each polling place, but Johnson lost. Although the reformers suspected that there had been irregularities and fraud they did not have enough evidence to challenge the political organization.[40]

The next year the settlement club appointed four Democrats and four Republicans to work through their own parties for better aldermen. They invited all the candidates to speak at a meeting of the Civic Federation, and after hearing them the club members endorsed the Republican candidate, Magnus Knudson, a thirty-three-year-old Norwegian. This time the Federation's "reform candidate" won the election. Not long afterward, however, Knudson, along with his colleague from the seventeenth ward, voted with the "boodlers" on street railway franchises. The reformers immediately called a meeting, and the assembly room at the Commons was packed with interested citizens, as the "reform alderman" tried to explain his vote. The settlement had become a rallying point for reform in the ward.[41]

In 1897 the men's club, determined that they would not be "double-crossed" again, nominated one of their own members, James Walsh, on an independent ticket. Walsh lost by the narrowest of margins, but the settlement reformers charged that the returns had been illegally altered, and this time they had evidence to prove their case. They launched a public protest, and Graham Taylor presided over a large mass meeting which gave voice to the "indignation of hundreds of voters of the 17th ward." Their protest led to an official investigation and the arrest of two clerks and a precinct judge. James Walsh was declared the winner and alderman from the seventeenth ward. Walsh lived up to the expectations of the settlement workers who had fought hard to get him onto the City Council. He became one of the leaders in the fight against Yerkes's attempt to extend the franchise of the Chicago street railways. In fact, the election of Walsh marked the decline of the political boss and the rise of Chicago Commons as a real factor in ward politics.[42]

The excitement aroused by the attempt to extend the franchise and the resulting campaign for municipal ownership led to a new political organization in the seventeenth ward. With the aid of the settlement workers, some of the younger men in the ward organized the Municipal Club. The club had little success in promoting municipal ownership, but it did help elect an alderman from the seventeenth ward in 1901. The Municipal Club came on the scene at the same time that a reorganization of wards in Chicago greatly enlarged the size of the seventeenth to include a large number of Polish and German voters within its boundaries. The club, with the help of the settlement workers, organized a coalition of Polish, German, and Scandinavian voters that demanded the nomination of a Polish candidate and then elected John Smulski to a seat on the City Council.[43]

After the successful ward campaign of 1901, the Municipal Club, together with the remnants of the Civic Federation and with several residents of Chicago Commons, organized the Seventeenth Ward Community Club with headquarters at the settlement. It was explicitly designed as a nonpartisan, local political organization. "There is no high tariff nor free silver way of running the municipal affairs of the city of Chicago . . . ," the constitution of the Community Club announced. "The purpose of the club is to unite men of common interests for action in neighborhood and civic affairs." The settlement club played a large part in influencing the politics in the ward for the next fifteen years.[44]

Graham Taylor was the major reason that Chicago Commons became a political force in its ward. He had a rare ability to organize and inspire those around him. A professor at the University of Chicago, and member of the Municipal Voters' League, the City Club, and a dozen other organizations, Taylor had influence in many quarters of the city. Through his weekly editorials in the *Chicago Daily News* and his monthly articles in the *Commons*, he publicized the needs of the seventeenth ward throughout the city. He was respected, if not admired, by all who knew him. On occasion, he could behave like the hardened, practical politician, but he was a minister, and always carried himself with an air of reserve that some took for aloofness.[45] Taylor could not have made the Community Club an effective political organization alone, and he was fortunate in having at the Commons a number of young men who enjoyed the excitement of ward politics.

Herman Hegner was in the first group to live at Chicago Commons. He threw himself into the political fight with an ardor that belied his theological training. John Palmer Gavit gave up a job as a newspaper writer to go to live at Chicago Commons. He edited the *Commons* in its first four years, and also found time to play an active role in several political campaigns. James Mullenbach, who originally came to Chicago Commons to learn about the slums so that he could be a minister in an institutional church, stayed on for more than ten years. He managed the city's Municipal Lodging House, but also attended meetings of the Community Club and took part in all their attempts to clean up the ward. Allen T. Burns came from his graduate work at the University of Chicago to the settlement and immediately threw himself into the activities of the Community Club. For Burns, as for a great many other bright young men, these campaigns served as an apprenticeship in practical reform techniques, and he spent a lifetime applying the things he learned in the seventeenth ward.[46]

None of the residents of Chicago Commons, not even Graham Taylor, exerted a greater influence on politics in the seventeenth ward than did Raymond Robins. Robins wandered into Chicago Commons in February 1901, and offered to remain at his own expense. In spite of his youth, he had a background of practical experience that proved a valuable asset in the give-and-take of ward politics, and Robins was soon accepted by the local citizens because he had none of the reserve that sometimes proved a handicap to

Graham Taylor. Robins had the ability to command without antagonizing. He helped organize the Community Club and became one of its most active members. It was not long before Taylor realized that he had a "past master of ward politics." [47]

In 1902 Robins and Taylor persuaded William Dever, a young Irishman who had studied law at night while working in a tannery during the day, to run on the Democratic ticket for alderman of the seventeenth ward. In 1901 the seventeenth ward had elected a Republican alderman; the following year the settlement club, with the endorsement of the Municipal Voters' League, swung the balance of power to Dever, and after an energetic campaign led by the Seventeenth Ward Community Club, he was elected.[48]

In 1903 the Community Club selected Republican Lewis Sitts as an ideal alderman, and they were able to secure his nomination. A basement room at the Commons served as headquarters for the campaign. Members of the settlement club sent out circulars to all the registered voters in the ward, comparing Sitts's record with that of his rival. They organized mass meetings and torch parades and showered the ward with posters, placards, and handbills. Taylor and Robins secured the endorsement of the Municipal Voters' League and the support of much of the press. On election day the Community Club provided poll watchers at every polling place in the ward. Sitts was elected by a large majority in spite of the fact that the Democratic candidate for mayor carried the ward. After the election of 1903, Taylor concluded, with justification, that in the seventeenth ward the settlement had replaced the saloon as a rallying place for local politics, and the Community Club had replaced the ward boss in controlling the balance of power in the ward.[49]

Shortly after the election of 1903, Robins accepted a position as head resident of Northwestern University Settlement. One of his first activities was to organize a Civic Club patterned after the Community Club of Chicago Commons. The two settlements cooperated in many reform campaigns, strengthening the independent political organization in the ward.[50] The crisis of 1906 was a good example. Just three weeks before the election William Dever voted for an ordinance that provided an increased fee for saloon licenses. In a ward where there were over four hundred saloons, this would have been political suicide in 1896, but in 1906, with the Community Club and the Civic Club supporting him, Dever was re-elected alderman by a large majority. By serving as a rallying point for municipal reform and by controlling the balance of power in the ward, Chicago Commons, along with Northwestern Settlement, in effect dictated the outcome of fourteen consecutive alderman's elections in the ward.[51]

Success in electing aldermen encouraged Taylor and Robins to extend the influence of the settlement, having learned, as did all civic reformers, that reform in the ward was closely related to reform in the city, and that municipal reform meant little without reform in the state. Taylor was more reluctant than Robins to extend the political influence of the settlement beyond the ward, but they could agree that it was part of the settlement's responsibility to elect good senators and representatives from the settlement's own district.[52]

In 1902, Taylor and several other prominent Chicago citizens urged Robins to run for senator from the twenty-first senatorial district (which included the seventeenth ward) in an attempt to defeat two especially corrupt candidates. Robins, however, preferred to work behind the scenes in promoting reform. He supported the candidacy of John J. McManaman, who was nominated on an independent ticket. Robins enlisted Clarence Darrow's help in the campaign. The Seventeenth Ward Community Club and the Municipal Voters' League joined the fight, and McManaman defeated both regular party candidates in a district where an independent had never won before.[53]

In 1904 the settlement club again entered a state campaign. Cooperating with the Municipal Voters' League, the reformers joined a city-wide attempt to upset the plans of the boss-controlled Republican and Democratic organizations in Chicago. The independent settlement organization in the seventeenth ward nominated Walter Elphinsone, president of the local shoemakers' union and for three years president of the Seventeenth Ward Community Club, as an independent candidate for the Illinois House of Representatives. Elphinsone had the support of the press; and the settlement clubs, led by Raymond Robins, carried on an aggressive campaign. But Robins had realized from the start that it was a "forlorn hope." The three regular party candidates were elected in the twenty-first district, with Elphinsone a poor fourth. Robins and Taylor learned the hard way that it was much more difficult to control an election in a congressional district than to hold the balance of power in one ward.[54] Defeat, however, did not dim the luster of the reformers' political importance, for in one ward Raymond Robins and Graham Taylor had made the settlement an antidote to boss rule in ward politics.

The settlement workers' impact on local politics in the seventeenth ward in Chicago was impressive and unusual, but whether they were participants in local politics or merely observers, and regardless of whether they defeated the ward boss or were defeated by him, the settlement workers invariably came to appreciate the usefulness of the politician and to learn from him, even as they despaired his lack of honesty and civic pride. They were among the first to analyze the source of the bosses' strength.[55] But they also learned that little could be accomplished in a single ward, and they were led to participate in a variety of city-wide reform campaigns.

9

The Settlement Movement
and Municipal Reform

The people who knew the city best were usually "the priests, the politicians, and the settlement residents," Mary Simkhovitch once recalled. Of these, the settlement workers were the most accessible and most eager to share their knowledge. At Hull House the residents took turns "toting" visitors around the neighborhood, showing them the sights and sounds of a crowded industrial city. Many of those who came were interested only in collecting local color; yet there were some who were seriously concerned with studying the city and finding answers to its problems. For these, the settlement house often served as a source of knowledge and a base for reform.[1]

In the progressive era urban sociology and the study of urban politics and economics were closely linked to the social gospel, the settlement movement, and municipal reform.[2] Charles Zueblin, social gospel minister, pioneer sociologist, and civic reformer, founded Northwestern University Settlement in Chicago in 1891 as a laboratory to study the city, and as a beachhead in the movement to try to change it. Frank Goodnow, a professor of administrative law and political science at Columbia University and author of several books on the city and its problems, served on the council of

University Settlement in New York and was strongly influenced by the settlement idea of neighborhood reconstruction. Economists Richard T. Ely, John R. Commons, and Edward Bemis were frequent visitors at several settlements, and Ely helped to found the University of Wisconsin Settlement in Milwaukee. Frank Parsons, author of *The City for the People*, was for many years connected with the work of Civic Service House in Boston.[3] Frederick C. Howe, one of Mayor Tom Johnson's reform lieutenants in Cleveland and the author of *The City: The Hope of Democracy*, was a resident for a brief period at Goodrich House in Cleveland. Later in an autobiography written at the peak of the postwar reaction against reform, Howe described his disenchantment with the settlement movement. He remembered how uncomfortable he felt when he visited tenements and organized clubs, and especially when he danced with the heavy-footed immigrant women. He recalled how he conducted investigations, and made charts and reports that no one read. Howe found his settlement experience "anything but fruitful." Charles Beard, historian and expert on municipal government, however, was profoundly influenced by his stay at a settlement. "I was introduced to a new world at meetings in the Hull House in the summer of 1896," he later recalled.[4] Those interested in municipal reform in the progressive era sometimes criticized the social workers for their methods and idealism, but they did not often ignore the settlement movement.

Few people may have bothered to read the reports and charts prepared at Goodrich House, but those interested in reforming the city did not overlook the stream of articles and books written by settlement workers in Boston, Chicago, and New York. These books and articles often provided the only information available on various aspects of urban living in the late nineteenth and early twentieth centuries. Many of the early settlement workers were influenced by Charles Booth's *Life and Labour of the People of London*, and they set out to emulate his painstaking research and to gather statistics about urban life, first in their neighborhood, then in the city. They investigated child labor, tenement houses, and tuberculosis, and they were interested in studying the problems of the city in all its aspects. The Hull House residents made a careful survey of a small area near the settlement; the residents of South End House studied sections of Boston and published their findings in *City Wilderness* and *Americans in Process*. They also made another study called "The Zone of Emergence," which together with Graham Romeyn Taylor's *Satellite Cities* (1915) marked the first attempt to analyze the new suburbs already beginning to grow around American cities in the first decade of the twentieth century. The settlement workers' reports became more detailed and more sophisticated as they gained experience. Despite the charts and graphs and statistics, however, their studies were hardly objective. They often made moral judgments about what they saw, and they did not hide the fact that they felt the major reason for investigation was to prepare the way for reform. They believed that despite grave problems and difficulties, there was hope for the American city.[5]

The settlement workers were not alone in studying the city. Especially in the early years of the twentieth century, many other groups investigated various aspects of urban living.[6] In 1905, the same year that the settlement and charity organization periodicals merged to form *Charities and the Commons*, settlement workers and other reformers organized the Charities Publication Committee specifically to sponsor social investigations. Jane Addams, Margaret Dreier Robins, and Jacob Riis were among those on the committee that immediately began two studies, one on the lot of the Negro in northern cities, the other on conditions of life, labor, and education in Washington, D. C. The success of these investigations and financial support from the newly organized Russell Sage Foundation inspired a much more ambitious project—the Pittsburgh Survey.[7]

The Pittsburgh Survey attempted to study one industrial city as carefully and as thoroughly as possible. It was directed by Paul Kellogg, a young man of twenty-eight who had given up a job as city editor on the newspaper in his home town of Kalamazoo, Michigan, to come to New York. There he found many outlets for his editorial and organizing ability. He resided for a time at Mary Simkhovitch's Greenwich House; he worked on the various publications of the New York Charity Organization Society and became an expert at social research. The Pittsburgh Survey was a co-operative project utilizing the aid and advice of a large group of experts and "social engineers" from many cities, but it built directly on the results and experiences of the settlement movement. Robert Woods, Florence Kelley, and John R. Commons served as an informal advisory committee. The Pittsburgh settlement workers, especially William Mathews of Kingsley House, provided valuable assistance and information to the visiting investigators. Crystal Eastman, a beautiful, vibrant girl with a law degree from New York University who had received some research training while a resident of Greenwich House, worked on the volume in the final report on *Work Accidents and the Law*. The Pittsburgh Survey, published in six volumes from 1909 to 1914, revealed the cost and the consequences of low wages and poor pay, of preventable diseases and industrial accidents, of ramshackle tenements and little planning. With indisputable statistics and page after page of factual description, the investigators documented the appalling human waste and misery, and drove home the need of reform, regulation, and planning in the industrial city. The Pittsburgh Survey was read, summarized, and discussed around the country. It inspired other surveys and investigations. It also fed the fires of reform.[8]

Reform and investigation were interrelated for the settlement workers, who often had an exaggerated conception of the power of statistics, and an idealistic belief that if people could be told the truth reform would follow naturally. Yet their base in a working-class neighborhood did serve to temper their idealism and make them realize the need for practical organization to promote reform in the city. The settlement workers were more skeptical than most reformers about the advantages of defeating corrupt mayors or revising inadequate charters. They had learned in their neighborhoods that mere opposition was not enough, but they remained interested in politics. "I never go into a tenement without longing for a better city government," Jane Robbins once remarked.[9]

Many settlement workers, especially in the first decade of the twentieth century, joined municipal reform movements led and inspired by business and professional men who were primarily inter-

ested in honest and efficient city government, and if possible, in a
lower tax rate. Settlement workers in Boston, Chicago, and New
York often co-operated with businessmen in attempts to defeat corrupt politicians and to revise antiquated charters. Yet they did
more than acquiesce in these municipal reform movements begun
by others. Although they did not often run for political office, they
did serve as advisers and campaign managers and as experts and
brain-trusters. In the process they helped to move municipal reform, in a few cities at least, from opposition to charters and bosses
to promotion of social welfare.

II

Robert Woods, head resident of South End House in Boston, was
an unlikely municipal reformer. Always immaculately dressed, he
often gave the impression of ministerial aloofness, even though he
wanted desperately to become friends with the immigrant neighbors. He did not delude himself into thinking that the immigrants
would accept the reformers as their "own kind." "The relation between the settlements and their neighbors is an artificial one. I
don't know that it can ever be otherwise," he remarked at one
point. He opposed a partisan stand in ward politics, but believed
that settlement workers ought to publicize the needs of their neighborhoods.[10]

A public bath was one of the most obvious needs of an area
where fifty thousand people were crowded into a square mile of
squalid tenements. Beginning in 1892, the residents of South End
House made regular trips to City Hall to appeal to the Boston City
Council. Each year the politicians listened to the settlement workers' pleas, but refused to appropriate the necessary money. In 1895,
however, when Josiah Quincy, III, decided to follow in his ances-
tor's footsteps and become mayor, he remembered the settlement
workers' descriptions of the needs of the South End. He consulted
Robert Woods, and on his advice included the erection of municipal bathhouses in his campaign promises.[11]

Quincy was elected Mayor of Boston in 1895 and re-elected in

1897. One of his first acts was to appoint Woods the chairman of a committee that effectively demonstrated the need for bathhouses in several sections of the city. This time an appropriations bill passed the Council. A few months later the first municipally owned bathhouses in the country opened at Dover Street near South End House.[12] The city also took over several other facilities, including several gymnasiums and playgrounds begun by settlements. Quincy optimistically predicted that the new bathhouses would cause a drop in the death and disease rate and solve the problem of "filthy tenement houses." He also seemed relieved that the unwashed slum dwellers would no longer be a "menace to their fellow citizens whom they come in contact with on the cars and in the streets." Whatever his motives may have been, Quincy sought the advice of the settlement workers and they helped him make Boston the leading American city as far as extending municipal government to the area of public welfare.[13]

The settlement workers' influence was unfortunately short-lived because a succession of Irish-Catholic politicians followed Josiah Quincy, and the reformers no longer had easy access to the mayor's office. But they continued to support "a municipal platform calling for playgrounds, public baths, public gymnasiums, public libraries, popular lectures, and concerts in the tenement house districts. . . ." They investigated the problems of the working-class districts and published their findings in books and articles and reports. They organized the South End Social Union and the Boston Social Union to promote reform and prevent duplication of effort. They continued their frequent trips to City Hall, to lobby and to testify before committee and Council. Settlement workers in Boston tried to avoid the "role of opposition" in attempting to make Boston a better place in which to live, but despite their professed nonpartisanship they did join several reform campaigns.[14]

The rising tide of municipal reform in Boston in the first decade of the twentieth century had many sources: it built on the accomplishments of Mayor Quincy, was influenced by other reform movements in New York, Chicago, and Cleveland, and was affected by ethnic and religious prejudice against Irish immigrants. It was organized by a group of public-minded businessmen, led by Edward A. Filene, and by civic organizations such as the Public School Association and the Twentieth Century Club. The settlement workers helped arouse businessmen to action and played an active role in the organization of the Good Government Association and the City Club.[15]

The Good Government Association, organized in 1903 and immediately dubbed the "Goo Goos" by the politicians, actively opposed Democrat John Fitzgerald in the mayoralty election in 1905. The fact that Robert Woods had earlier exposed Fitzgerald's political tactics did not prevent his victory. Boston was in a "peculiarly unfortunate position" in the national movement for municipal reform, Woods decided after the election. With artificial boundaries cutting off most of the suburban population from the city, Boston's government was in "full control of the downtown districts." This situation convinced Woods that the settlement house was a "clearly indispensable agency for effectively representing . . . the better public sentiment of the local districts . . . ." Woods, even before 1905, had begun to realize that the settlement idea of promoting reform from within the neighborhood needed modification. It was difficult to produce an enlightened electorate in a depressed area where the natural leaders moved away as soon as they were able. Reform in the neighborhood was not possible without the support and co-operation of "the public spirited people throughout the city." In the first decade of the twentieth century the settlement workers joined these public-spirited people in a variety of attempts to reform the neighborhood by emancipating the city from the grasp of corrupt politicians.[16]

The residents at South End House made it very clear in their studies of the political structure of the downtown districts that local political corruption depended largely on the entrée to the city treasury by way of the board of aldermen. Well-organized machines and the solidarity of the Irish voters made many of the aldermen unbeatable and the City Council a bulwark against reform. The settlement workers' analysis of the political situation in Boston, reinforced by the conviction of many municipal reformers in other cities, led to a change in the method of electing aldermen in Boston. Other cities were gradually reducing the power of the City Council, hoping that this would help clear the way for municipal reform, but Boston was one of the first to elect its aldermen at-large. After 1905 the reformers were able to concentrate their support on a few candidates throughout the city.[17]

Ironically, it was a commission appointed by Mayor Fitzgerald that crystallized the reform movement and brought it to a climax in the years 1907 to 1910. Fitzgerald, hoping to take some of the bite out of the charges that his administration was the most corrupt in Boston's history, appointed a Finance Commission composed largely of members of the Good Government Association, with former Mayor Nathan Mathews as chairman, to investigate waste and extravagance in the city government. Given this unexpected chance, the reformers did much more than pinpoint waste and inefficiency; they proceeded to examine and overhaul the city charter.[18] Fitzgerald was defeated in 1907, and Woods, who only two years before had been discouraged by the failure of the reformers to produce an enlightened electorate, credited the settlements with helping engineer the revolution that caused twenty thousand Democratic voters to mark their ballots against Fitzgerald, their party's candidate. He believed the settlements had "much to do with creating the mental and moral attitude among the rank and file of the city's electorate without which even the work of the Finance Commission would have been comparatively meaningless and barren." Woods's jubilation over Fitzgerald's defeat caused him to over-emphasize his own importance in influencing the rank and file of the city's voters (Fitzgerald, for example, carried the ward in which South End House was located); but undeniably the settlement workers' exposure of Fitzgerald helped bring about his defeat. The victory over Fitzgerald in 1907 was, however, a shallow one. The new mayor, George Hibbard, was of such dubious quality that the Good Government Association had refused to endorse his candidacy.[19]

The reformers were confident, nevertheless, that they could elect a reform mayor, and many of their recommendations for changes in the city charter were designed to concentrate more power in that office. They submitted two proposals to the people of Boston on November 2, 1909. Plan One called for a mayor elected for two years and a legislature with nine members elected at-large; and Plan Two was similar except that the mayor would be elected for four years. Plan Two, which was favored by the Good Government Association and the settlement workers, also provided that the nominations for mayor be made by a petition containing five thousand signatures, and that all party designations be excluded from the ballot.[20]

Robert Woods, Meyer Bloomfield, and many other settlement workers campaigned for the acceptance of Plan Two. Together with other members of the Good Government Association, they confidently believed that the plan would "abolish the municipal boss, . . . the money-bought nomination, . . . the irresponsibly large council, the wasteful division of public funds, . . . and place power in the people. . . ." Plan Two won by a narrow margin, partly because of the energetic campaign carried on by the reformers, and partly because political bosses Fitzgerald, Donovan, and Curley also decided to support that plan.[21]

Plan Two called for a mayoralty election early in January, giving the reformers barely two months to find a candidate and organize a campaign against Fitzgerald, who would certainly be a nominee even if under the new system he carried no label. Meyer Bloomfield, the head resident of Civic Service House, was secretary of the Good Government Association committee that had the responsibility of selecting the reform candidate. Bloomfield's committee, dubbed the "mayor makers" by one of the newspapers, finally decided on James J. Storrow, a prominent young Boston businessman and civic leader.[22] He was a partner in the brokerage firm Lee, Higginson & Company, had served on the Boston School Committee, and had helped to organize the City Club. He was not only acquainted with many of the settlement workers and a good friend of Robert Woods, he was an experienced worker himself, having founded West Side House, a settlement centered around the activity of a boys' club.[23]

Faced for the first time with a campaign for political office, Storrow depended on the advice and counsel of his settlement friends in selecting the men to help him. Woods, who had previously maintained that a settlement should never take a partisan stand in a political campaign, decided in 1909 that with "the removal of party designations and the appearance of two so sharply contrasted candidates, the question was simply that of the best interests of the city." [24] Woods stumped the city in support of Storrow, but he was not an effective public speaker. His real influence was more subtle. He was primarily responsible for surrounding Storrow with a brain-trust of young settlement workers—Edmund Billings, Robert Bottomley, William Prest, and David Howie.

Edmund Billings, who did not remain a settlement worker for long, was then the superintendent of the Wells Memorial Institute (an organization dedicated to the education of workingmen) located only two blocks from South End House. Woods and Billings had cooperated on many projects to improve the lot of workingmen in the area. Billings was secretary of the Good Government Association when on Woods's advice he resigned to become Storrow's campaign manager. [25]

Billings's replacement in the Association was Robert Bottomley, a towering, six-foot four-inch Amherst graduate, whom boss Martin Lomasney called "the sweet-smelling geranium of reform." Bottomley had spent two years at South End House and with Woods's help became active in the Good Government Association soon after its organization; he remained closely associated with Woods and other settlement workers in Boston long after he gave up being a resident for a career in municipal reform. He was secretary of the committee that campaigned for the adoption of Plan Two and chief coordinator of the Storrow campaign in 1910. [26]

William Prest was a lawyer living at South End House who, four nights a week, gave free legal advice to anyone who cared to come to the settlement. He became Storrow's assistant campaign manager and treasurer of the campaign committee. David Howie, a young Harvard graduate and a resident of South End House, served as Storrow's private secretary and trouble-shooter during the campaign, and Storrow came to depend on Howie's judgment and initiative.[27]

The settlement workers remained in the background, but they helped Storrow and the Good Government Association carry on an aggressive campaign. The newspapers commented on the "clockwork" precision of the reform organization, but efficient organization could not overcome the shrewdness of a practical Irish politician, and Storrow lost by a narrow margin. Woods found some solace in the returns from the usually Democratic ninth ward (the ward in which the South End House was located); there Storrow led Fitzgerald by more than three hundred votes.[28] But this did not take the sting out of the defeat in 1910—a defeat made more bitter because the reformed charter made Fitzgerald mayor for four rather than two years. Although Woods and the others were disappointed, they continued to investigate urban problems and to work for reform in the city. They even convinced Fitzgerald of the need of another small park in the South End. But the frustrating results of municipal reform efforts helped reinforce their conviction that a program of social welfare could only be accomplished by national legislation and national reform.[29]

III

There was, in New York as well as in Boston, a group of settlement workers interested in political reform for the city. "Go into politics," James B. Reynolds urged a group of residents in 1896. "Be earnest, practical, and be active. Political reform is the great moral opportunity of our day." Settlement workers, Reynolds decided, ought to study municipal government, formulate a program of reform, perfect a political organization, and consider not only how to "sow the seeds of right" but also how to win a majority at the polls.[30] With Reynolds taking the lead, they played a significant part in programs for political and social reform in New York City in the last decade of the nineteenth century. Municipal reform in New York became by necessity an anti-Tammany movement. Settlement workers took part in several campaigns against Tammany candidates and got caught up in the spirit of the battle, but they also looked beyond elections to their major goal of humanizing the industrial city.

From the day he became head resident of University Settlement in 1893, Reynolds sought to make the settlement an influence in civic affairs. He was one of the leading members of the Committee of Seventy, formed in 1893 to challenge the political dominance of Tammany Hall and promote municipal home rule and honest government in New York. He was also an active participant in the successful reform campaign that put William Strong in the mayor's office in 1894. During Strong's administration he served on many committees and commissions and was a school trustee from the tenth ward.[31]

The election of Mayor William Strong through nonpartisan action convinced a group of reformers, including many settlement residents, that a permanent nonpartisan political organization was needed. "Good city government cannot be secured through the agency of existing parties organized upon national and state issues," the Committee of Seventy decided, and the Citizens' Union was born. Reynolds became one of its most active members; he was chairman of the executive committee and a persuasive advocate for the nomination of an independent candidate for mayor in 1897.[32]

The Citizens' Union considered the election of 1897 a crucial test for municipal reform in New York; it was the first under the new charter that had added Brooklyn to Greater New York and separated municipal from state and national elections. The reformers sought a strong candidate to challenge the dominance of Tammany Hall and finally decided on Seth Low, who had served two terms as mayor of Brooklyn before he became president of Columbia University. Low was also a member of the council of University Settlement and a good friend of Reynolds, who was primarily responsible for drafting him as a reform candidate.[33]

Low was disturbed by the attitude of many of the members of the Citizens' Union; they seemed to him, like the prohibitionists, to be merely "running a ticket for the fun of it," but he respected Reynolds and depended upon his advice and counsel. Reynolds worked behind the scenes to manage Low's reform campaign. He approved the candidate's speeches before they were delivered, answered letters, made statements to the press, suggested candidates for the other offices, and planned the campaign.[34] An integral part of Reynolds's strategy was to use his friends in the settlements as ward heelers for the reform organization. Lillian Wald at Henry Street Settlement and Elizabeth Williams at College Settlement helped to organize support for Low on the East Side. Felix Adler, Jacob Riis, and Josephine Shaw Lowell, all friends of the settlement movement, joined the campaign. Reynolds enlisted the clubs at University Settlement and Everett Wheeler obtained the support of the residents of East Side House. Even the small boys at the settlements distributed handbills and acted as messengers. A decade later a resident of Henry Street remembered "Miss Wald in blue-checked dress giving final instruction to her corps of assistants, and sending them forth with their printed sheets . . . to help secure a clean mayoralty for our great city." [35]

The reform campaign in New York in 1897 was complicated by many factors. The Citizens' Union and the settlement workers aimed their attack at the Tammany candidate, Robert C. Van Wyck, but the Republicans refused to accept Low as their candidate and nominated Benjamin Tracy. To add to the confusion of candidates and issues, Henry George, the single-tax reform advocate, decided to run on the Independent Democratic ticket. The energy and hard work of James B. Reynolds in organizing the Citizens' Union campaign and the enthusiastic support of the other settlement workers were not enough to offset the Tammany organization in an election where the opposition was split, and Seth Low went down to defeat in 1897.[36]

Four years later the reformers and Seth Low tried again. Reynolds resumed his role as campaign manager and strategist, and the settlement workers, with the Women's Municipal League and the City Club and helped by Justice William Travers Jerome, made effective use of statistics and stories exposing the connections between organized vice and politics in New York.[37] Again, as in 1897, the settlements played an important part in the ward organization of the reform campaign, and Everett Wheeler used his influence with lawyers in the city to develop an effective system of district poll watchers.[38]

One of the most active organizers in the reform campaign on the Lower East Side in 1901 was Henry Moskowitz, a young man who had attended classes and clubs at Neighborhood Guild and University Settlement as a boy. He had graduated from City College in 1899 and was taking graduate work at Columbia, but he maintained his interest in settlement work and political reform through Madison House. In Brooklyn one of the leading reform campaigners was Raymond Ingersoll, a young Amherst graduate who had been a resident of University Settlement while attending New York University Law School. When he graduated in 1900 he moved to Brooklyn and lived at Maxwell House. In 1901 Ingersoll campaigned for Seth Low and himself ran for the position of police magistrate.[39] This time the anti-Tammany forces all agreed to support the Citizens' Union candidate, and Seth Low was elected. One of Low's first actions on taking office was to appoint settlement worker James Reynolds as his private secretary.[40]

For two years Reynolds served as the "outside man" and the "listening post" for the reform administration. With tact, patience, and sympathy he heard the grievances and the visionary schemes of the thousands who had advice to give the reformers. Reynolds also headed an informal brain-trust of social workers who worked closely with Mayor Low in extending the public welfare functions of the city government.[41] For two years the settlement workers and other reformers used their direct line to the Mayor to promote better housing laws, more parks and playgrounds, a reorganized Health Department, and a city-supported system of visiting nurses in the public schools.[42]

The Mayor did not always follow the social workers' advice; he refused to appoint Lawrence Veiller tenement commissioner because he thought Veiller was too radical, and his relationship with organized labor was strained, to say the least. "The administration of Mayor Low may not have been perfect . . ." Lincoln Steffens decided, "nevertheless for an American city it has been not only honest but able, undeniably one of the best in the whole country."

There were critics, but many observers agreed with Steffens's analysis of the Low administration, although this did not save the reformers from a defeat in 1903.[43]

There were many reasons for the defeat of reform in New York in 1903. Low, a Republican, had angered some of his Democratic and independent supporters by speaking for the Republican state ticket in 1902. He often gave the impression of being aloof and dignified, too much concerned with efficiency, too little with reform; and his insistence on supporting the Sunday closing of saloons contributed to his downfall. The primary cause of defeat, however, was the inability of a reform administration in a brief two years to build up an organization that could compete on equal terms with Tammany Hall.[44] The settlement workers studied the methods and techniques of the Tammany politicians and utilized what they learned in managing the reform campaign, but they were handicapped by lack of money and too many scruples in their attempt to maintain an organization between elections. Henry Moskowitz and others dreamed of a settlement house in every ward and a close-knit political organization designed to counteract the influence of Tammany Hall. This dream never became a reality; instead, the settlement workers had to depend on more frustrating, spasmodic methods for reforming the city.[45]

Despite the settlement workers' part in making New York a cleaner, safer, more pleasant place during Mayor Low's administration, they were disappointed by the small impact of their efforts; yet they continued their campaign even after Low's defeat. Lillian Wald, Mary Simkhovitch, Jane Robbins, and others made frequent trips to Albany and City Hall; they testified before committees and commissions, wrote letters to aldermen, assemblymen, mayors, and governors, and played a part in influencing legislation on garbage collection, parks and playgrounds, kindergarten training, reorganization of the police department, taxation and the city budget, workmen's compensation, and many other matters relating to the improvement of living and working conditions in New York City.[46]

The settlement workers' influence was not dependent on success at the polls, but they did not give up hope for political reform. In

1909 Moskowitz, then the head resident of Madison House and Raymond Ingersoll, head resident of Maxwell House in Brooklyn, played prominent parts in another anti-Tammany reform campaign. Moskowitz was the chairman of a small group that appointed a committee of one hundred to conduct the campaign. Both men were members of this larger committee, and Ingersoll was chairman of the executive committee and campaign manager for the fusion ticket headed by Otto T. Bannard, a banker and philanthropist. Bannard was defeated largely because William Randolph Hearst, who refused to support the fusion ticket, ran as an independent and split the reform vote. The reformers, however, did elect their candidates to almost every major office except that of mayor.[47] And the settlement workers had cause to applaud William Gaynor, the successful Tammany candidate for mayor in 1909. One of his first actions was to appoint Charles B. Stover, settlement worker and crusader for parks and playgrounds, to the position of Park Commissioner—a fitting tribute to a man who had devoted twenty years to the campaign to provide the children of New York with adequate and safe places to play.[48]

Despite the excitement of political campaigns, the settlements' greatest contribution to municipal reform in New York and in other cities was probably their education of a generation of young men in the tactics of reform and the training of a group of experts in city administration. Henry Bruère and Raymond Fosdick were among those who were inspired by their settlement experience to do something about the problems of the city, and both contributed to the movement for municipal efficiency and scientific management.[49]

Henry Bruère was a resident at Denison House in Boston, but he made frequent visits to the New York settlements and was especially influenced by Robert Hunter, the outspoken young radical who replaced Reynolds as head resident of University Settlement. At the settlement, Bruère met Stanley McCormick, who talked him into coming to Chicago in 1903 to apply settlement methods to the problems of a large industrial plant. The experiment was not altogether successful, but Bruère profited from his association with Raymond Robins, Jane Addams, Graham Taylor, and the rest of the settlement workers in Chicago. He studied their methods of investigation and reform and returned to New York in 1905 ready to begin his own personal attack on the problems of the city.[50]

Bruère sought out Robert Hunter, who introduced him to William H. Allen, an agent for the Association for Improving the Condition of the Poor, and to Robert Fulton Cutting, an official of the Citizens' Union. These men talked to Bruère about municipal reform and hired him to set up a Bureau of City Betterment. He set out to apply his idea that municipal reform must be based on facts, organization, and management, rather than on reform campaigns. He made a study of public baths and then a study of the borough president and the Health Department. He uncovered enough information on corruption and inefficiency to cause the removal of John Ahearn, the borough president. In 1907, the Bureau of City Betterment was made permanent and renamed the Bureau of Municipal Research. Bruère and other social workers remained the driving force behind this new organization which went a long way toward introducing administrative efficiency into the government of American cities.[51]

As director of the Bureau of Municipal Research, Henry Bruère met John Purroy Mitchel, a young and able lawyer who served during Mayor George B. McClellan's second administration (1906–1910) as Commissioner of Accounts. He also met Mitchel's young assistant, Raymond Fosdick, who had been a resident at Henry Street Settlement and had also helped to organize the campaign for the re-election of District Attorney William Travers Jerome in 1905. Fosdick became Assistant Commissioner of Accounts, and later under Mayor Gaynor, Chief Commissioner of Accounts. He co-operated with Bruère in investigating graft and promoting efficiency in New York City government.[52]

In 1913 John Purroy Mitchel was elected Mayor of New York City and, with the advice and guidance of men like Bruère and Fosdick, he surrounded himself with a cabinet of social workers. Mitchel appointed Bruère to the position of City Chamberlain, and Bruère served, in effect, as the prime minister of the reform administration. Henry Moskowitz became president of the Civil

Service Commission. Katharine B. Davis, who had been for five years head resident of College Settlement in Philadelphia before becoming a prison reformer, was appointed by Mitchel to the position of Commissioner of Correction. Raymond Ingersoll became Brooklyn Park Commissioner. John Kingsbury, general agent of the Association for Improving the Condition of the Poor and a close friend of the settlement workers, was made Commissioner of Charities. In the background other settlement workers worked hard to promote reform during Mitchel's administration.[53]

From Mayor William Strong to Mayor John Purroy Mitchel, over a period of twenty years, settlement workers played important roles in municipal reform in New York City. They helped in the reform campaigns, but their influence as advisers, investigators, administrators, and originators was more important.

IV

The pattern of municipal reform in Chicago was different from that in either Boston or New York; there was less emphasis on increasing the power of the mayor and more concentration on electing able and honest aldermen. "Chicago should be celebrated among American cities for reform," decided Lincoln Steffens in 1903.[54] The social settlements, especially Hull House and Chicago Commons, were partly responsible for this reputation.

The municipal reform movement in Chicago had many sources, but the 1893 World's Columbian Exposition, for one, united the various reform efforts. The settlement workers held a conference in conjunction with the fair, and their speeches and exhibits helped to point up the contrast between the "ideal" White City at the Exposition and the real Chicago of slums, disease, and corrupt politics.[55] It was William T. Stead, the crusading editor of the London *Review of Reviews*, who really triggered the reform movement in Chicago. Stead came for the fair and stayed to look at the rest of Chicago. He visited brothels and tenements, jails and flop houses, and often dropped in at Hull House to sip hot chocolate and talk to the settlement workers about his experiences. "The best hope for Chicago is the multiplication of Hull Houses . . . in all the slum districts of the city," he remarked. But Stead was not content to wait for the multiplication of settlements. He hired the Central Music Hall, and in the afternoon and evening of November 12, 1893, he told the citizens of Chicago what he had seen in their city and called for a religious and civic revival. Later he was to put some of his observations and moral indignation into a book, *If Christ Came to Chicago,* but at that time he suggested a reform organization. The citizens responded by electing Jane Addams and Edward Bemis, as well as a labor leader, a minister, and a millionaire lumber dealer to a committee. They selected a larger group of forty that became the nucleus of the Civic Federation, a nonpolitical, nonsectarian organization designed to make Chicago "the best governed, the healthiest city in this country." [56]

Miss Addams, Julia Lathrop, and Graham Taylor played important roles, along with a group of business and professional men, in organizing the Civic Federation. They set up departments of political action, philanthropy, moral improvement, and legislation, and immediately went to work to relieve some of the suffering caused by the depression winter of 1893–94. The Federation conducted a campaign to promote cleaner streets in Chicago, organized vacation summer schools, and also campaigned in favor of the extension of civil service laws and against gambling and the sale of pornography. Jane Addams chaired one committee that conducted an investigation of the town of Pullman during the strike in 1894; another committee protested against the extension of the gas ordinances. In 1900 Ralph M. Easley, one of the leaders of the Chicago Civic Federation, with the co-operation of Mark Hanna and Samuel Gompers, organized the National Civic Federation primarily to promote the peaceful settlement of labor disputes. Despite the whirlwind activity of the diverse groups of businessmen, society women, labor leaders, and settlement workers who made up the membership of the national organization, it failed to live up to the idealistic goals of the founders.[57]

One of the original aims set by the founders of the Chicago Civic Federation was to drive "the boodlers" out of the City Council. The plans called for the establishment of a branch of the Civic Federation in each of the thirty-four wards, but the seventeenth ward branch at Chicago Commons was the only active one. In 1896, however, another nonpartisan organization grew out of the failure of the Civic Federation to become a force for political reform in Chicago. The Municipal Voters' League, as the new organization was called, was designed explicitly "to secure the nomination and election of aggressively honest and capable men for all city offices." There was certainly need for reform of the City Council, where men like "Bathhouse John" Coughlin, "Hinky Dink" Kenna, Mike Ryan, and Johnny Powers held sway and made fortunes in bribes for granting street and utility franchises.[58]

A group of Chicago business leaders and professional men was the driving force behind the Municipal Voters' League, but settlement workers and settlement experience were also important. Graham Taylor was a member of the Council of Nine (the governing body of the Municipal Voters' League), and he was able to offer advice based upon his political experience in the seventeenth ward. Allen B. Pond, a trustee of Hull House and a frequent visitor at the settlement, was also one of the Council of Nine. His experience in the nineteenth ward had convinced him of the unity of politics and the need for an organization like the Municipal Voters' League. William Kent, alderman from the thirty-second ward, served on the advisory group of the Municipal Voters' League, and he profited similarly from his experience with the political situation in the nineteenth ward.[59]

Soon after the League was organized in 1896, the members began their self-appointed task of improving the caliber of the men in the City Council. Settlement workers co-operated in an investigation of incumbent aldermen which led to announcements in the press and at mass meetings that fifty-seven of the sixty-eight aldermen were "thieves." The Municipal Voters' League condemned twenty-six of the thirty-four aldermen whose terms expired in 1896, and the League's mark of disapproval helped prevent the nomination of sixteen. Of the remaining ten, only six were re-elected. Publishing the record of a man like Johnny Powers of the nineteenth ward had little effect on the elections in the ward, but by 1900 the Municipal Voters' League could claim with justification that two thirds of the aldermen were honest, if not enlightened.[60]

The settlements provided an able group of young reformers who became expert at ferreting out the records of the candidates for city offices, and in some cases they were able to provide local organization to make the recommendations of the Municipal Voters' League effective. The prime example of the success of the Municipal Voters' League was the seventeenth ward, where settlement workers at Chicago Commons and Northwestern Settlement controlled the balance of power in the alderman's elections. To Lincoln Steffens the story of the accomplishments of the Municipal Voters' League seemed incomprehensible and unbelievable until he learned how a normally Democratic ward like the seventeenth gave a 1300-vote plurality to a Republican one year, and then turned around and voted for a Democrat the next. The story of reform in the seventeenth ward convinced Steffens that in Chicago the reformers had borrowed the methods of the politicians.[61]

By concentrating on the City Council rather than on the mayor's office, the Chicago reformers were able to win concessions from the mayor. Steffens, who visited Chicago in 1903, and William English Walling, who stopped at Hull House for a few weeks in the spring of 1904, both agreed that the reformers had forced Mayor Carter Harrison to clean up some of the worst of the "wiggling grafters" in the municipal departments.[62]

With the City Council in the hands of honest and able aldermen, the Chicago reformers began to think in terms of a positive reform program, one that would include the municipal ownership of street railways. Municipal ownership was, in fact, an important issue in most major cities during the progressive era. In Cleveland the settlement workers seemed to have opposed or ignored Tom Johnson's appeals for municipal socialism. James B. Reynolds supported municipal ownership in New York in principle, but Low's administration did next to nothing to aid the cause. Robert Woods supported Mayor Quincy's plan for city ownership of the Boston subways, and

Joseph Eastman, a South End House resident, became a leading member of the Public Franchise League, which led the fight against the traction interests in Boston.[63] In Chicago, partly because of the sprawling nature of the city and partly because of the power of Charles Yerkes, municipal ownership of street railways was needed more than in most cities. Hull House was the center of much of the agitation and protest against Yerkes's attempts to extend the street-car franchises to ninety-nine and then in 1897 to fifty years. The celebrated group of Chicago settlement workers made trips to Springfield to lobby against the bills, held mass meetings, and organized a protest; then they joined the fight to defeat the Chicago legislators who had voted for extension.[64]

The settlement workers, however, did not stop with campaigns for short-term franchises granted fairly without bribes. In 1903 the Hull House group invited Henry Demarest Lloyd to come to Chicago and make the settlement the headquarters for a city-wide campaign for municipal ownership. Lloyd accepted the invitation and spent the last days of his life at Hull House working to organize the campaign that attracted the prominent settlement leaders in the city. The campaign was successful, for in the spring of 1904 a referendum of voters in Chicago showed that an overwhelming majority favored municipal ownership, and the vote was especially heavy in the working-class wards.[65]

There was no more persuasive advocate of municipal ownership than Raymond Robins, dubbed the "oracle of the settlements" by a Chicago newspaper. He became a master of ward politics through his activities with the Community Club of Chicago Commons in the seventeenth ward, but he was not content to confine his influence to one ward. He became an active investigator for the Municipal Voters' League, expert at investigating the records of candidates for office. Robins, furthermore, toured all the wards in the city, urging interested groups to take part in "practical politics" in order to defeat the bosses at their own game. He encouraged a careful study of the precinct vote, a knowledge of the local situation, friendship with the voters, and then co-operation with the

politicians in order to elect the best candidate or, at least, a reasonably good one. Above all, he urged people to become interested in
politics, which was to him the only road to reform.[66]

Robins followed his own advice and was active in the mayoralty
campaign of 1905. John Harlan, who had run on an independent
ticket for mayor in 1897, was the Republican candidate. Edward
Dunne, a genial Irish judge, was the Democratic choice. Both men
supported municipal socialism during the campaign, but Dunne attracted more attention with his plan for immediate municipal
ownership. George Hooker and Charles Zueblin supported Dunne,
but Robins backed Harlan. Together with Allen T. Burns, a recent graduate of the University of Chicago, and Harold Ickes, a
young lawyer who helped manage the campaign, Robins stumped
the city giving speeches for Harlan.[67] Despite the active support of
Robins, Burns, and Ickes, Harlan was defeated by Dunne in
1905. Defeat, however, did not deter Raymond Robins. In an open
letter to the new mayor he pledged his support. "I wish to be considered as a volunteer in readiness for any demand within my
power," he wrote Dunne, and the Mayor took this "aggressive, po-
litical-minded social worker" at his word. He appointed Robins to
the school board, made him a member of several committees, and
utilized his talents and his settlement experience by making him
chairman of a committee to investigate the records and qualifica-
tions of the Democratic candidates for aldermen.[68]

Robins launched an investigation that nearly cost him his life. A
few days after he filed his final report, he was attacked and severely
beaten by three men. The *Chicago Tribune* was outraged at this
open attack on a well-known "settlement worker and city reformer," and blamed the attack on "Ed" Carrol, a gangster and
former labor leader who had been denounced as "utterly unfit" in
Robins's report, "in a ward where such a report practically meant
his defeat in the primaries." Robins recovered from the beating but
the incident was a good demonstration of the importance attached
to this settlement worker's investigation.[69]

Mayor Dunne had many, probably too many, advisers, in his attempt to make municipal ownership a reality in Chicago, but Rob-

ins was one of his chief strategists in the fight against the traction interests. He made speeches and helped win the support of organized labor. He prepared and circulated petitions and referendums. He also helped plan the strategy for the campaign, which was troubled by endless litigation, opposition in the Council, and dwindling public support. The plan was finally defeated in the courts in 1907, but the ten-year battle for municipal ownership, in which settlement workers played a prominent part, was responsible for stopping some of the graft and for improving service on the Chicago streetcar lines.[70]

During the progressive era, municipal reform in Chicago, as well as in New York, Boston, and other cities, was a frustrating struggle filled with defeats and setbacks, broken only occasionally by partial victory. Settlement workers participated in movements that took halting steps toward improving life in the city. They did not often initiate the reform movements in these cities, and sometimes they seemed to underestimate all that was needed, but the settlement houses served as clearing houses for urban reform and meeting places for reformers. Settlement workers helped move municipal reform from mere opposition to positive programs of social welfare; yet they became frustrated by the small results of municipal reform and became persuaded that reform at the national level was necessary.

10

The Progressive Crusade

Many settlement workers thought the Progressive party of 1912 was the climax to their long struggle for social justice, and in many ways they were right. For more than two decades they had campaigned for better housing laws, for shorter hours and safer working conditions, for parks and playgrounds, and for other reforms in the city. Through publicity and petitions, through lobbying and political pressure, they had tried to correct the abuses they saw all around them; occasionally they had joined political reform movements, but altogether they were disappointed with the results. Their reform efforts had often been frustrated by unco-operative courts and politicians, and even when they had managed to elect an official or pass a reform bill, they had remained dissatisfied and disturbed by the problems remaining. By 1912 many settlement workers believed that reform had to be carried to the national level. They had helped organize the National Child Labor Committee, the National Women's Trade Union League, the National Association for the Advancement of Colored People, and the National Playground Association, as well as a National Conference on City Planning. They had lobbied for a federal investigation of women and children in industry, and had organized the National Federation of Settlements.

Settlement workers had often talked of the need for a larger reform movement, for a "great cause" to unite the various national and local reform groups. Some of them had even spoken of the need for a new political party.[1] Theodore Roosevelt walked out of the Republican Convention in 1912, and that made a new party possible; but settlement workers, along with other reformers, played an important part in making the new party stand for social reform. They supported the Progressive party not because of Roosevelt, or because of a theory of New Nationalism, but because of the social and industrial planks of the party's platform, which they helped to draft.[2]

The social and industrial planks of the Progressive party platform had their origin in a committee meeting of social workers appointed at the National Conference of Charities and Correction; they were the direct result of settlement experience and of the growing co-operation between settlement residents and charity workers in the first decades of the twentieth century. The hostility toward settlement work that had prompted Jane Addams in 1897 to apologize for being at the conference at all had changed to warm regard, and the philosophy of the conference moved from correction to prevention, from charity to social reform. A number of charity experts, especially in New York, caught some of the spirit of reform that permeated the best settlements, and in the twentieth century settlement workers began to take a larger and larger part in the annual conference. The growing concern of the Conference of Charities and Correction for reform and the growing co-operation with the settlement movement were symbolized in 1909 by the election of Jane Addams as president, and by the appointment of a committee on occupational standards to make a systematic study of "certain minimum requirements of well being" in an industrial society.[3]

Not every member of the National Conference approved the settlement idea of reform, but Paul Kellogg, the chairman of the new committee, was certainly a reformer and friend of the settlement movement. Kellogg was genial and urbane; he also was a tough-minded realist and organizer who worked behind the scenes in a dozen reform movements. In a preliminary report to the social work conference in 1910, he outlined the desperate need for the enforcement of reasonable standards of hours, health, safety, and wages in industry. In 1911 the chairman of the committee was Florence Kelley, resident of Henry Street Settlement and general secretary of the National Consumers' League. The following year when the conference met in Cleveland, Owen Lovejoy, the secretary of the National Child Labor Committee was chairman and Margaret Dreier Robins, president of the National Women's Trade Union League, was vice-chairman. Many settlement workers contributed to the discussions and investigations of the committee. In 1912, the committee decided that the time had arrived to summarize three years of work by formulating a program of minimum standards to help "direct public thought and secure official action." [4]

The social workers drafted a minimum platform which they called "Social Standards for Industry." Among other things they demanded an eight-hour day in continuous twenty-four industries, a six-day week for all, the abolition of tenement manufacture, the improvement of housing conditions, the prohibition of child labor under sixteen, and the careful regulation of employment for women. They also called for a federal system of accident, old age, and unemployment insurance. This was not a list of ideals, Lovejoy insisted, but minimum standards for any community "interested in self preservation." [5]

When the National Conference of Charities and Correction adjourned on June 19, 1912, some of the reform-minded social workers stayed on to meet informally and discuss how their minmum platform could be made relevant to the presidential campaign. One way to make their point of view count, they decided, was to go to Chicago, where the Republican National Convention was already in session. John Kingsbury, general agent of the New York Association for Improving the Conditions of the Poor and a good friend of the settlement work group in New York; Samuel McCune Lindsay, former director of the New York School of Philanthropy; and Homer Folks, secretary of the New York State Charities Aid Association, along with Kellogg and a few others, went to Chicago, where they applauded Roosevelt and presented their "Platform of Industrial Minimums" to the platform committee of the Republican party. The platform committee rejected their proposals in short order, but Roosevelt seemed interested.[6]

Roosevelt's interest took on more meaning after he bolted the Republican party. A small group of social workers including Henry Moskowitz, Kingsbury, and Kellogg traveled to Oyster Bay in mid-July to confer with him. They presented to him their proposals of minimum social standards for industry and talked about the meaning of the new Progressive party. Roosevelt "took over the Cleveland program of standards of life and labor practically bodily . . . ," Paul Kellogg later reported.[7]

There were a large number of social workers on hand at the Progressive Convention in Chicago a few weeks later when Roosevelt used many of their ideas in his acceptance speech. Henry Moskowitz, who saw the address a few days before it was delivered, reported to Lillian Wald: "It's the biggest utterance along these lines ever spoken by a statesman of national influence. . . . It means something to have Lovejoy's program at the National Conference used as a political asset." [8] The platform committee of the Progressive party, which included among its members or advisers such friends of the social workers as George W. Kirchway of Columbia University, Charles Merriam of the University of Chicago, and Charles McCarthy of the Wisconsin Legislative Reference Bureau, proved much more receptive to their suggestions than had the Republicans. In fact much of the "Social Standards for Industry" was taken over and incorporated into the Progessive party platform.[9]

The settlement workers and the other social workers contributed to the religious-revival atmosphere of the Chicago Convention. They organized a "Jane Addams Chorus" and joined in the singing of "Onward Christian Soldiers" and the "Battle Hymn of the Republic." But the convention was more than a revival meeting. It reminded Jane Addams of a meeting of the American Sociological

Association or a Conference of Charities and Correction because she saw so many familiar faces. It was also something like a circus. A group of social workers led by Kellogg and Kingsbury had passed out red bandannas to the delegates at the Republican Convention in a futile attempt to cheer Roosevelt to the nomination. Now the brightly colored bandanna became the mark of a Progressive.[10]

The social workers and the others had a chance to wave their bandannas when Jane Addams, dressed simply in white, seconded the nomination of Theodore Roosevelt, and "not even the Colonel got more rousing cheers." Judge Benjamin B. Lindsey of Denver, a pioneer of the juvenile court, also seconded Roosevelt's nomination; and Raymond Robins seconded the nomination of Hiram Johnson for vice president.[11]

II

Roosevelt and the Progressives adopted the social workers' platform; they also endorsed woman suffrage, and the combination proved irresistible to many social reformers.[12] "Just think of having all the world listen to our story of social and industrial injustice and have them told that it can be righted," one social worker remarked excitedly. "The Roosevelt platform is tremendously attractive," another reformer wrote. "It embodies all the dreams and aspirations which have been a large part of our lives." "The Progressive Platform contains all the things I have been fighting for for more than a decade," Jane Addams announced.[13]

Miss Addams, however, was not being quite accurate; there were some things she believed in that the Progressive party did not stand for. She believed in peace, and the Progressive platform advocated the building of two battleships each year. "I confess that I found it very difficult to swallow those two battleships," she later remarked.[14] She found it even more difficult to swallow Roosevelt's decision to prevent the seating of Negro delegates from several southern states. There were Negro delegates from some northern states, but those social workers who had played a part in the founding of the NAACP protested vigorously against making the Progressive party a "lily white party" in the South. They also fought for the inclusion of a plank recognizing the equality of the Negro in the platform, but their efforts were in vain.[15]

Despite the battleships and the failure to seat the southern Negro delegates, many settlement workers were tremendously excited by the new party in 1912, and many who had usually voted for the Democratic party switched their allegiance to the Progressives. Cornelia Bradford, head resident of Whittier House in Jersey City and a leader in the child labor and housing reform movements in New Jersey, had supported Woodrow Wilson for Governor in 1910, and for President in 1912 until after the Progressive convention, when she switched to Roosevelt. "The platform of the third party, with the men and women supporting it; also the need for such a party must control me . . . ," she decided.[16] Lillian Wald was disturbed by the conservatives around Wilson, by the cold academic essays he delivered for speeches, and by the failure of the Democrats to endorse woman suffrage. Eventually she forsook the Democrats to support the Progressives.[17] Henry Moskowitz switched his support to the Progressives in part because he saw the Democrats handicapped by a reactionary South and by corrupt local leaders.[18] Raymond Robins, who had been an active campaigner for William Jennings Bryan, agreed with Moskowitz that the Democratic party was "an impossible instrument for social reform." Roosevelt's leaving the Republican party seemed to Robins, as it seemed to many social workers, a perfect opportunity "to make a new cleavage in American political life and to unite people of common purpose all over the country in behalf of a program for economic and social justice." [19]

A great many important and vocal social workers joined the Progressive party. Not all settlement workers, however, were Progressives in 1912. Some, like Sophonisba Breckinridge, felt that a social worker ought to remain neutral in national politics; a few, like Alice Hamilton and Henry Morgenthau, formerly a resident of Henry Street Settlement, supported Wilson and the Democrats. A number of former settlement workers, including William English Walling,

J. G. Phelps Stokes, and Robert Hunter, supported Eugene Debs and the Socialists. Benjamin Marsh, a believer in the single tax, refused to support the Progressives for the reason that "the land question is more important than Col. Roosevelt, and T. R. does not understand the land question." [20] Despite Roosevelt's enunciations of the need for a sweeping program of social welfare legislation, despite his sympathetic co-operation with the social workers in their attempts to promote child labor and housing reform, many social workers distrusted him in 1912. It was the social and industrial planks of the platform rather than Roosevelt that appealed to most of them. Indeed, they accepted the Progressive party in spite of, rather than because of, the fiery Progressive leader. "I look upon the movement as more important than any personality be it Roosevelt or La Follette," Henry Moskowitz wrote Lillian Wald. "It is not his movement," Graham Taylor of Chicago Commons announced, "He is only one of its men. It would have come—not so fast and so far—but it would have come without him, and it will survive him." "I cannot bring myself to believe in the genuineness of Mr. Roosevelt . . . ," a settlement worker admitted to Jane Addams.[21] Even Raymond Robins, a great admirer of Roosevelt, confessed that he wished the new party had been formed over the issue of the platform rather than over Roosevelt's failure to win the Republican nomination, but he maintained that Roosevelt's personality and motives were "unimportant in the present situation except as it helps to make the situation possible and the cleavage real." "I deplore the fact of T. R.'s leadership," another settlement worker admitted, "and yet I feel that he will give an impetus to the movement which without him could not be achieved without a social unheaval." Henry Moskowitz, in arguing that social workers should support the Progressive party, even if they disapproved of the candidate, said simply, "Social Reform has the services of America's first publicity man. . . ." [22]

To the social workers, the Progressive party, however, meant more than Roosevelt, no matter how good an agent for reform he was. It meant more than woman suffrage, more than a policy of business regulation, or a philosophy of New Nationalism. To many, the Progressive party was the culmination of a crusade for social reform; it was thus the climax of a movement bigger than candidates or platforms.

III

The same social workers who played a part in turning the Progressive Convention into a religious revival meeting set to work after it was over to organize a new political party. They were idealists and crusaders, they were even sentimental, but they could also be practical. In New York, Henry Moskowitz, who had taken part in many local and city reform movements, took the lead in organizing the Lower East Side in the Progressive cause. He was aided by men like Leo Arnstein, secretary of the Borough of Manhattan and once a resident of Henry Street Settlement, and Hamilton Holt, editor of the *Independent* and for a time a resident of University Settlement. Moskowitz was more than an organizer, however; he had been a delegate to the Progressive Convention, and he ran for Congress on the Progressive ticket to represent an East Side district; he was also a close adviser of Oscar Straus, the party's candidate for Governor of New York.[23]

Moskowitz organized the Progressive party in New York with help from Frances Kellor, a tireless organizer with a sharp tongue. She had investigated employment bureaus while a settlement worker at the New York College Settlement, then had become a member of the Inter-municipal Research Committee and secretary of the New York State Bureau of Industries and Immigration. She had investigated urban social problems, drafted legislation, and helped lobby for bills. In 1912, like many other social workers, Miss Kellor transferred her activities from social investigation to work for the Progressive party. She served on the New York State Progressive Committee and was director of the publicity and research department of the National Progressive Committee. She helped to prepare Roosevelt's labor record for use as a a campaign document and drafted letters to enlist the support of women and social workers for the Progressive cause.[24]

It was not necessary to enlist many of the social work group in New York; they volunteered. Mary Dreier, the president of the New York Women's Trade Union League, had been a delegate to the Progressive Convention and an active worker for the party in New York. Paul Kellogg used the pages of the *Survey* and other more subtle means to advance the Progressive cause. Walter Weyl, once a resident of University Settlement in New York and in 1912 a successful writer and author of *The New Democracy*, was a member of the National Progressive Committee and traveled with Roosevelt on a campaign tour. He spent most of his time, however, organizing a Progressive educational campaign for the immigrant population in New York. Frederic Almy, secretary of the Buffalo Charity Organization Society, Homer Folks, Owen Lovejoy, Mary Simkhovitch, and Samuel McCune Lindsay were others active in the Progressive campaign.[25] There was also John Kingsbury, who was associate Progressive leader of his ward, chairman of the New York City Progressive Committee, a member of the New York State Progressive Committee, and a volunteer assistant at the National Progressive headquarters. He helped draft letters to be sent out to social workers, and spent all his spare time campaigning or organizing for the Progressive party. He summed up the feeling of many other social workers when he remarked to Raymond Robins, "I declare I never got so completely involved in any big enterprise in so short a time, as I am involved in the Progressive Movement at this moment." [26]

In Massachusetts Philip Davis and Robert Woods supported the new party, but the settlement workers in Illinois were more active. Raymond and Margaret Robins were in the center of the whirlwind attempt to organize the Progressive party in the Midwest. Robins had resigned as head resident of Northwestern University Settlement in 1907, but he remained in close touch with the movement. Years of experience in organizing and campaigning in the seventeenth ward paid off when Robins joined his old friend Harold Ickes in working for the Progressive organization in the state. He became a member of the Illinois Progressive Committee and chairman of the Cook County Progressive Convention. He took charge of much of the Progressive organization and campaign outside of Chicago. He was in contact with the National Progressive Committee and on several occasions was called away from Illinois to make speeches in various parts of the country. "I have never before in politics felt that I was standing upon more than half truths and advancing other than uncertain political fortunes," Robins wrote in the middle of the campaign. "Now I am sure that whole result of this struggle shall be for the social welfare and moral strength of the country." [27]

Margaret Robins, president of the National Women's Trade Union League, was a member of the Executive Committee of the Illinois Progressive party and a candidate on the Progressive ticket for trustee of the University of Illinois. She actively campaigned for the Progressive party throughout the Midwest. George Hooker, secretary of the Chicago City Club and a resident of Hull House, was a candidate for presidential elector on the Progressive ticket Graham Taylor remained dubious about the advisability of a Progressive ticket on the state level, but he supported the Progressive platform in his editorials in the *Chicago Daily News*. Mary McDowell, head resident of the University of Chicago Settlement, was on the Illinois Progressive Committee. Harriet Vittum, head resident of Northwestern University Settlement, Mrs. Joseph Bowen, a longtime friend of Hull House, Edith and Grace Abbott, and many others helped out when they could. Few of those close to the settlement movement in Chicago remained untouched by the Progressive crusade.[28]

Despite the dedication of the others, Jane Addams was the most famous and in many ways the most effective social worker in the 1912 Progressive campaign. She did far more than second Roosevelt's nomination at the convention; she was a member of the National Progressive Committee, the Illinois State Progressive Committee, and the Cook County Progressive Committee. She also wrote a series of six articles, syndicated in newspapers across the country, to attract attention to the Progressive party platform.[29] During the last month of the campaign, she covered thousands of miles in a speaking tour that sometimes called for as many as three

speeches a day. She spoke in New York and Boston and all the
major cities of the Midwest. She got as far south as Oklahoma and
spent the last few days before the election in Denver and Kansas
City. But she was nevertheless able to satisfy only a small percentage of the requests that poured in to her during the campaign. One
of the other Progressive campaigners remarked, "Wherever I went
I heard nothing but talk of Jane Addams, I suppose other political
speakers had been out there, but you never would have guessed it
from what people had to say." [30]

Perhaps Jane Addams's biggest contribution to the Progressive
party was the example she set for other women and social workers.
She was the most famous woman in America in 1912; her open and
active support of the new party was an important factor in attract-
ing votes and the support of those who could not vote. But Jane
Addams was more than a figurehead, or a prize display. Partly because the press always gave her addresses top billing, she was often
chosen to make rejoinders to Democratic attacks. Her support of
the Progressives attracted so much attention that the Democratic
National Committee tried to persuade Lillian Wald to come out
publicly in support of Wilson "to counteract Jane Addams' support
of the Progressive Party." [31]

During her long career Jane Addams had been criticized at times
for being too cautious and too careful and not willing enough to
commit herself in a reform movement; but she did not hesitate in
1912. "I never doubted for a moment that my place was inside,
where there was a chance to help on such a program as this one,"
she wrote Lillian Wald during the campaign. And her enthusiasm
never lagged; on one occasion after six consecutive nights on the
train she returned to Hull House weary and uncomfortable, but she
stayed up half the night regaling the residents with her campaign
experiences. [32]

Although most social workers admired and supported Jane Addams's active participation in the Progressive campaign, there were
some who disapproved. Edward T. Devine announced in the *Survey* that it was "the first political duty of social workers to be per-
sistently and aggressively non-partisan to maintain such relations

with men of social goodwill in all parties as will insure their cooperation in specific measures for the promotion of the common good. . . ." And Graham Taylor decided a few years after the campaign that by taking part in a partisan campaign Jane Addams had "lost the heeding if not the hearing of the whole city which she had before. . . ." [33]

Jane Addams's most bitter critic during the campaign was Miss Mabel Boardman, president of the National Red Cross. "The great moral questions for whose furtherance the country owes a debt of gratitude to Miss Addams," Miss Boardman announced, "should not be handicapped by the limitations of party affiliation nor trammelled by becoming involved in the bitterness of controversies over condidates and utterly irrelevant policies." To a great many social workers, including Jane Addams, working for the Progressive party was not the same as taking part in an ordinary political campaign—it was the natural result and end of years of struggling for social and economic justice. Nor were the issues irrelevant. "When the ideas and measures we have long been advocating become part of a political campaign . . . ," Jane Addams wrote, "would we not be the victims of a curious self-consciousness if we failed to follow them there?" [34]

Despite the eagerness with which the social workers threw themselves into the campaign, few had any illusions about the outcome of the election; they joked about moving to Washington, but they knew they could not win. "I shall be very happy if Wilson comes in first and Roosevelt second . . . ," Henry Moskowitz admitted; and most of the others agreed with him. They viewed the campaign as a great opportunity to educate the public. Sometimes they compared the Progressive party in 1912 to the Republicans in 1856: they expected to replace the Republicans as the Republicans had replaced the Whigs, and to win in 1916 as the Republicans had in 1860. [35]

The social workers were convinced, in effect, that the election of 1912 was merely the first step in a long educational campaign, and the beginning of a new political era. This conviction led them to increased efforts to broaden the Progressive party even after the results of the election were in. [36] They poured most of their energy into building an elaborate organization which they called the National Progressive Service.

IV

The Progressive Service was designed to apply the principles and techniques of social work and social research to the organization of a political party, especially to separate the tasks of writing platforms, drafting laws, and educating voters from the more mundane job of electing individuals to office. Frances Kellor, the principal author of the elaborate plan, defined its major purpose as an attempt "to bring the interest, enthusiasm and organization of the progressive movement into the service of the people to be used by them for their welfare and advancement." Jane Addams argued for the acceptance of the Progressive Service idea at the meeting of the National Progressive Committee on December 10, 1912, and despite the hostility and skepticism of some of the politicians, the Committee voted to allow the social workers to go ahead with their plans.[37]

The Progressive Service was divided into two bureaus and four departments, each with many subdivisions designed to increase the Progressive party's contact with the people and implement the social justice planks of the Progressive platform. Gifford Pinchot directed the Department of Conservation, George Record, the Department of Popular Government, and Charles Bird and Jane Addams, the Department of Social and Industrial Justice. Donald Richberg headed a Legislative Reference Bureau to co-ordinate all the information gathered by the other departments, and to supervise the drafting of progressive bills at the state as well as the national level. There was also a Speakers' Bureau to send out speakers and propaganda all over the country.[38]

Frances Kellor was chief of the entire Progressive Service. Jane Addams was one of the members of the general committee, and she, together with Walter Weyl and Benjamin Lindsey, was on the Legislative Reference Bureau. Other members of the social work group were scattered throughout the entire organization. But it was especially the various branches of Miss Addams's committee on social and industrial justice that most social workers found a place to continue their political activity. Henry Moskowitz headed a subcommittee on Men's labor that included Raymond Robins among its members and Mary McDowell was chairman of the corresponding subcommittee on women's labor on which Margaret Robins and Edith Abbott served. Frances Kellor temporarily took the chairmanship of the committee on immigration with members Emily Greene Balch, Grace Abbott, and Jacob Riis. Frederic Almy was a member of a committee on social insurance that had Paul Kellogg as its head.[39]

The National Progressive Service encouraged states, counties, cities, and even towns to set up Progressive Service organizations. In Illinois Jane Addams, Mary McDowell, Graham Taylor, and Mrs. Joseph Bowen were among the group that formed an active state Progressive Service, and by 1914 twenty-one states in all had Progressive Service organizations. For a time after the election it seemed as if defeat had infused a new vigor into the Progressive organization.[40]

The social workers' enthusiasm even attracted a few who had not been active during the campaign. Katherine Coman, a Wellesley professor, frequent resident and long-time friend of Denison House in Boston, resigned her professorship and offered her services to the Progressive party. "In this one cause seems [sic] to be embodied most of the interests that are dearest to me . . . ;" she wrote Jane Addams. Lillian Wald, who had remained silent during the campaign, became an active Progressive soon after the election. Partly because of the pressure exerted by Henry Moskowitz and other settlement workers, she accepted a position on the New York Legislative Reference Committee. She also became a member of the executive committee of the New York State Progressive party, and a member of the immigration committee in Jane Addams's department of the Progressive Service. For a few months after the election the future seemed bright for the Progressive party and for social reform.[41]

V

The settlement workers did not devote all of their time and energy to organizing the Progressive party and the National Progressive Service. Many of the same men and women who jointed the Progressive crusade were simultaneously engaged in a less exciting campaign for an industrial relations commission, a campaign that resulted from the settlement workers' twenty-year struggle to aid the workingman and to promote industrial peace, just as the Progressive party climaxed two decades of dedication to political reform and social justice. In both campaigns the settlement workers drew from experience gained from work in the neighborhood and the city, and in a number of national reform movements, and they co-operated with charity workers and other reformers.

The campaign for an industrial relations commission began in late 1911. A group of social workers were annoyed because the everyday industrial problems of wages and working conditions were being overshadowed by sensational headlines about labor violence. They were especially upset by the adverse publicity given to the labor movement stemming from the dynamiting of the *Los Angeles Times* building in October 1910, and by the admission of guilt from John J. McNamara, a union official, and his brother. A few days before the McNamaras were sentenced (one to life, one to fifteen years) in mid-December 1911, a small group of social workers met in New York for the first of a series of informal meetings to discuss what they might do to counteract the damage done by the McNamara case. Jane Addams presided at the meetings that were held either at the *Survey* offices or at Henry Street Settlement. The participants included: Paul Kellogg, Lillian Wald, Mary Simkhovitch, Florence Kelley, Henry Moskowitz, John Kingsbury, and Samuel McCune Lindsay; also Edward T. Devine, the editor of *Survey*, Owen Lovejoy of the National Child Labor Committee, James B. Reynolds, formerly head resident of University Settlement and in 1911 the Assistant District Attorney for New York County, Rabbi Stephen Wise of the Free Synagogue of New York, and the Rev-

erend John Haynes Holmes, a Unitarian clergyman and minister of
the Church of the Messiah in New York. Out of these meetings
came a symposium published in *Survey* on "The Larger Bearings
of the McNamara Case," and the idea for the industrial relations
commission.[42]

It was natural that this group should think in terms of a federal
investigating commission. Their faith in facts and research as necessary parts of reform had been strengthened by their experience
with the Pittsburgh Survey and many lesser investigations. As settlement workers, most of them had gained first-hand experience
with social research and had an exaggerated impression of its usefulness. They believed that one of the great barriers to solving the
problems of industrial unrest was a lack of accurate knowledge
about the real causes of disagreements and disputes, of strikes and
violence. They expected that an industrial relations commission
would provide the facts and clear the way for reform.[43]

The actual campaign for an industrial relations commission began with the drafting of a communication which a delegation of
social workers presented to President Taft on December 30, 1911.
"The case of the State of California *vs.* the McNamaras is legally
closed," the communication began, "but what happens from now
on to the McNamaras in San Quentin prison does not concern the
American people so profoundly as what happened, is happening
and may happen to workmen who did not and would not use dynamite as a method to secure their ends. . . ." The social workers
went on to describe some of the unsafe and unsanitary working
conditions still existing in the United States and warned that if
workingmen were not given better wages, better working conditions, and a chance to bargain collectively, the nation could expect
more violence and more dynamite. One way to prevent this, they
suggested, would be to create a commission, "with as great scientific competence, staff resources and power to compel testimony as
the Interstate Commerce Commission," to investigate the causes of
strikes, the conditions of labor, and the role of trade unions and
employer associations in a number of key industries. The social
workers wanted government investigation and government action

in the area of industrial relations, and they strengthened their case by adding the signatures of some prominent economists and sociologists to those already supporting the proposal. Edward Ross of Wisconsin, W. F. Wilcox of Cornell, Edwin R. A. Seligman of Columbia, Ernest Freund of Chicago, and Simon Patten of Pennsylvania, who happened to be attending the joint meetings of the American Economic and Sociological associations in Washington, were among those who added their names to the communication before it was presented to President Taft.[44]

Taft was impressed with the social workers' request, and in a message to Congress on February 2, 1912, he paraphrased their words. "The extraordinary growth of industry in the past ten decades and its revolutionary changes have raised new and vital questions as to the relations between employers and wage earners, which have become matters of pressing public concern," he announced, and went on to urge that Congress pass a bill providing for a Federal Commission on Industrial Relations.[45]

Taft's message to Congress was the signal for the social workers to go into action. They had seen too many bills defeated or quietly tabled in committee to be overconfident. They were particularly concerned that nearly six years had passed since they had sponsored a bill to create a Children's Bureau, and nothing had yet happened. They were determined to organize a vigorous campaign to follow up their suggestion for an industrial relations commission. They picked New York and the *Survey* offices as the headquarters for the campaign; they chose Edward T. Devine as chairman, Adolph Lewisohn, a businessman who had given $5000 to help with the campaign, as vice chairman, and Lillian Wald as treasurer of the industrial relations committee. They also enlisted the help of two young settlement workers, Graham Romeyn Taylor and Allen T. Burns, who agreed to devote full time to the campaign. Taylor, who had grown up at Chicago Commons, was then a young man of thirty-two. After graduating from Harvard he had been employed by a newspaper for a year before returning to Chicago to work on the staff of the *Commons,* and its successors *Charities and the Commons* and the *Survey.* Through his father he had met most of the men and women who now called themselves the industrial relations committee, and he was thus a good choice for secretary to the committee, with the task of keeping in contact with the scattered members.[46]

The industrial relations committee borrowed Allen T. Burns, a young man of thirty-six, from his duties as secretary of the Pittsburgh Civic Commission and gave him the task of lobbying for the bill in Washington. He had been a resident of Hull House, assistant warden of Chicago Commons, active in industrial Y.M.C.A. work, and a leading campaigner for John Harlan in the Chicago mayoralty election of 1905 before going to Pittsburgh in 1907. There Burns had served as liaison between the politicians and the social workers engaged in the Pittsburgh Survey. He had been successful in promoting an intensive study of transportation and land allotment, and had co-operated, as well, in changing the housing laws and tax structure. His wide range of experience in Chicago and Pittsburgh had brought him into contact with politicians, social workers, and labor leaders. In effect, he had been a lobbyist for reform on the municipal level; now he transferred his operations to Washington on behalf of the industrial relations commission.[47]

In Chicago, Jane Addams called a meeting to enlist support for the campaign. Besides settlement workers like Mary McDowell and Graham Taylor there were also Julius Rosenwald of Sears, Roebuck and Company, Harold Ickes, and Mrs. Emmons Blaine, daughter of Cyrus McCormick, a close friend of the settlement work group in Chicago, and an active participant in a wide variety of reforms. These men and women were the nucleus of the Chicago branch of the industrial relations committee. With Graham R. Taylor and Allen T. Burns operating as lobbyists and organizers, the social workers set out to translate their idea into legislation.[48]

They prepared a draft bill which Burns carried to Washington and gave to Senator William Borah of Idaho and Representative William Hughes of New Jersey. These congressmen introduced the social workers' draft with few changes early in March 1912, and the industrial relations committee set out to marshal support for their brainchild. Graham R. Taylor urged all committee members to write to their congressmen and to get others, especially prominent businessmen, to support the Hughes-Borah bill. The editors of the *Survey* began a special series of articles on industrial relations and the need of a commission that appeared once a week for ten weeks in fifty of the leading newspapers in the country. Samuel Gompers offered the support of the American Federation of Labor, and the National Civic Federation endorsed the bill at their meeting early in March.[49] Burns marshaled his forces in Washington and got labor leaders, manufacturers, and social workers from all over the country to testify before the House Committee of Labor on March 22. Late in April Burns and Taylor requested that the New York and Chicago social workers obtain letters from a few prominent men to be directed to the key individuals on the House Committee. The tactics were successful, for the House Committee approved the Hughes-Borah bill in mid-May.[50]

The prospects for passage of the bill dwindled during the summer. In June Samuel McCune Lindsay replaced Devine as chairman. After conferring with Burns and with some members of Congress in Washington, he reported that it was doubtful whether the bill could be brought to a vote before Congress adjourned. But during the summer, while the Progressive party was being organized, the social workers continued their campaign. When the committee ran out of money, Jane Addams, an experienced fund-raiser, talked Mrs. Blaine and Julius Rosenwald into contributing $500 each. Burns conferred almost daily with several members of Congress, especially Borah in the Senate and William Wilson of Pennsylvania, a former labor leader and champion of the bill in the House. The social workers continued to write letters and exert pressure and persuasion where Taylor and Burns told them it would do the most good. Their efforts were not in vain, for the bill was finally passed and signed by the President late in August, three days before Congress adjourned.[51]

The bill provided for a commission composed of three representatives from labor, three from industry, and three who would represent the public. Immediately, a group of three social workers traveled to Beverly, Massachusetts, to confer with President Taft and give him their recommendations for the commission. When a government official informed the Chicago social workers that a Chicago businessman who had opposed employer liability and workmens' compensation laws was being considered as a possible member of the commission, they appealed to friends in Washington, to prominent industrialists and others, to influence Taft against the businessman.[52] Their protest was successful, but they were disappointed with the selections made by President Taft in December 1912, especially since there were no women or distinguished sociologists or economists among Taft's nominations.

The industrial relations committee met the day after the nominations were announced and decided to start a delaying action in the hope that President-elect Wilson would improve upon Taft's selections. Chairman Lindsay urged all members of the committee to do everything in their power "through local publicity channels and by personal conference or letters and telegrams to your senators . . . to make our protest effective." Again the social workers were successful; Taft's nominations did not come before the Senate for ratification during the "lame duck" Congress, and on June 26, 1913 Wilson nominated his candidates for the Industrial Relations Commission. The social workers were not overjoyed by most of the selections, but Wilson's naming of John R. Commons, economist and close friend of most of the social workers, to the Commission was enough to restore their faith in it. The *Survey* published a symposium on what the Industrial Relations Commission should actually do. Not all of the contributors agreed, of course, but they all looked ahead confidently to important discoveries and important reforms.[53]

VI

The social workers were also optimistic about the future of the Progressive party and the National Progressive Service for the first few months after the election of 1912. They wrote briefs, reports, letters, and speeches, and looked ahead hopefully to 1914 and the congressional elections. In the spring of 1913 Paul Kellogg, Frances

Kellor, and Samuel McCune Lindsay traveled to Washington to confer with progressives from all parties. They agreed upon a limited program of "well thought out national bills that would include accident compensation, child labor and an eight-hour day for women." When Wilson appointed the Industrial Relations Commission, a committee from the Progressive Service submitted a list of industrial problems that needed investigation. But little came of their efforts, and gradually some of the enthusiasm began to die.[54]

Even as the social workers enthusiastically organized the Progressive Service, they saw ominous signs. They worried about the men Roosevelt seemed to turn to for advice. "Defeat has thrown him clear back into the lap of the most conservative counselors of our party . . . ," John Kingsbury decided early in 1913.[55] They worried especially about the growing power and influence of George Perkins, a partner in J. P. Morgan Company, organizer of the International Harvester Company, and a controversial Progressive party leader. The social workers had been observers rather than participants in the bitter struggle over the antitrust planks in the Progressive party platform. Regulating trusts did not seem as vital to most of them as legislating social justice, but the legacy of resentment and hate toward Perkins had its effect even on the social workers. They were not as bitter as Amos and Gifford Pinchot who, immediately after the election, demanded that Roosevelt ask Perkins to resign, but most social workers found themselves ideologically much closer to the Pinchots than to Perkins. A few days before Christmas in 1912, a group of New York social workers including Homer Folks, Paul Kellogg, John Kingsbury, and Samuel Lindsay met with George Record and Amos Pinchot and agreed that the Progressive party should stand for the public ownership of utilities as well as for social justice. The New York group of Progressives, including many social workers, met several times in the next few weeks to attempt to outline a program and map a strategy that would overcome Perkins's influence over Roosevelt. They agreed that "The Colonel has become suspicious of the whole social worker crowd except Jane Addams, and he is afraid of her, and we must depend on her to save the situation." [56]

Jane Addams, however, was unwilling to try to save the situation if it meant becoming involved in the factional struggle within the party. Several times in the next two years she tried to resign from her positions in the Progressive Service organization and from the Executive Committee of the Progressive party. But "the extreme wing," which felt that she was "the greatest asset which the real Progressive cause has at this time," would not hear of it. She remained on the committees, but devoted less and less time to the party and the Progressive Service.[57]

Personal squabbles and factional strife even affected the Progressive Service organization, and many loyal workers resented the strict control and petty rules enforced on the organization by Miss Kellor. Raymond Robins, too, had to admit in the spring of 1914 that the Progressive Service was "over organized"; what was really needed, Robins decided, was "organization from the precincts up." More than any other social worker, he tried to prevent the Progressive party from dissolving into factions; he urged Frances Kellor to remember that "Mr. Perkins is the most important and powerful single personality in our movement [besides Roosevelt]; it is necessary for us to come to an understanding with him." A short time later he was advising Roosevelt to insist that Perkins resign either from his positions on the board of directors of U. S. Steel and International Harvester or from his position in the Progressive party.[58] Roosevelt refused to ask Perkins to resign, and probably classified most of the social workers as part of the "lunatic fringe" of the movement, but he did attempt to smooth the differences between Perkins and the social workers. On one occasion in 1913 he reminded Perkins that the social and industrial plank of the Progressive platform ("our best plank, the plank which has really given our party its distinctive character . . .") had been drafted by the social workers: "They are doing literally invaluable work and I want you to know this and to take it into account when dealing with them." The attempts by Robins and Roosevelt to iron out the differences between the social workers and the Perkins wing of the party, and to prevent the outbreak of factional strife, had little effect. The Progressive party seemed less and less like the climax to a lifetime struggle for social justice, and many social workers, following Jane Addams's example, slowly drifted away. A large group began to turn toward the Democrats, in part because Woodrow Wilson was beginning to demonstrate that his party could stand for social reform.[59]

Raymond Robins was still not convinced by Wilson; he ran for the Senate on the Progressive ticket in Illinois in 1914, but like most Progressives in 1914, he lost. Robins and a few others remained loyal, but to most it was obvious by late 1913—or surely by 1914— that they had failed to create a new political alignment, and they began to be disillusioned about reform.[60]

VII

Dissension and disagreements plagued the work of the Industrial Relations Commission as well as the Progressive party, and the disagreements were exacerbated by the flamboyant and headline-seeking tactics of Frank Walsh, the chairman of the Commission. The Commission used two approaches in studying the underlying causes of industrial conflict—the public hearing and research by experts. Walsh spent most of the Commission's money on a long series of public hearings held in cities from Boston to San Francisco, with many hearings receiving wide publicity. Among other things, Walsh and his aides tried to establish the responsibility of the Rockefeller interests (and John D. Rockefeller, Jr., personally) for the "Ludlow Massacre" during the 1914 Colorado mine-workers' strike, and accused many educational and philanthropic foundations of being allied with the big-business interests.[61]

The research side of the Commission's work received little publicity and little support, but if the Commission contributed anything of permanent value, it was in this area. Commons persuaded Charles McCarthy, the director of the Wisconsin Legislative Reference Library, to co-ordinate the research, and McCarthy set up headquarters in Chicago with a well-trained staff. Settlement workers Crystal Eastman and Gertrude Barnum were among the research experts, who also included Selig Perlman, a young Wisconsin labor economist, and Basil Manly, an economist from the Bureau of Labor Statistics. Disagreements with Walsh, however, caused the dismissal of McCarthy and the sudden abandonment of most of the research begun by his staff. The disagreement within the Commission was so strong that when its work was completed in 1916, among its findings—published in eleven volumes—were three separate sets of recommendations instead of one.[62]

By 1916 most of the settlement workers and social workers who had been responsible for the creation of the Industrial Relations Commission had become disillusioned with it and equally discouraged about the prospects of the Progressive party. They did not completely abandon their fight for social justice and political reform, but by 1916 they shifted some of their concern to international affairs. The shift was caused in part by the collapse of their expectations for political and social reform; it was also caused by the outbreak of World War I in Europe.

11

Epilogue: World War I and After

The outbreak of war in Europe in 1914 came as a shock to most settlement workers. Many had traveled abroad, and some were actively involved in the peace movement. Though aware of the growing tensions in Europe, they were, like most Americans, totally unprepared for war. Their hopes of promoting social justice at the national level had been dimmed if not demolished by the limited success of and the internal dissension within their own Progressive party and the Industrial Relations Commission. Now the news from Europe added to their disillusionment, and their immediate reaction was similar to that of John Haynes Holmes, a liberal clergyman, who felt that the war had ended the social movement.

> We are three thousand miles away from the smoke and flame of combat and have not a single regiment or battleship involved. And yet who in these United States is thinking at this moment of recreation centers, improved housing or the minimum wage? Who is going to fight the battle of widows' pensions, push the campaign against child labor or study exhaustively the problem of unemployment? Where is the strike in Colorado and the Industrial Relations Commission?

Lillian Wald echoed the same feeling in her remark, "War is the doom of all that has taken years of peace to build up." [1]

Some of the disillusionment and discouragement remained, but the shock wore off quickly. Most of the settlement workers were too committed to action to stand back and wring their hands in despair. They continued to work for social reform at home, or at least to hold the line so that the hysteria of wartime would not destroy the accomplishments of twenty years' work for social justice. The outbreak of war, however, if it did nothing else, diverted a large part of their energy and attention from domestic reform to international affairs. On August 29, 1914, Lillian Wald helped lead a parade of 1200 women down Fifth Avenue in protest against war. A few weeks later at Henry Street Settlement Jane Addams presided over a meeting of social workers and reformers concerned with the implications of war and their responsibilities to promote peace. It was much the same group that had met three years before to plan the movement for the Industrial Relations Commission, but now they were not so much concerned with preventing industrial strife as with promoting international peace. Out of this meeting came the American Union Against Militarism, and eventually, the Civil Liberties Union. [2]

Lillian Wald was the first president of the American Union Against Militarism, and Jane Addams was chairman of the Women's Peace Party and later president of the Women's International League for Peace and Freedom. Others close to the settlement movement played prominent roles in the growing protest against war. [3] Jane Addams, Alice Hamilton, Emily Greene Balch, and Grace Abbott attended the International Congress of Women at the Hague in 1915, and Miss Addams and Miss Balch were members of the delegations which visited European capitals. They talked to prime ministers and leaders, urging them to end the war through negotiation and to support a league of neutral nations. [4] In December 1915, when President Wilson submitted his National Defense bill asking for an expanded army, Paul Kellogg, Lillian Wald, Florence Kelley, and many others joined the protest and helped organize an "Anti-preparedness Committee." [5] In the spring of 1916, when the most immediate threat of United States involvement in war came not from Europe but from Mexico, Lillian Wald, Paul Kellogg, and other members of the American Union Against Militarism worked to calm the situation. On one occasion late in 1916 Miss Wald and Kellogg, together with Henry Bruère (who had left the Bureau of Municipal Research to become a representative of the American Metals and Mining Company), were summoned to Washington to testify before a joint commission that was trying to arrange a settlement of the disagreements between the two countries. [6]

II

Not all settlement workers agreed with John Haynes Holmes that the primary job of the social worker in wartime was to become a "peace fanatic," and not all settlement workers were as absorbed in the problems of international crisis as Jane Addams and Lillian Wald; but the war and its implications touched nearly all those connected with the settlement movement. The daily round of clubs, classes, lunches, and conferences continued, of course, and there was still time to work for the enforcement of tenement house and child labor laws. Settlement workers also continued to use pressure and persuasion on mayors and legislatures. They approved Senator Robert La Follette's Seaman's bill and early in 1916 helped force a reluctant Wilson into supporting a national child labor bill. [7]

The majority of the social work group which had supported Roosevelt in 1912, shifted their allegiance to the Democrats in 1916. In large part this was due to Wilson's support of the child labor bill, along with his work for peace. To most of this group the Progressive party in 1916 seemed a forlorn hope with a platform that subordinated industrial justice to preparedness, but there was not universal agreement on this point. Raymond Robins, still not convinced that Wilson was a progressive, served as chairman and keynote speaker at the Progessive Convention in 1916. When Roosevelt refused to accept the Progressive nomination, Robins supported Charles Evans Hughes, believing that the Republican party was then the best hope for progressivism. Harriet Vittum and a few other settlement workers also campaigned for the Republican Hughes in 1916. "Never have I known those hitherto closely bound together by their community of interests so divided," Graham Taylor remarked about the settlement workers in Chicago in 1916.[8]

A much more serious disagreement came in the spring of 1917 when the United States finally abandoned neutrality and entered the war. "It is almost demonical," Helena Dudley wrote Jane Addams, "the sweep toward conscription and these enormous war loans which Wall Street is eager to heap on: and labor so passive and the socialists broken up, and the social workers lining up with the bankers." Alice Hamilton, Lillian Wald, and Florence Kelley, among others, agreed and remained consistent pacifists, while Jeannette Rankin, a representative from Montana and a former resident of Hull House, voted against the war resolution in Congress. The majority of settlement leaders, however, including Mary Simkhovitch, Paul Kellogg, and Robert Woods, supported America's entry into the war, and the National Federation of Settlements adopted a resolution supporting American participation. "America cannot hold aloof . . . it cannot stand apart, but must rather die that the world may live," Mary Simkhovitch announced in explaining her break with Jane Addams.[9]

Yet even at Hull House several of the young residents enlisted in the army, and a contingent of the Hull House band went overseas to entertain the troops. Many settlements collected money for war relief, helped to operate the selective service system, organized neighborhood defense councils, and tried to care for the families of men who had been called to military service. Indeed, a few of the settlement workers threw themselves into the war effort so strenuously that some of the leaders feared they would give up all activities not related to the war.[10]

III

The war came as a great shock to the social workers; at first it seemed to spell the end of social reform. Yet gradually, to their own surprise, many of them came to view the war, despite its horror and its danger, as a stimulus to their promotion of social justice in America. At least in the beginning, few of them saw the war as a great crusade to make the world safe for democracy, but they were soon caught up in the feverish activity that marked the first months of the war. Part of the excitement came from the thrill of being listened to after years of frustration, of plotting and planning and lobbying. "Enthusiasm for social service is epidemic . . . ," Edward T. Devine wrote in the summer of 1917; "A luxuriant crop of new agencies is springing up. We scurry back and forth to the national capital; we stock offices with typewriters and new letterheads; we telephone feverishly, regardless of expense, and resort to all the devices of efficient 'publicity work.' . . . It is all very exhilarating, stimulating, intoxicating." [11]

John Andrews, secretary of the American Association for Labor Legislation, went to Washington in October 1917 to lobby for a bill, already passed by the Senate, to provide workmen's compensation for longshoremen. Andrews's organization had often cooperated with settlement workers in their campaigns for social legislation, but now with Congress ready to adjourn everyone assured him that there was no chance for passage. Nevertheless, he went to see President Wilson and the next day the bill passed the House under the unanimous consent rule. Andrews was amazed and found himself with a great stack of unused facts and statistics. "Usually before our bills are passed, we wear our facts threadbare," he remarked, and went on: "Perhaps this is not the most democratic way to secure urgently needed labor laws, but it is effective." [12]

Settlement workers were especially cheered during the war by the rights labor gained. The National War Labor Board, the War Labor Policies Board, the United States Employment Service, and other wartime agencies recognized collective bargaining, the minimum wage, the eight-hour day, and improved conditions of work, and they reduced the exploitation of women and children in industry. "One of the paradoxes of the war is the stimulus it is giving to human conservation," a writer in *Survey* noted.[13] The settlement workers spent a large amount of time making sure that labor standards were not weakened, and that women and children were not exploited. Yet even the invalidation of the national child labor law by the Supreme Court failed to dim their enthusiasm. The National Child Labor Committee set to work to design another and better law, and Congress responded by passing a bill that levied a 10 per cent tax on products produced by children under fourteen. A Supreme Court decision did not seem very important when Secretary of War Newton Baker and other members of the Wilson administration were saying publicly, "We cannot afford, when we are losing boys in France to lose children in the United States at the same time . . . , we cannot afford when this nation is having a drain upon the life of its young manhood . . . , to have the life of women workers of the United States depressed." [14]

The crisis of war also brought the first national experiment with public housing. Borrowing something from the English example and spurred to action by the crucial need for housing war workers, the federal government, operating through the United States Shipping Board and the Department of Labor, built or controlled dozens of housing projects during the war years. For the settlement workers, who had been working to improve housing conditions for decades, the government experiments appeared to be a realization of their dreams. Lawrence Veiller drew up the "Standards for Permanent Industrial Housing Developments" that were followed by government agencies. As a result, the projects were much better designed and safer than those built by commercial builders. In addition, the architects of the developments, influenced by the English Garden City Movement and by the settlement ideal of neighborhood unity, experimented with row houses, curved streets, and recreation and shopping areas.[15]

The war also provided a culmination to the social insurance movement. Most states had passed workmen's compensation laws between 1910 and 1917, but many were inadequate and filled with loopholes, and the philosophy of the movement was only gradually being accepted by many reformers, let alone the general public, when the United States became involved in World War I. Consequently, settlement workers hailed as a great victory the Military and Naval Insurance Act, which became law October 6, 1917. The act, which was drawn up by Judge Julian Mack with the aid of experts Lee Frankel and Julia Lathrop, provided compensation in case of death or disability, re-education in case of crippling injury, and a voluntary insurance plan for death and total disability. The architects of the plan hoped that it would take the place of demands for pensions and bonuses that had followed every American war, but most important to those who had supported social insurance was the fact that the government had assumed the extra hazard involved in military service and guaranteed a minimum standard of subsistence to the soldier's family.[16]

Health insurance, which a group of social workers picked as "the next step in social progress" in 1915, aroused the opposition of too many groups, but the move to improve the nation's health seemed to be stimulated by the war. "War makes sanitation a common cause," Alice Hamilton announced. "We suddenly discovered that health is not a personal matter, but a social obligation," Owen Lovejoy remarked.[17] Early fears that the war, by drawing doctors and nurses into the army, would lead to a rise in infant mortality, tuberculosis, and other diseases, proved groundless as the federal government and a variety of agencies, including the settlements, rallied to the cause. Lillian Wald, who opposed American participation in the war, served on the Red Cross Advisory Committee, traveled frequently to Washington as a consultant on health matters, and labored long and hard to keep the district nurses in New York functioning at top efficiency even during the influenza epidemic at the end of the war.[18]

Settlement workers also applauded other developments during the war. They approved the use of industrial education in rehabilitation work, and the use of psychiatrists and psychiatric tests by the army. They co-operated with the Council of National Defense in the use of schools as community centers, for long a goal of the school social center movement. They aided community councils and the war chest drives which stimulated community organization and led to the acceptance of the federated fund drive.[19] They also cheered the progress of women's rights. Women entered hundreds of occupations formerly closed to them, and brought about establishment of the Women in Industry Service and ultimately the Women's Bureau of the Department of Labor. The war also seemed to accelerate the movement for woman suffrage. Eight additional states gave women the vote, at least on some issues, during 1917; then Wilson came out in favor of votes for women, and the House of Representatives passed a woman suffrage amendment in January 1918.[20]

Many of the diverse progressive movements that the settlements had been promoting for years seemed to win acceptance during the war, but some of the most impressive victories were won by the Commission on Training Camp Activities. Raymond Fosdick was chairman of the commission, and he picked men like Joseph Lee of the Playground Association, Lee Hanner of the Russell Sage Foundation, and John Mott of the Y.M.C.A. to serve with him. With the aid of other private agencies the commission set out to apply the techniques of social work, recreation, and community organization to the problems of mobilizing, entertaining, and protecting the American serviceman at home and abroad. They organized community singing and baseball, post exchanges and theatres, and even provided university extension courses for the troops. Moving out into the communities near the military bases, they in effect tried to create a massive settlement house around each camp. No army had ever seen anything like it before, but it was an outgrowth of the recreation and community organization movement, and a victory for those who had been arguing for the creative use of leisure time.[21]

The Commission on Training Camp Activities also continued the progressive crusades against alcohol and prostitution. It became patriotic to support prohibition in order to save grain for food, and in 1917 the National Conference of Charities and Corrections (which changed its name in that year to the National Conference of Social Work) came out for the first time in favor of prohibition. But this endorsement was due to more than patriotism, for to many social workers prohibition seemed one key to social advance, and those who had doubts were swept along. Edward T. Devine announced, after returning from Russia in 1917, that "the social revolution which followed the prohibition of vodka was more profoundly important and more likely to be permanent than the political revolution which abolished autocracy." And Robert Woods, long an advocate of prohibition, predicted in 1919 that the Eighteenth Amendment would reduce poverty, nearly wipe out prostitution and crime, improve labor organization, and "substantially increase our national resources by setting free vast suppressed human potentialities." [22]

Progressive attitudes toward alcohol and prostitution were written into sections twelve and thirteen of the Military Draft Act, which established zones around military camps where prostitutes would be prohibited, and outlawed the sale of liquor to men in uniform. There was opposition from a few military commanders, a number of city officials, and from at least one irate citizen, who protested that red light districts were "God-provided means for prevention of the violations of innocent girls, by men who are exercising their 'God-given passions.'" But Fosdick, with the full cooperation of the government, launched a major crusade to wipe out sin in the service; "Fit to Fight" became the motto. It was a typical progressive effort which combined a large amount of moral indignation with the use of the most scientific prophylaxis. The crusade was successful, for by the end of 1917 every major red light district in the country had been closed, and the venereal disease rate had been lowered so that there existed what one man called "the cleanest army since Cromwell's day." [23]

Though settlement workers took part in the moral crusades of the war years, they often gave in to the racist hysteria that accompanied the war. They tried to protect the radicals and pacifists who were harrassed during the war, but sometimes they were overwhelmed by the bitterness of public opinion. The increasing numbers of southern Negroes lured to northern cities by jobs in wartime industries received their help, but they often acquiesced in segregated facilities and inferior treatment for the Negro soldier in the training camps. Most settlement workers also accepted the passage in February 1917 of the first immigration bill requiring a literacy test. There had always been disagreement over immigration restriction, but in 1917 not even the Immigrant Protective League launched an effective protest against the bill. A number of settlement workers joined the National Committee for Constructive Immigration Legislation, formed in 1918, but they tried only to soften and define the restrictive legislation.[24]

The war had the effect of ending debate and opposition. And the settlement workers, like many other reformers, deluded themselves into thinking that the social experiments and social action of the war years would lead to even greater accomplishments in the reconstruction years ahead. Robert Woods surveyed the positive actions of the federal government in the spring of 1918 and asked, "Why should it not always be so? Why not continue in the years of peace this close, vast, wholesome organism of service, of fellowship, of constructive creative power?" Even Jane Addams, who saw much less that was constructive in war than did many of her colleagues, lectured for Herbert Hoover's Food Administration, and looked ahead with confidence and hope for the future. Paul Kellogg also mirrored some of these hopes when he wrote to *Survey* subscribers in September 1918:

> With hundreds of people for the first time shaken out of their narrow round of family and business interests and responding to public service as patriotic call, with American help going out to the far ends of the earth as at no time since the early stages of the missionary movement; with federal action affecting housing, labor relations, community life as never before; with reconstruction plans afoot in England and France . . . we feel that the *Survey* has never before faced such a great obligation and such a great opportunity.[25]

IV

Kellogg also hoped the war would wrench social workers out of their provincialism. "Whether we recognize it or not, whether we want it or not," he wrote in 1919, "those of us who deal with problems of individual and social well being will, in the years of reconstruction ahead . . . , be called upon to render service in wider and wider spheres of activity." [26] A number of settlement workers did become more interested in the international scene after the war. Eleanor McMain of Kingsley House in New Orleans went to France for a year to help found a social settlement in Paris. Several Americans helped organize an international settlement conference in 1922, and an International Federation of Settlements in 1926. [27]

A few social workers were fascinated also by the Russian Revolution. A number, especially in New York, were members of organizations like "The Friends of Russian Freedom," and several of the energetic group of young residents of University Settlement, including Arthur Bullard, Ernest Poole, and William English Walling, had gone to Russia during the abortive revolution of 1905. At first the revolution of 1917 seemed to many social workers, including Jane Addams, "the greatest social experiment in history." Although some of them became disillusioned with the rise of the Bolsheviks, others saw the Soviet experiment as a fulfillment of their dreams of social justice. Raymond Robins led the American Red Cross Expedition to Russia in 1917 and became the leading American defender of the Bolsheviks. Lillian Wald traveled in the Soviet Union in 1924 and praised their achievement in the field of public health. Mrs. Robert La Follette was even more extravagant. "All the reforms that Florence Kelley and the Consumers' League have been working for these long years," she remarked, "have been achieved under the Soviet Republic. . . ." [28]

The social experiments in the Soviet Union seemed attractive in part because of the failure of social reform at home, for the hopes raised by the war were quickly shattered. The Wilson administration lost interest in human conservation and reform; it abandoned public housing and social insurance, and withdrew government participation in many areas. The gains of labor during the war proved ephemeral, and all that remained were prohibition, immigration restriction, and increased racist hysteria. Woman suffrage and the other rights won by women during the war had little effect on the mood of the country. The hopes that women would usually vote for progress and that a generation of young men would be transformed by their army and training camp experience proved groundless. The settlement workers' relationship with organized labor also deteriorated badly during the 'twenties; labor was more confident and more conservative, and the reformers more timid. But the settlement workers were especially upset and discouraged by the rejection of the second national child labor law by the Supreme Court.[29]

Inevitably, the settlement movement was influenced by what Jane Addams called "the political and social sag" that was one of the legacies of the war. Many settlement boards and councils became hypercritical of any activity that could be interpreted as radical (even clubs and classes for immigrants), and the fact that several prominent settlement leaders had been pacifists or sympathetic to the Russian Revolution left them wide open to attack.[30] Of course there had been animosity and disagreement between the residents and the settlement boards before. Helena Dudley had resigned as head resident of Denison House in Boston in 1912 because she felt her radical position endangered the settlement's financial support. In the spring of 1914 the residents of University Settlement in New York went on strike until they were allowed a representative on the settlement's council. But the war, and especially the "Red Scare" after the war, made the disagreements between the residents and board members more frequent and more acute.[31] A few settlement workers courageously defended individual liberties and the right of free speech. Several of their number were founders of the American Civil Liberties Union, whose director, Roger Baldwin, had begun his career in public service as a settlement worker in St. Louis. Others reiterated the need for better housing, more playgrounds, and better working conditions. Yet inevitably there was retrenchment and retreat. "I believe as you do," remarked Charles Cooper, the head resident of Kingsley House in Pittsburgh, to Jane Addams in 1922, "that in the Great War and in the troubled years that followed, the settlement movement had its measure of failure. I likewise feel that government failed, that culture failed, that education failed, that religion itself failed." Somehow, Cooper decided, "people believed that civilization was founded on too secure a rock of righteousness for such a devastating war. . . ." [32]

The conservative reaction to the war forced the settlements to restrict their reform activities, but other factors also influenced the situation. Old neighborhoods were changing; the prosperity of the 'twenties gave many families the opportunity to move to better sections of the city or to the suburbs. They were replaced by Negroes, Latin Americans, and other groups who forced the settlements to change their programs and alter their approaches or become obsolete. Racial equality had always been one of the goals of the settlements, but now, with Mexicans feuding with Italians and Poles, and the Negro snubbed by all immigrant groups, the problem became more complex. Financial difficulties also troubled the settlements. After 1900 new buildings, expensive equipment, and large staffs of paid workers made most settlements increasingly dependent upon gifts from philanthropists. In fact, leaders like Robert Woods, Jane Addams, and Graham Taylor spent a large portion of their time in fund-raising. The war, with its Liberty Bond drives and appeals from the Red Cross, siphoned money away from the settlements. Only the response of former club members and residents saved University Settlement in New York from being turned over to the Associated Jewish Charities in 1917, and every settlement felt the reduction in funds in one way or another.[33] These financial difficulties increased rather than diminished after the war. Regular contributors died each year, and the prosperity of the 'twenties lulled many into thinking the problem of poverty had been solved. It also became more difficult to attract funds for work with Negroes than it had been for work with Jews and East Europeans. Robert Woods and Graham Taylor tried to build up endowment funds, but even their settlements were forced to reduce their staff and curtail some of their activities. Eventually, most houses found it expedient to join the Community Chest campaigns, and they thus became to many donors just one of many charitable agencies worthy of support. Moreover, they often felt the need to stress service to the community rather than reform.[34]

Even more important than the failure to attract financial support was the failure after the war to attract large numbers of dedicated young reformers. Financial difficulties forced the abandonment of most of the settlement fellowships and thus reduced the number of young people who could afford to spend a year or two in a settlement after college. Other young men and women found teaching in Africa or serving with the Red Cross in France or living in Greenwich Village more exciting than becoming a social worker. Because settlements were "entirely accredited, thoroughly established," Vida Scudder wrote in 1917, "they present no appeal to the chivalry of youth. . . ." Just as important as the loss of new recruits was the drifting away of old residents and long-time supporters such as Vida Scudder, Raymond Robins, and James Reynolds. Of course, some had become disinterested before the war, and there were exceptions. In the 'twenties Lea Taylor replaced her father as head resident at Chicago Commons; a young an named Adolph Berle, later a member of Franklin Roosevelt's brain-trust, became a resident of Henry Street Settlement; and young Amelia Earhart went to live at Denison House in Boston. Paul Kellogg and Bruno Lasker, a German intellectual who had lived at Henry Street before the war, maintained their contact and concern with the movement though they were primarily journalists and social critics.[35]

In general, most of those who chose to become settlement workers in the 'twenties thought of themselves as social workers rather than social reformers, and many were graduates of professional schools of social work. They thus came trained as case workers or recreation experts, and they gradually began to speak of the people they were helping not so much as their neighbors as their clients. They brought a professional attitude, and often the belief that there was a scientific basis for social work. Critical of traditional practices that seemed sentimental and haphazard, the new breed of social workers even challenged the idea that residence was indispensable, and they saw no value in the settlement workers' gathering around the dinner table at night with the head worker mixing the salad. The old ways lingered in most settlements, but the new workers desired changes both because of their professional training and backgrounds. Many were the sons and daughters of immigrants, and some had, themselves, been brought up in the slums. They were interested neither in living in a working-class neighborhood nor in remaining at the settlement in the evening to attend meetings of labor unions or reform organizations. They often wanted a home in the suburbs and other trappings of status that earlier residents had taken for granted. Looking at settlement work as a job, they tried consciously to make their work professional. By stripping away much of the sentimental and emotional tradition that had developed in the movement, they lost in the process some of the crusading zeal of the progressive era.[36]

V

These changes in the settlement movement in the early 1920's were not as drastic or as complete as they at first seemed. The war had not ended the reform movement, but it had changed attitudes. There was less optimism and less faith that one could solve the problems of the industrial city with statistics. Still, despite the social and political reaction and their own doubts, many settlement workers continued to make surveys, file reports, and lobby for legislation. In New York, Belle Moskowitz, a former settlement worker herself and the wife of Henry Moskowitz, became "the Colonel House of the Smith administration" and a close adviser of Governor Al Smith, especially in matters of social welfare.[37] In Chicago, when a bitter and bloody race riot broke out in the summer of 1919, Graham Taylor and Harriet Vittum were among the small group that called a conference of the leaders of both races to calm the tension and prevent more bloodshed. Graham Romeyn Taylor played a significant role in compiling the final report of the Chicago Commission on Race Relations, which became an important contribution to the understanding of urban racial tensions. Others, individually or through the NAACP and the Urban League, worked hard to aid the growing numbers of Negroes trying to find their way in northern cities.[38]

Also, the election of William Dever as Mayor of Chicago in 1923 provided a certain justification for many years of settlement struggle to improve government in that city. Ever since Dever had begun his political career in 1902 by running for alderman at the urging of Raymond Robins and Graham Taylor, he had been a close friend of the settlement workers in Chicago. He showed his respect for them by appointing Mary McDowell commissioner of the Department of Public Welfare. Miss McDowell turned the department into what Paul Kellogg called the "eyes of the city." She set up a Bureau of Employment to find jobs for some of the many unemployed in the city, reactivated the Bureau of Social Surveys, and urged Mayor Dever to appoint a permanent Housing Commission. Though she did not solve all of Chicago's welfare problems, by working closely with the mayor she was able to convince a few that the city had a responsibility to help citizens who were old or sick or unemployed.[39]

Not many settlement workers in the 1920's had the opportunity that Mary McDowell had in Chicago to translate their theories into action. For most, the early 'twenties were a time of discouragement, self-conscious reappraisal, and doubt.[40] Charles Cooper, who traveled widely in 1922 and visited many different settlements, reported to Jane Addams: "I have not found an unwillingness to meet the issues of life today, what I have found is an uncertain vision and a bewildered attempt at comprehending the awful problems of the war and its aftermath." [41] Some of the doubt, some of the uncertain vision was caused by the settlement workers' uneasiness as to their exact role and function in the postwar world. They had always been self-conscious about their special role and had justified their existence in part by joining a variety of reform movements. Now that reform was in retreat they wondered where they should turn. They had helped to organize the Women's Trade Union League and the National Child Labor Committee; they had co-operated with the Consumers' League and with a dozen other organizations. Now there seemed to be no more organizing to do. They had co-operated with charity workers and other social workers in promoting social and political reform, but in the 1920's social work was becoming more specialized as it became more professional. They had created the National Federation of Settlements in 1911, but for several years they continued to meet jointly with the National Conference of Charities and Correction. And sometimes they felt uncomfortable even with other social workers who increasingly gave more attention to individual problems and psychiatric adjustment than to social reform. "The drama of people's insides rather than the pageantry of their group contacts and common needs seemed to dominate the profession," one observer remarked. As social workers divided into case workers, group workers, and community organizers, the settlement workers wondered exactly where they fit in. Whereas they had formerly considered themselves the general practitioners of social work, in an age of specialization this role seemed to have little status or meaning. "The role of the settlement is in the middle ground," Jane Addams had once remarked, but in the years after the war it was hard to tell where the middle ground was.[42]

Part of the settlement workers' problem in the 1920's resulted from their own success. College Settlement in New York was typical. A Carnegie library two blocks away had made the settlement library unnecessary; a public bath had replaced the settlement bath; two public parks had made the settlement playground obsolete; a Penny Provident Bank down the street had relieved the settlement of another responsibility; and, with the city museum open on Sunday, it no longer needed to sponsor picture exhibitions. Although settlement workers had contributed toward each of those improvements, with the shifting population in the area, it was easy for them to conclude that their job was done.[43]

Indeed, there had been a few critics who had declared the settlement unnecessary even before the war, but in the 'twenties, with school centers, recreation centers, and community councils doing some of the work formerly done by the settlements, and with sociologists becoming the new authorities on the city and the neighborhood, the criticism seemed more justified. The settlements, of course, had pioneered in the community center movement, and after the war men trained in settlements led the movement. Edward Burchard, the first male resident of Hull House, was secretary of the National Community Center Association and an associate editor of *Community Center* during the 1920's. In addition, sociologists Robert Park, Louis Wirth, and Ernest Burgess built on settlement studies of the neighborhood and the city, even as they criticized the emotional and unscientific nature of the research. The settlements could be proud of their influence, but success led to self-doubt.[44]

Some of the questioning and doubt within the movement was a product of the tensions and disagreements between two generations of settlement workers. Many of the pioneers were getting old and set in their ways, and the new breed, in any case, had a different spirit and different goals. They often resented the small recognition they got for their work, and felt they did not have a large enough part in forming policy for the National Federation. Isabel Taylor, one of the younger leaders, remarked: "a movement needs good followers as well as good leaders, but after thirty or forty years it is time for new leadership to develop." She confessed, however, that the new workers were often overwhelmed and confused by the complexity and size of the job: "The founders of the settlement had higher hopes than we who have lived through the war can have." [45]

VI

Robert Woods and Albert Kennedy published a full length appraisal of the settlement movement in 1922, which they optimistically called *The Settlement Horizon*. The book revealed very little of the tension and disagreement within the movement. It was glowing in its praise of settlement accomplishments, but was of limited use as a blueprint for the future. Woods was the first of the pioneers to die three years later, but Kennedy, a tall and spirited graduate of Harvard and Rochester Theological School, emerged as one of the leaders of the movement in the 'twenties. He had been a resident of South End House and had served as an assistant and collaborator of Woods's on many projects. He became secretary of the National Federation of Settlements in 1914, and succeeded Woods as head resident of South End House before taking a similar post at University Settlement in New York in 1928. Kennedy had immense energy and strong convictions; he also had the capacity to antagonize those who worked with him.[46]

Kennedy was convinced that settlement leaders should concentrate on developing cultural programs. The settlements had, of course, been pioneers in the movement to bring art to the people, but Kennedy believed that with the specialization of social work and with the growth of community centers and other agencies, the settlements could make their greatest contribution in the areas of art, drama, and music rather than by social action. In 1930 the leaders of College Settlement in New York, carrying Kennedy's idea to its logical conclusion, closed the settlement and transformed it into an art workshop uptown. Faced with a shifting population and new problems, they decided their primary responsibility was to provide creative leisure activities and to teach art and dramatics to all who were interested.[47]

The idea that the settlement should be primarily a cultural center did not go unchallenged, however. Paul Kellogg wrote to Kennedy in February 1928, suggesting that the settlements were putting too much emphasis on cultural activities, on art, music, and drama, and too little on "civic functions." He warned that they were losing their position of leadership in social and political matters to Jewish organizations and the Y.M.C.A. If the current trend continued, he charged, the settlements were likely "to become more like abbeys and monasteries than like missionary posts." Kennedy made the contents of the letter public at the spring meeting of the National Federation and took it as a request to resign his position as secretary. There was a lively debate at that meeting, as at other times, over the relative merits of cultural versus civic concerns. The very fact that one could stir up a good argument seemed to indicate to some observers that a little of the prewar reform spirit was returning to the movement.[48]

Some of the returning concern for social problems was evident at the Conference of the National Federation in 1926, when the settlement workers appointed Lillian Wald chairman of a committee to investigate the social effects of prohibition at a time when no private foundation or government agency had bothered to make an inquiry. Many settlement workers supported prohibition, but few of them were fanatics, and they drew the fire of the temperance workers for not devoting more time to wiping out the use of liquor. The settlement study was begun in 1926 because of the suspicion that prohibition was breaking down. Martha Bensley Bruère, writer and artist, directed the study, which was financed in part by the National Federation of Settlements. Using data supplied largely by the individual houses, a staff of workers studied the effects of the Eighteenth Amendment in cities in all sections of the country. There was widespread agreement among the social workers that prohibition had really worked between 1920 and 1923. It had not stopped drinking, of course, but it had cut down on alcoholism and improved life in tenement neighborhoods; but as enforcement became lax and bootleg liquor safer and more plentiful, the situation had changed in many communities. Yet the study concluded that "all the things hoped for by the advocates of prohibition are being realized in some places and even where the law is least observed some of them have come true." [49]

Paul Kellogg was unhappy that the settlements did not follow up their study and use their information to influence government policy. "The trend of the times," he wrote in 1928, "is not any more adverse to social adventure and espousal today than it was when the settlements loosed their dynamite in the nineties." There was a desperate need, he told Jane Addams, for real leadership in the movement, so that "the testimony of settlement folk on such issues as prohibition, immigration, race relations, unemployment, capital punishment and the like can be pooled in ways which will promote public understanding, spread what you once called Compunction and engage the spirit of social adventure." [50]

Kellogg found a few allies in his campaign to make the settlements once more the instruments of social reform, but there were many who were reluctant to "engage the spirit of social adventure." It was obvious, nevertheless, that vitality was returning to the movement. It was marked by the launching of a new settlement periodical, the *Neighborhood*, in January 1928.[51] And it was apparent at the settlement convention in 1928, when those concerned with social reform were drafted to appoint a committee to study unemployment. Helen Hall, the head worker of University Settlement in Philadelphia and one of the younger leaders committed to social reform, was made the chairman. Eighteen months before the stock market crash, settlement workers were documenting the effects of unemployment on health and family life, and on the dignity and self-esteem of the man who could not get work. Two books came out of the investigation: one, *Case Studies of Unemployment*, documented the human tragedy of unemployed men, and the other, a more popular account written by Clinch Calkins, *Some Folks Won't Work*, was published just as the depression broke and it went through four printings. Helen Hall also wrote several articles and reports and Senator Robert F. Wagner used much of the material, personal accounts as well as the statistics, in the successful fight for social security and unemployment insurance. On one occasion in 1931 Senator Wagner read one of Miss Hall's articles into the *Congressional Record*. Miss Hall, who came to Henry Street Settlement as Lillian Wald's successor in 1933, also participated in the fight for a state unemployment law in New York, testified before congressional committees, and helped marshal testimony from the residents of the Lower East Side.[52]

The depression that began officially in 1929 got a running start in many tenement neighborhoods, and the crisis of the 'thirties forced many settlement workers to concentrate on relieving suffering rather than promoting reform or bringing art and culture to the people. One settlement worker explained the impact of depression on the neighborhood when she described the game the nursery school children played. "They're playing eviction. They don't play keeping house any more or even having-tonsils-out. Sometimes they play Relief, but Eviction is the favorite—it has more action and they all know how to play." [53]

One of the most discouraging experiences, especially for the older workers, was to look around their neighborhoods and to realize that forty years of struggle had not really improved conditions. It was especially depressing for them to examine urban housing, which seemed equally as bad as it had in the 'nineties, despite the fact that many settlement workers had continued the struggle to improve housing. The National Federation of Settlements drew up an elaborate set of goals in 1922, and the United Neighborhood Houses of New York constantly collected data and agitated for reform. The United Neighborhood Houses was the central organization, made up of most of the settlements in the city. The same organization with a different name (the Association of Neighborhood Workers) had played a prominent part in the child labor and tenement house reform movements of the first decade of the century. In 1929 the housing committee of the United Neighborhood Houses, under the direction of John L. Elliot of Hudson Guild, was successful in getting a new multiple dwelling law to replace the Tenement House Law of 1901, but it was eight more years before the committee won all the provisions it thought necessary. Playing a prominent part in the struggle for minimum standards in housing in New York was Stanley M. Isaacs, president of the United Neighborhood Houses, for many years the only Republican member of the City Council, and in the late 'thirties the borough president of Manhattan. Isaacs came by his interest in the settlement movement naturally; his father had been the founder of the Educational Alliance. Isaacs himself had been actively engaged in politics since he joined the local Republican club at sixteen in 1898, and he had been an ardent campaigner for Roosevelt in 1912.[54]

The settlements contributed indirectly to other attempts to solve the problem of urban housing in the 1920's. Through their impact on Clarence Stein, Alexander Bing, and Clarence Perry they helped to influence the development of planned suburban communities and the neighborhood unit plan. Bing, an enlightened realtor, and Stein, an architect, were both closely associated with Hudson Guild in New York. Bing became especially aware of the housing problem through his work at the settlement, and in 1924 he organized the City Housing Corporation, a limited-dividend corporation that built Sunnyside Gardens and Radburn in New Jersey, both planned communities, designed by Clarence Stein and Henry Wright, that combined row houses with garden courts to form superblock neighborhoods. Stein admitted that these communities were not the solution to the problem of the slums, but thought perhaps they would forestall the growth of new slums and gradually attract city dwellers to the less congested areas. Stein and Bing were both influenced by the English Garden City Movement and the planned community inaugurated in 1909 at Forest Hills, Long Island, by the Russell Sage Foundation; they were also moved by the neighborhood idea they had acquired at Hudson Guild. In a sense, however, they perverted the settlement idea, for instead of re-creating urban neighborhoods they sought to build self-contained suburban neighborhoods in order to draw people away from the city.[55]

Clarence Perry, a leader in the school social center movement, was employed by the Russell Sage Foundation after 1909. The settlement idea was one ingredient in his neighborhood unit plan, formulated first in the early 'twenties and published in detail in 1929 as "The Neighborhood Unit: A Scheme of Arrangement for The Family Community," part of the *Regional Survey of New York and Its Environs.* The neighborhood unit ideally would have a school at its core, a shopping center, parks, and playgrounds, and highways to divert most of the traffic away from the living areas of the neighborhood. Perry, like the early settlement workers, hoped to instill pride in the local community and to build neighborhood spirit. He believed that his plan could be used to rebuild the slums as well as to develop new areas. Perry's neighborhood unit became an important influence on housing reform and city planning, having a strong impact on the greenbelt towns of the 1930's for example, but it did not solve the problem of slum tenements.[56]

Discouragement with the small results of forty years of housing reform led Mary Simkhovitch to decide that the only answer was low-rent housing built at government expense. She was one of a handful of reformers who organized the Public Housing Conference in New York in 1931. The next year the organization became national in scope, and Mrs. Simkhovitch became its president and Helen Alfred, another settlement worker, its secretary. The group tried without success to get a public housing provision written into the Federal Relief and Reconstruction Act of 1932. After Roosevelt was elected, however, Mrs. Simkhovitch and a few others approached Senator Robert Wagner, Harold Ickes, Hugh Johnson, and Mrs. Roosevelt in Washington and convinced them that public housing was the only solution to the problem. Mrs. Simkhovitch and Miss Alfred, with the help of others, were primarily responsible for obtaining the public housing provision of the National Industrial Recovery Act; for convincing Harold Ickes to include housing in the PWA projects; and for drafting the bill that finally passed Congress in 1937 as the Wagner-Steagall Housing Act. Mrs. Simkhovitch served on the advisory committee in the Public Works Administration and on the New York Housing Authority after it was created in 1934. Her work for public housing was the capstone of a long career in behalf of social legislation.[57]

The Wagner-Steagall Act that set up the United States Housing Authority in 1937 did not solve the housing problems in most settlement neighborhoods. The residents of Henry Street Settlement discovered that their area of the city was not eligible for public housing in 1937 because it was assumed that the land values were too high. A survey of the area initiated by the Settlement Housing Committee demonstrated that the land value had indeed dropped, and an appeal to Mayor Fiorello H. La Guardia made possible the construction of a large housing project, which was named after B. Charney Vladeck, an immigrant leader on the Lower East Side.[58]

Public low-rent housing was just one of the many ways that the New Deal affected life in settlement neighborhoods, but the settlements also had their impact on the New Deal. Helen Hall and Mary Simkhovitch were two of the more prominent settlement workers who served with a government agency. Mark A. McClos-

key and Helen M. Harris worked with the National Youth Administration, and almost every settlement worker co-operated with the
WPA or the Temporary Emergency Relief Association.[59]

VI

Perhaps the most important settlement contribution to the New
Deal and to the larger movement for social justice in America was
the effect upon a group of young men and women whose minds
were changed significantly and their ideals altered by spending a
year or two in a settlement house. Vida Scudder often remarked
that in the long run it was the impact of the settlement on the
resident rather than the impact of the resident on the neighborhood
that was most important. "It often surprises me how fundamentally
and powerfully those two years have shaped my ideals and ambitions, and my general attitudes toward life," a resident of South
End House remarked. "I gained a more sympathetic knowledge of
the laboring man in general and trade unions in particular," a
young woman from one of the college settlements reported. "Even
a short residence at a social settlement affects people's character in
a most remarkable way," Bruno Lasker recalled.[60] Of course it was
possible to live in a settlement and ignore the social and economic
conditions that made people poor; and it even happened occasionally that settlement experience made young men, like J. G. Phelps
Stokes and William English Walling, into socialists. Robert Hunter
and Philip Davis, on the other hand, claimed that their settlement
experience kept their radicalism in check. More typical was Raymond Fosdick, who credited Lillian Wald and Henry Street with
making him a liberal. "The incredible poverty and degradation
matched with public lethargy and insensibility" he encountered influenced his ideas permanently. And Louis Pink, housing reformer
and advocate of social insurance, remembered Lillian Wald and
Mary Simkhovitch: "These dynamic people were a ferment, a yeast
in the community—trying to make people realize the necessity for a
different world, a better community. . . ."[61]

Settlement experience altered more than the ideas of the residents; it changed their goals and their occupations. As Jane Addams remarked, it turned a generation of young Americans from philanthropists into reformers. And reformers many of them remained. Some of them became college teachers or newspaper reporters, a few went into business or another branch of social work, while a large number became public servants. They served in federal agencies, on state government commissions, and on local investigating committees. They supervised private foundations and staffed the bureaus of municipal research and the urban planning commissions. Many turned up in New Deal agencies at the state and national level.[62]

Rufus Miles was an Amherst graduate who had spent two years at South End House during the early part of the century before becoming head resident of Goodrich House in Cleveland. During the 'twenties Miles worked for the New York and Cincinnati bureaus of Municipal Research, and in the 'thirties he directed the work of the PWA in Ohio and was secretary of the Governor's Welfare Commission. The author of many books and articles on the problems of municipal organization, Miles's career as an organizer and administrator was directly related to his settlement experience.[63]

Another Amherst graduate, Joseph Eastman, went from a Boston settlement to the Public Franchise League, and after this apprenticeship in public service, worked for the Massachusetts Public Service Commission. In 1919 Woodrow Wilson appointed him to the Interstate Commerce Commission, and he turned his attention from the state to the nation. In 1933 President Roosevelt named Eastman Federal Coordinator of Transportation. Throughout the New Deal period and until his death in 1944, Eastman wielded great power and influence as a transportation expert. His career as a public servant, his conception of the responsibility of the government to the people—his life's work, in fact—began at South End House.[64]

William H. Mathews left Kingsley House in Pittsburgh in 1910. He ran a ranch in Idaho and investigated labor conditions for U. S. Steel before going to work for the New York Association for Improving the Conditions of the Poor in 1913. As early as 1915, along with Harry Hopkins, a member of his staff, he experimented with work relief projects to combat some of the misery and hopelessness of unemployment. In the early 'twenties Mathews, with the backing of the A.I.C.P., used work relief to ease the burden of depression. When the great depression struck in 1929 he created the Emergency Work Bureau (a private organization under the auspices of the A.I.C.P.), and between 1930 and 1933 he directed the spending of about thirty million dollars in relief wages. He served on several state commissions while Roosevelt was governor, always advocating work relief when possible. Thus, William Mathews, himself strongly influenced by his settlement experiences, had a direct impact on Hopkins and Roosevelt and on the relief policies of the New Deal.[65]

Harry Hopkins had once been a settlement worker at Chistadora House in New York, and many others who held positions of power during the New Deal received an education in social responsibility at a settlement house. Frances Perkins had been a resident at both Hull House and Chicago Commons; Henry Morgenthau, Jr., Herbert Lehman, and Adolph Berle were associated with Henry Street Settlement; the president of General Electric, Gerard Swope, whom Roosevelt consulted on such diverse matters as housing, social security, and the NRA, was a former resident of Hull House and a friend of many settlement workers. An even more direct influence on government policy came through the President's wife, who had long supported the Women's Trade Union League and the Consumers' League in New York. After a visit to the White House early in the New Deal, Lillian Wald reported, "Mrs. R[oosevelt] acts truly as if she had been brought up in the settlement." [66]

In many subtle and persistent ways the settlement movement influenced the social justice movement in America. Settlement workers fought for educational reforms, for better housing, for the protection of the working woman and child, for more parks and playgrounds. They tried to understand the complex problems of the people who lived near them, and to re-create the neighborhood in the city. Their books and articles, based upon careful research, documented the need for reform and helped to convince at least a portion of the American people that social environment, not individual weakness, was the greatest cause of poverty, that the color of a man's skin, or the sound of his accent, was no just basis for treating him as inferior. They demonstrated that private charity and philanthropy were not enough, that action by the government at all levels was necessary to combat the massive problems of urban, industrial America.

Settlement workers usually combined an idealistic faith in the future with a hard-headed realism about how change is accomplished in a democracy. Their fight was a frustrating one, for success came slowly, and battles that seemed to be won had to be fought over and over again. It would be easy to conclude that the settlements failed, but they did win victories and change attitudes. All those who today join the war on poverty or try to rehabilitate the nation's cities are influenced, whether they know it or not, by a generation of settlement workers who dared to dream that American cities could be safe and stimulating for all citizens, and who worked from their bases in urban neighborhoods to make a part of that dream come true.

A Note on Sources

Since the primary purpose of this book is to trace the impact and outward reach of the settlement movement it would be impossible, or at least presumptuous, to list all the materials I have used. I have tried to give complete citations in the footnotes. The following is a discussion of the sources, especially the unpublished and out-of-the-way material, that proved most useful to me.

When I first started research on this project in the late 1950's there had been no systematic attempt to preserve manuscripts or reports of the early social workers. I spent a great deal of time trying to locate material, and then, in attics and closets of settlement houses and other organizations, picking out what was most useful. Fortunately, the attitude toward the early history of social work has changed and libraries and other institutions are preserving and organizing collections. Of course, in some cases it is too late. Especially encouraging is the development of the Social Welfare History Archives at the University of Minnesota, under the direction of Clarke Chambers.

MANUSCRIPTS

Jane Addams Papers (Swarthmore College Peace Collection). This collection incorporates the correspondence originally deposited in the Library of Congress, and the material that I used at Hull House. It is a large and well-organized collection including correspondence both to and from Jane Addams (although, unfortunately, not too much of the latter for the early years). There are also reports, speeches, and a huge and almost unused clipping collection. The correspondence in the collection has been microfilmed and is available at several centers around the country.

Annita McCormick (Mrs. Emons) Blaine Papers (McCormick Collection, Wisconsin State Historical Society), is a huge and important collection with 84 four-drawer file cabinets full of material. The collection is arranged according to correspondent and can be used easily. It is a mine of information on all aspects of twentieth-century reform, for Mrs. Blaine was a participant in, as well as a financial supporter of, many movements.

Sophonisba Breckinridge Papers (Library of Congress) are disappointing for a study of the settlement movement, but there are many letters addressed to Jane Addams in the collection, especially in 1912 when Miss Breckinridge answered much of Miss Addams's correspondence.

Alice Hamilton Papers (Schlesinger Library, Radcliffe College) are thin, but more of Dr. Hamilton's papers will be added at a later date.

Mary McDowell Papers (Chicago Historical Society) are sparse and contain very little correspondence. But there are portions of an unpublished autobiography and considerable material relating to the stockyards strike of 1904.

National Federation of Settlements Records (now at Social Welfare History Archives, University of Minnesota). I used this material, including the morgue files, clippings, correspondence, articles, biographical sketches, and so on, at the NFS headquarters in New York. The collection is stronger after 1920, but contains some material that antedates the founding of the organization in 1911.

Raymond Robins Papers (Wisconsin State Historical Society) are a major collection for the study of American social reform after 1901. They are especially good for municipal reform in Chicago and for the rise and fall of the Progressive Party.

South End House (20 Union Park, Boston) holds an important collection of reports, articles, books, correspondence, and other material, including the records of the Boston Social Union, relating to the early history of South End House and the settlement movement. I dug much of this material out of boxes and from closets at the settlement. It is now organized for easy use in a special room. Some of this material will be soon transferred to Houghton Library, Harvard University, and incorporated with the material already there. In 1952 Mrs. Robert Woods gave Houghton Library the Woods Papers she had used to write the biography of her husband; however, Houghton lost or misplaced this material and all my attempts between 1957 and 1962 to have them find it were in vain. The Woods Papers have been located recently, but they are not yet catalogued. There are two boxes and seventeen packets. See "Papers of Robert A. Woods," *Social Service Review*, xxxix (Dec. 1965), 476–77.

Mary K. Simkhovitch Papers (Schlesinger Library, Radcliffe College) are sparse and contain little correspondence. There are some handwritten and typed drafts of speeches and articles. But I got the impression from Vladimir Simkhovitch, in a conversation shortly before his death, that there are more manuscripts.

Ellen Gates Starr Papers (Sophia Smith Collection, Smith College) are important principally for the correspondence with Jane Addams, although there are other letters, clippings, etc.

J. G. Phelps Stokes Papers (now in Special Collection, Columbia University Library). I used these papers when they were still in the author's possession in an office on the third floor of his Greenwich Village home. They contain correspondence, clippings, and fragments of an autobiography. They are a major source for a study of the settlement movement, New York reform, and many other liberal and radical movements in the progressive era.

Survey Associates Papers (now at Social Welfare History Archives, University of Minnesota). I used these papers when they were in the Annex of the New York School of Social Work. It was research under exotic but trying conditions and I was able to dip into the collection only here and there. Its strength is in the 1920's and 1930's but must be ranked as one of the best collections anywhere for the study of social reform in the twentieth century. Also now at Minnesota are the personal papers of Paul Kellogg.

Graham Taylor Papers (Newberry Library, Chicago) are a major source for the study of the settlement movement and Chicago reform, as well as for various national reform movements. There is extensive correspondence, clippings, copies of articles, speeches, and other materials.

United Neighborhood Houses Records (now at Social Welfare History Archives, University of Minnesota) contain minutes, correspondence, and clippings of one of the most important city settlement federations.

William English Walling Papers (Wisconsin State Historical Society) are disappointing but contain copies of articles, clippings, and some correspondence. Mrs. Walling, before her death, showed me additional material but its whereabouts now is uncertain.

Lillian Wald Papers (New York Public Library) are a large and valuable collection for a study of the settlement movement and all aspects of social reform. The collection, which gets stronger in the 1920's, proved one of the most valuable sources for this study.

OTHER COLLECTIONS

The Radcliffe Women's Archives, recently renamed the Arthur and Elizabeth Schlesinger Library, contains several collections that proved valuable: the Leonora O'Reilly Papers are important for an understanding of the early settlement movement in New York and for the story of the Women's Trade Union League; also there are records, files, and correspondence of the League (which supplement the main collection at the Library of Congress), the unpublished autobiography of Mary Kenny O'Sullivan, and the papers of Mary Anderson. Radcliffe Archives has also the papers of settlement workers Eva Whiting White and Maryal Knox, although both of these collections are disappointing for the progressive period.

The Library of Congress has the Papers of the Women's Trade Union League. The Jacob Riis Papers are scant, but among them is some interesting correspondence with settlement worker Jane Robbins. The John Kingsbury Papers are thin, too, but have some interesting material on early social work and on the Progressive party. The Harold Ickes Papers, while very weak for the Chicago period, have some material on the Progressive party. I also consulted the Theodore Roosevelt Papers and the Albert Beveridge Papers at specific points.

The New York Public Library, in addition to the Lillian Wald papers, holds the papers of Everett Wheeler, founder of East Side House. The collection is unorganized but important for some aspects of reform in New York. In the Columbia Special Collections are the papers of Seth Low. When I used them they were in an unorganized state in the Low Library. The records of the Citizens' Union are at Columbia, but they are of no use for the early period; in addition, the Papers of Lawrence Veiller are on film.

The Papers of Mark A. De Wolf Howe and of Oswald Garrison Villard at Houghton Library, Harvard, proved useful for some details. The Journals of George Hodges at the Episcopal Theological School in Cambridge provided some information on an important early settlement and social gospel leader. The Papers of William Jewett Tucker at Dartmouth were of little use. Yale holds the Papers of William Kent and Frank Parsons, which proved useful but on the whole disappointing. The Sophia Smith Collection at Smith College has some interesting articles and clippings relating to the settlement movement, and an important journal kept by Mrs. Florence L. Cross Kitchet, an early resident of the college settlement. The Chicago Historical Society holds the Papers of Agnes Nester, an early leader of the Women's Trade Union League, and of William Dever, a politician and mayor of Chicago who began his career in the 17th ward; but neither collection was of much use for this study. The Emily Greene Balch Papers at Swarthmore are concerned mostly with her peace activities. The Julia Lathrop Papers at Rockford College, Illinois, are unorganized; they deal primarily with her activities with the Children's Bureau. Mrs. Ralph Albertson of Washington allowed me to read the fascinating unpublished autobiography of her husband.

The Vida Scudder Papers, cited by Arthur Mann in *Yankee Reformers*, have apparently disappeared. And the Florence Kelley Papers seem, at this writing, to be lost forever. I dipped at random into the papers and records of University Settlement when they were in the possession of Albert Kennedy. I saw enough to convince me that this could be a valuable collection if properly organized. A few other collections that might have proved valuable were not consulted either because they were not available at the time I did the research for this study or because I was unaware of their existence: the Grace and Edith Abbott Papers at the University of Chicago; the Catheryne Cooke Gilman Papers, Minnesota Historical Society; and the Charles Bernheimer Papers, the New York Historical Society.

ORAL HISTORY

I used the following typescripts of interviews in the Oral History Project, Columbia University: Henry Bruère, Homer Folks, Bruno Lasker, Louis Pink, and Lawrence Veiller.

I also interviewed a number of people connected in one way or another with the settlement movement. While I usually gained little in specific information, I learned a great deal about the spirit of the times. The most valuable interviews were, perhaps, those with J. G. Phelps Stokes. I talked with him several times over a period of about six weeks in his home while I was going through his manuscripts. Mrs. William English Walling and Dr. Alice Hamilton helped me and related their experiences with great gusto. Also helpful were Albert Kennedy, Eva Whiting White, John Gaus, and David Howie. Of the many contemporary settlement workers whom I troubled with my problems, Margaret Berry of the National Federation of Settlements and Charles Fraggos of South End House were most helpful.

REPORTS, BULLETINS, PERIODICALS

The settlement workers turned out an incredible quantity of reports and bulletins, but since many were designed primarily to attract contributions, they must be used with care. Most valuable to me were the reports of South End House, Greenwich House, University Settlement, Lincoln House (Boston), and East Side House; others proved useful at specific points. The Twentieth and Twenty-fifth Anniversary Reports of Henry Street Settlement were especially helpful, and *Hull House Bulletin*, published monthly between 1896 and 1910, provided a valuable record of the activities of that settlement. *The Settlement Journal*, published spasmodically between 1904 and 1914, provided a similar record for Henry Street. *The University Settlement Studies Quarterly*, 1904–07, served as an outlet for articles written by the residents of that settlement.

The annual reports of the National Federation of Settlements also provide important information on the development of the movement after 1913. In addition, there is a large amount of ephemeral pamphlet literature published by individual settlements and by various settlement organizations. There is no easy way of locating collections of these reports, bulletins, and pamphlets, but the Widener Library at Harvard, the New York Public Library, and the files of the National Federation of Settlements have good collections. I used the annual reports of a number of organizations: the National Child Labor Committee, National Women's Trade Union League, Chicago Municipal Voters' League, and various other reform organizations. Also useful were the *Proceedings of the National Conference of Charities and Correction*, which in 1917 became the Conference of Social Work.

More significant, however, than annual reports were the periodicals. The most important journal for the early settlement movement is the *Commons*, 1896–1905. It was published by Chicago Commons, but for most of its nine years it served as the unofficial organ of the movement. There is an index to the *Commons*, 1896–1905, prepared by Harriet Peck and published by the Training Center, National Federation of Settlements and Neighborhood Centers, 72 E. Eleventh Street, Chicago. *Charities and the Commons*, 1904–09, and the *Survey*, 1909–52, are also important for following the course of the settlement movement and all aspects of social reform. *Neighborhood*, 1928–32, is useful for the later movement. Articles on the settlement movement and on social reform appeared, of course, in a wide range of periodicals, both scholarly and popular.

AUTOBIOGRAPHIES

Like many others of their generation, the settlement workers wrote autobiographies and memoirs. Although they must be used with care, they are an aid to the study of social reform and the impulse that made people reformers in the progressive era. The most famous of these memoirs are by Jane Addams, *Twenty Years at Hull House* (New York, 1910) and *The Second Twenty Years at Hull House* (New York, 1930). Jane Addams seldom mentions a name or a date, but her volumes capture some of the spirit of the movement. Graham Taylor's two volumes, *Pioneering on Social Frontiers* (Chicago, 1930) and *Chicago Commons Through Forty Years* (Chicago, 1936), while not as charmingly written as Jane Addams's, are more useful to the historian. Mary K. Simkhovitch, *Neighborhood: My Story of Greenwich House* (New York, 1938), and Lillian Wald's two volumes, *The House on Henry Street* (New York, 1915) and *Windows on Henry Street* (Boston, 1934), are indispensable for a study of the reform movements in New York. Alice Hamilton's autobiography, *Exploring the Dangerous Trades* (Boston, 1943), paints a colorful picture of the Hull House group and is especially important for a study of the settlement workers' role in support of organized labor. In many ways the most charming and perspective of all the autobiographies is Vida Scudder's *On Journey* (New York, 1937).

Some of the following are less well known, but worthwhile: Ernest Poole, *The Bridge: My Own Story* (New York, 1940); Philip Davis, *And Crown Thy Good* (New York, 1952); Gregory Weinstein, *The Ardent Eighties: Reminiscences of an Interesting Decade* (New York, 1928); William H. Mathews, *Adventures in Giving* (New York, 1939); Raymond Fosdick, *Chronicle of a Generation: An Autobiography* (New York, 1958). Also Charles Bernheimer, *Half a Century of Community Service* (New York, 1917); Benjamin Marsh, *Lobbyist for the People* (Washington, 1953); and Mary W. Ovington, *The Walls Came Tumbling Down* (New York, 1947). Florence Kelley published her autobiography in four installments in *Survey Graphic*, LVII (Oct. 1, 1926, Feb. 1, 1927), 8 ff, 55 ff, and LVIII (April 1, 1927, June 1, 1927), 31 ff, 271 ff. Others include: Esther G. Barrows, *Neighbors All: A Settlement Notebook* (Boston, 1929); Frederick C. Howe, *Confessions of a Reformer* (New York, 1925); and William J. Tucker, *My Generation* (Boston, 1919). Some autobiographies of those close to the settlement movement are: Harold Ickes, *The Autobiography of a Curmudgeon* (New York, 1943); Jacob Riis, *The Making of an American* (New York, 1901);

Edward T. Devine, *When Social Work Was Young* (New York, 1939); Stephen Wise, *Challenging Years: The Autobiography of Stephen Wise* (New York, 1949); and Robert Morss Lovett, *All Our Years* (New York, 1945).

BIOGRAPHIES (primary)

In addition to the many autobiographies listed above, there are many memorial volumes and biographies written by friends and relatives of settlement workers that contain primary source material for a study of the settlement movement. Eleanor Woods, *Robert A. Woods: Champion of Democracy* (Boston, 1929), reproduces many letters and other items written by Woods that are unavailable elsewhere. Mary E. Dreier, *Margaret Dreier Robins: Her Life, Letters and Work* (New York, 1950), is a sister's tribute that contains many letters. Jane Addams, *My Friend, Julia Lathrop* (New York, 1935), and Josephine Goldmark, *Impatient Crusader* (Urbana, Illinois, 1953), are human portraits of Julia Lathrop and Florence Kelley drawn by lifetime friends. *James Bronson Reynolds, March 17, 1861–January 1, 1924: A Memorial* (New York, 1927), James K. Paulding, *Charles B. Stover, July 14, 1861–April 24, 1929: His Life and Personality* (New York, 1938), and *Carola Woerishoffer: Her Life and Work* (Philadelphia, 1912), are uncritical, but provide valuable information on these social reformers and settlement workers. *A Heart That Held the World: An Appraisal of the Life of Helena Stuart Dudley and a Memorial to Her Work* (pamphlet, 1939) is an important sketch of a little-known Boston settlement worker. Edith Abbott wrote her sister's story in a series of articles, "Grace Abbott and Hull House, 1908–21," *SSR*, xxiv (Sept., Dec. 1950), 374–94, 493–518; "Grace Abbott: A Sister's Memories," *SSR*, xiii (Sept. 1939), 351–407.

BIOGRAPHIES

The best biography of a settlement leader is Louise C. Wade, *Graham Taylor: Pioneer for Social Justice* (Chicago, 1964). Robert L. Duffus, *Lillian Wald: Neighbor and Crusader* (New York, 1938) is better than James W. Linn, *Jane Addams: A Biography* (New York, 1935); however, both are undocumented and largely uncritical, although occasionally useful. Howard E. Wilson, *Mary McDowell: Neighbor* (Chicago, 1928), and Isabella Dubroca, *Good Neighbor: Eleanor McMain of Kingsley House* (New Orleans, 1955), are sketchy and superficial. Mercedes M. Randall, *Improper Bostonian: Emile Greene Balch* (New

York, 1964), and Tay Hohoff, *Ministry to Man: The Life of John Love-joy Elliot* (New York, 1959), are somewhat better. Biographical information on many of the lesser settlement figures is difficult to find and is often limited to contemporary sketches or obituaries.

SOCIAL WORK AND SOCIAL REFORM

The best place to begin an investigation is with Robert Bremner, *From the Depths: The Discovery of Poverty in the United States* (New York, 1956), and Clarke Chambers, *Seedtime of Reform: American Social Service and Social Action* (Minneapolis, 1963). Both are excellent works with extensive bibliographies. Agnes F. Young and E. T. Acton, *British Social Work in the Nineteenth Century* (London, 1956), provides an introduction to the English background. Robert Woods and Albert Kennedy, *Handbook of Settlements* (New York, 1911), and *Settlement Horizon* (New York, 1922), still provide the starting place for the study of the American movement. Christopher Lasch, ed., *The Social Thought of Jane Addams* (New York, 1965), contains a convenient collection of Jane Addams's writings. See also Anne F. Scott, ed., *Jane Addams, Democracy and Social Ethics* (Cambridge, 1964). Robert A. Woods, *The Neighborhood in Nation Building* (Boston, 1923), is a collection of his articles. Lorene M. Pacey, ed., *Readings in the Development of Settlement Work* (New York, 1950), is a useful collection of articles. Arthur Hillman, *Neighborhood Centers Today: Action Programs for a Rapidly Changing World* (New York, 1960), is a contemporary survey of the movement. Sidney Dillick, *Community Organization for Neighborhood Development—Past and Present* (New York, 1953), is the best introduction to community organization. Roy Lubove, *The Professional Altruist: The Emergence of Social Work as a Career, 1880–1930* (Cambridge, 1965), is the best study of the development of social work as a profession, although interestingly he does not deal with the settlement workers, the most unprofessional of all social workers. Ralph E. and Muriel W. Pumphrey, *The Heritage of American Social Work* (New York, 1961), provides another easy introduction to the whole range of the movement. I will not attempt to list the growing literature on all aspects of social reform in the progressive era, but I have profited by it and note what I have used in each chapter. Critical bibliographies may be found in George E. Mowry, *The Era of Theodore Roosevelt, 1900–1912* (New York, 1958), and in Robert H. Wiebe, *The Search for Order, 1877–1920* (New York, 1967).

Bibliographical Addenda 1984

MANUSCRIPTS

In the last twenty years a great many archives and libraries have made major efforts to collect and preserve material relating to social welfare and the settlement movement. I cannot possibly list all the new collections. A major guide has been prepared by Andrea Hinding, Ames Sheldon Bower, Clarke Chambers, eds., *Women's History Sources: A Guide to Archives and Manuscript Collections in the United States*, 2 vols. (New York, 1979) has 96 separate index references to settlements. The University Settlement (New York) material is now at the State Historical Society of Wisconsin. Columbia University has additional Lillian Wald manuscripts. The Henry Street Settlement Papers are now at the Social Welfare History Archives at the University of Minnesota, which remains one of the most important depositories for material relating to the history of the settlements and social reform. The Urban Archives at Temple University has a number of collections relating to social settlements and social reform in Philadelphia. The Library at the University of Illinois-Chicago has collected a wide variety of material relating to Hull House and Chicago reform movements. Perhaps the most important and complete settlement collection of all has been discovered recently at Greenwich House in New York, but at this writing it is not clear where it will be deposited, and it is currently not available for use by scholars. Several settlement collections have been microfilmed, but the most important project by far is Mary Lynn McCree, ed., *The Jane Addams Papers*, Microfilm Edition (Microfilm Corporation of America and University Microfilm International, 1984). This massive collection contains most of Jane Addams' writing as well as her letters and letters written to her.

SETTLEMENT MOVEMENT

On the English settlement movement see especially Gareth Stedman Jones, *Outcast London: A Study in the Relationship between Classes in Victorian Society* (Oxford, 1971). He is critical of the paternalism and class bias of the pioneer settlement workers, but his account is indispensable. On Hull House see Allen F. Davis and Mary Lynn McCree, eds., *Eighty Years at Hull House* (Chicago, 1969) and Allen F. Davis, *American Heroine: The Life and Legend of Jane Addams* (New York, 1973). For a more critical view of the Hull House reformers see Thomas Lee Philpott, *The Slum and the Ghetto: Neighborhood Deterioration and Middle-Class Reform, 1880–1930* (New York, 1978). Cynthia Grant Tucker, *A Woman's Ministry: Mary Collson's Search for Reform as a Unitarian Minister, A Hull House Social Worker and a Christian Science Practitioner* (Philadelphia, 1984) gives a perspective on Hull House from one of the lesser known residents. Judith Ann Trolander, *Settlement Houses and the Great Depression* (Detroit, 1975) is a solid work with a good discussion of sources. Two articles which raise important questions about the relationship of settlements to their immigrant neighbors are: Richard N. Juliani, "The Settlement House and the Italian Family," *The Italian Immigrant Woman in North America, Proceedings of the Tenth Annual Conference of the American Italian Historical Association*, edited by Betty Boyd Caroli, Robert F. Harney, Lydia F. Thomas (Toronto, 1978), 103–123; and Rivka Lissak, "Myth and Reality: the Patterns of Relationships Between the Hull House Circle and the 'New Immigrants' on Chicago's West Side, 1890–1919," *Journal of American Ethnic History* II (1983), 21–50. John J. Grabowski, *A Social Settlement in a Neighborhood in Transition: Hiram House: Cleveland Ohio, 1896–1926* (Cleveland, 1977), and Ruth Crocker, "Sympathy and Science: The Settlement Movement in Gary and Indianapolis to 1930," (Unpublished Ph.D. thesis, Purdue University, 1982) demonstrate that in other cities the success of the settlement movement was more limited than it was in Boston, Chicago and New York.

Several scholars have begun to evaluate the special importance of the settlement experience for women. Dolores Hayden has a provocative chapter, "Public Kitchens, Social Settlements, and the Cooperative Ideal," in *The Grand Domestic Revolution* (Cambridge, Mass., 1981). But also important are John P. Rousmaniere, "Cultural Hybrid in the Slums: The College Woman and the Settlement House, 1889–1894," *American Quarterly* XXII (Spring 1970), 45–66; Jill Kathryn Conway, "Women Reformers and American Culture, 1870–1930," *Journal of Social History* (Winter 1971–72), 164–182; Blanche Wiesen Cook, "Female Support Networks and Political Activism: Lillian Wald, Crystal Eastman, Emma Goldman," *Chrysalis* III (1977), 43–61; and Estelle Freedman, "Separatism as Strategy: Female Institution Building and American Feminism, 1870–1930," *Feminist Studies* V (Fall 1979), 512–529. We do not yet have successful biographies of many of the settlement leaders. Lela B. Costin, *Two Sisters for Social Justice: A Biography of Grace and Edith Abbott* (Urbana, 1983) is an important addition to the literature. Peter J. Frederick has an interesting chapter on Vida Scudder in *Knights of the Golden Rule* (Lexington, 1976). Elizabeth H. Carrell, "Reflections in A Mirror: The Progressive Woman and the Settlement Experience," (Unpublished Ph.D. thesis, University of Texas, Austin, 1981) makes useful comparisons between Ellen Starr and Vida Scudder. Biographies of Florence Kelley by Kathryn Kish Sklar, of Alice Hamilton by Barbara Sicherman, and of Mary McDowell by Louise Wade are in preparation.

SOCIAL REFORM

The writing about progressivism in all its aspects has been voluminous since 1967. The best place to begin an examination of the literature about this fascinating movement is with the works of Arthur S. Link and Richard L. McCormick, *Progressivism* (Arlington Heights, Illinois, 1983) and Daniel T. Rodgers, "In Search of Progressivism," *Reviews in American History* (Dec. 1982), 113–132. Two important recent interpretations are: Paul Boyer, *Urban Masses and Moral Order in America, 1820–1920* (Cambridge, Mass., 1978) and Robert M. Crunden, *Ministers of Reform: The Progressive Achievement in American Civilization, 1889–1920* (New York, 1982). Michael B. Katz, *Poverty and Policy in American History* (New York, 1983) is an important attempt to refocus social welfare history.

Many books and articles have been published on subjects I dealt with briefly in *Spearheads for Reform*. Among the more important are: Clarke A. Chambers, *Paul U. Kellogg and the Survey: Voices for Social Welfare and Social Justice* (Minneapolis, 1971); Ruth Rosen, *The Lost Sisterhood: Prostitution in America, 1900–1918* (Baltimore, 1982); Nancy Schrom Dye, *As Equals and As Sisters: Feminism, the Labor Movement and the Women's Trade Union League of New York* (Columbia, Mo., 1980); Alice Kessler-Harris, *Out to Work: A History of Wage-Earning Women in the United States* (New York, 1982); David M. Kennedy, *Over Here: The First World War and American Society* (New York, 1980); J. Stanley Lemons, *The Woman Citizen: Social Feminism in the 1920s* (Urbana, 1973); Dominick Cavallo, *Muscles and Morals: Organized Playgrounds and Urban Reform, 1880–1920* (Philadelphia, 1981). John F. McClymer, *War and Welfare: Social Engineering in America, 1890–1925* (Westport, Conn., 1980) takes exception to a number of my interpretations.

Abbreviations used in Notes

AHR   *American Historical Review*
Annals   *Annals of the American Academy of Political and Social Science*
BPL   Rare Books Room, Boston Public Library
DAB   *Dictionary of American Biography*
JAH   *Journal of American History*
MVHR   *Mississippi Valley Historical Review*
NCAB   *National Cyclopedia of American Biography*
NCCC   Proceedings of the National Conference of Charities and Correction
NCSW   Proceedings of the National Conference of Social Work
NFS   National Federation of Settlements. Material now at Social Welfare History Archives, University of Minnesota.
OHP   Oral History Project, Columbia University
SAP   Survey Associates Papers. Material now at Social Welfare History Archives, University of Minnesota.
SEH   South End House
SSR   *Social Service Review*
SL   The Arthur and Elizabeth Schlesinger Library on The History of Women in America, Radcliffe College.
UNH   United Neighborhood Houses, New York. Material now at Social Welfare History Archives, University of Minnesota.
USSQ   *University Settlement Studies Quarterly*
WTUL   Women's Trade Union League

Notes

PREFACE

1. Robert H. Bremner, *From the Depths: The Discovery of Poverty in the United States* (New York, 1956), 201–3.
2. Arthur Schlesinger, Jr., *The Crisis of the Old Order* (Boston, 1957), 25.
3. Henry F. May, *The End of American Innocence: A Study of the First Years of Our Own Time, 1912–1917* (New York, 1959), 29.
4. Arthur S. Link, *American Epoch* (New York, 1955), 69–72; Bremner, *From the Depths*, 140–63. A recent book, Irwin Yellowitz, *Labor and the Progressive Movement in New York State, 1897–1916* (Ithaca, 1965), defines a similar group as "Social Progressives."
5. Samuel P. Hays, *The Response to Industrialism, 1885–1914* (Chicago, 1957), 85–6; George E. Mowry, *The Era of Theodore Roosevelt* (New York, 1958), 101–3.
6. Eric Goldman, *Rendezvous with Destiny* (New York, 1953), 77–9; C. Vann Woodward, *Origins of the New South* (Baton Rouge, 1951), 369–95.
7. Mowry, *The Era of Theodore Roosevelt*, 94–5; Morton and Lucia White, *The Intellectual Versus the City* (Cambridge, 1962), 139–54.
8. Goldman, *Rendezvous with Destiny.*
9. Morton White, *Social Thought in America: The Revolt Against Formalism* (New York, 1949).
10. Richard Hofstadter, *The Age of Reform* (New York, 1955), 131–72.
11. Michael Harrington, *The Other America: Poverty in the United States* (New York, 1963).
12. "What Is the Future for Settlements?" *Social Work*, VIII (April 1963), 41–7. For the change in one settlement see Jon A. Peterson, "From Social Settlement to Social Agency: Settlement Work in Columbus, Ohio, 1898–1958," *SSR*, XXXIX (June 1965), 191–208. The settlements have been vigorously attacked by sociologists who charged that they performed the function of a neighborhood institution very badly, and indeed, did not understand the people they tried to serve. See especially, William F. Whyte, *Street Corner Society: The Social Structure of an Italian Slum* (2nd edn., Chicago, 1955), 98–104; Herbert J. Gans, *The Urban Villagers: Group and*

Class in the Life of Italian Americans (New York, 1962), 142–62. It should be pointed out that both Whyte and Gans attack settlements which had long ceased to be concerned primarily with social reform.

13. See Arthur Hillmann, *Neighborhood Centers Today: Action Programs for a Rapidly Changing World* (New York, 1960); *Neighborhood Goals in a Rapidly Changing World: Action-Research Workshop Held at Arden House, Harriman, New York, Feb. 13–15, 1958* (New York, 1958); *Review and Revision: A Report of the Self-Study Committee of the National Federation of Settlements* (New York, 1960); *Neighborhood Work in the Space Age* (NFS Annual Report, 1957–58).

14. Quoted in *Neighborhood Goals,* 12.

CHAPTER 1

1. Henrietta O. Barnett, *Canon Barnett, His Life, Work and Friends,* 2 vols. (London, 1918), I, 312–13.

2. See Leonard E. Elliott-Binns, *Religion in the Victorian Era* (London, 1936), 144–6, 266–71, 346–8; Robert A. Woods, *English Social Movements* (New York, 1897), 79, 142.

3. On Ruskin see Raymond Williams, *Culture and Society, 1780–1950* (New York, Anchor Books, 1960), 140–60; John D. Rosenberg, *The Darkening Glass: A Portrait of Ruskin's Genius* (New York, 1961); Charles A. Beard, "Ruskin and the Babble of Tongues," *New Republic,* LXXXVII (Aug. 1936), 370–72. Quotation is from *The Stones of Venice,* quoted in Williams, *Culture and Society,* 153.

4. Quotation is from *Art and Socialism,* quoted in Williams, *Culture and Society,* 166.

5. See Agnes F. Young and E. T. Ashton, *British Social Work in the Nineteenth Century* (London, 1956), 115–25; Robert H. Bremner, " 'An Iron Scepter Twined with Roses': The Octavia Hill System of Housing Management," *SSR,* XXXIX (June 1965), 222–31.

6. Robert A. Woods and Albert Kennedy, *The Settlement Horizon* (New York, 1922), 17–24; Young and Ashton, *British Social Work,* 223–5.

7. Henrietta Barnett, *Canon Barnett,* I, 302–13.

8. Henrietta Barnett, *Canon Barnett,* I, 314–92. See also Werner Picht, *Toynbee Hall and the English Settlement Movement* (London, 1914).

9. Barnett, "Settlements of University Men in Great Towns," *Practicable Socialism* (London, 1915), 96–106; "Twenty-one Years of University Settlements," *Practicable Socialism,* 127, 165. Quotation from Canon and Mrs. Barnett, *Toward Social Reform* (New York, 1909), 12.

10. Samuel Mencher, "The Influence of Romanticism on Nineteenth

Century British Social Work," *SSR*, xxxviii (June 1964), 174–90; Woods, *English Social Movements*, 86–101; quotation from Woods, "The Social Awakening in London," *The Poor in Great Cities* (New York, 1895), 19.

11. Young and Ashton, *British Social Work*, 232–3; Henrietta Barnett, *Canon Barnett*, I, 152; statistics from Robert Woods and Albert Kennedy, *Handbook of Settlements* (New York, 1911), 305–8.

12. Woods, "The Social Awakening in London," *Poor in Great Cities*, 1–3. On the impact of English ideas on American reform see also Charles Zueblin, "The New Civic Spirit," *Chautauquan*, xxxviii (Sept. 1903), 55–9; and Arthur Mann, "British Social Thought and American Reformers," *MVHR*, xlii (March 1956), 672–9.

13. Stanton Coit, *Neighborhood Guilds: An Instrument of Social Reform* (London, 1891), quotations from 6, 7.

14. Charles B. Stover, "The Neighborhood Guild in New York," *USSQ*, ii (July 1906), 19–26.

15. Description of Stover is from Robert L. Duffus, *Lillian Wald: Neighbor and Crusader* (New York, 1938), 61. See also James K. Paulding, *Charles B. Stover, July 14, 1861–April 24, 1929: His Life and Personality* (New York, 1938).

16. Gregory Weinstein, "Memorial Address for Edward King, Delivered January 28, 1923," *The Ardent Eighties: Reminiscenses of an Interesting Decade* (New York, 1928), 166–72.

17. Weinstein, *The Ardent Eighties*, 7–81; James H. Hamilton, "Origin of the University Settlement," *USSQ*, ii (July 1906), 13–18.

18. Quotation from Edward King's review of Coit, *Neighborhood Guilds Charities Review*, i (Dec. 1891), 86. See also Hamilton, "Origin of the University Settlement," *USSQ*, ii (July 1906), 13–18.

19. Vida Scudder, *On Journey* (New York, 1937), 80–141; quotation, 140. Scudder, *Socialism and Character* (Boston, 1912), 16–20; Helen Rand Thayer, "Blazing the Settlement Trail," *Smith Alumnae Quarterly* (April 1911), 130–7.

20. Thayer, "Blazing the Settlement Trail," 131–2; quotation from Jane Robbins, "The First Year at the College Settlement," *Survey*, xxvii (Feb. 24, 1912), 1802. The College Settlement Association was officially organized May 1890; unofficially it dates to 1887. In 1892 the association founded Denison House in Boston and the College Settlement in Philadelphia.

21. Edward King to Leonora O'Reilly Feb. 18, 1887, April 17, 1889, O'Reilly MSS. See also Frances Hovey Howe, "Leonora O'Reilly: Socialist and Reformer," Unpublished honors thesis (Radcliffe College, 1952).

22. Lillian Wald, *House on Henry Street* (New York, 1915), 1–25; Duffus, *Lillian Wald*, 1–78.

23. Jane Addams, *Twenty Years at Hull House* (New York, 1910), 65–80; Ellen G. Starr to Mary Blaisdell, Feb. 23, 1889. Addams to

Starr, June 4, 1889, Starr MSS. Quotation from "Hull House, Chicago: An Effort Toward Social Democracy," *Forum*, XIV (Oct. 1892), 226.

24. Different people arrived at different counts depending in part on their definition of a settlement. See *Bibliographies of College, Social and University Settlements*, 1893, 1895, 1897, 1900, 1905. Cf. Woods and Kennedy, *Handbook*.

25. Tucker to Robert Woods, Dec. 30, 1916, SEH. On the social gospel movement see Henry May, *Protestant Churches and Industrial America* (New York, 1949). Also Louise C. Wade, "The Social Gospel Impulse and Chicago Settlement House Founders," *Chicago Theological Seminary Register*, LV (April 1965), 1–12.

26. Tucker, *My Generation* (Boston, 1917), 161–72, *Andover House Circular No. One*, Oct. 9, 1891. Tucker, "Twenty-five Years in Residence," *Atlantic Monthly*, CXIX (May 1917), 640–49.

27. Graham Taylor to Albert Kennedy, Sept. 20, 1912, Taylor MSS; Taylor, *Pioneering on Social Frontiers* (Chicago, 1930); Louise C. Wade, *Graham Taylor: Pioneer for Social Justice, 1851–1938* (Chicago, 1964).

28. George Hodges, "What Kingsley House Is For," clipping, Hodges Journal, Jan. 7, 1896; "A Letter from George Hodges," William Mathews, *The Meaning of the Settlement Movement* (Pittsburgh, 1909), 33–4.

29. "The Purposes of the House," Hodges Journal, March 1897; extracts from speech of Dean Hodges, South End House Annual Meeting, Jan. 2, 1917, SEH. Not long after founding Kingsley House, Hodges became dean of Episcopal Theological School in Cambridge, Mass., and was especially active in the affairs of South End House.

30. *East Side House Annual Report*, Jan. 1, 1916, 3; Everett P. Wheeler, *Sixty Years of American Life: Taylor to Roosevelt, 1850 to 1910* (New York, 1917), 470–71.

31. Quoted in *Commons*, II (Nov. 1897), 1–2.

32. Of 38 religious settlements established before 1900, 11 were Episcopalian. See Woods and Kennedy, *Handbook*, also Florence Winslow, "The Settlement Work of Grace Church," *Charities Review*, VIII (Nov. 1898), 418–25.

33. In 1910 of 167 religious settlements listed by Woods and Kennedy, *Handbook*, there were 31 Methodist, 29 Episcopal, 20 Presbyterian, 10 Congregational. Boris D. Bogan, *Jewish Philanthropy* (New York, 1917); "Settlement Work Among the Jews," *Charities*, X (Jan. 3, 1903), 1–2. The Educational Alliance in New York, although it had no residents, was perhaps the most important Jewish "settlement." See Moses Rischin, *The Promised City: New York Jews, 1870–1914* (Cambridge, 1962), 101.

34. Aaron I. Abell, *American Catholicism and Social Action* (New York, 1960), 155–66. Abell mentions the figure 2500, but Woods and

Kennedy list only 22 Catholic settlements in 1910. See also Grace O'Brien, "Catholic Settlement Work in Brooklyn," *Survey,* xxiv (May 7, 1910), 203–4.

35. John Gavit, "Missions and Settlements," *Commons,* ii (Feb. 1898), 1. Welcome Hall in Buffalo and Christodora House in New York were, perhaps, exceptions and for many years Chicago Commons maintained a precarious affiliation with a nearby Congregational church.

36. *SEH Report,* Dec. 1895, 1; Eleanor McMain, "Kingsley House, New Orleans," *Charities,* xi (Dec. 5, 1903), 549–53.

37. Samuel Barnett, "Twenty-one Years of Settlements," *Practicable Socialism,* 127; J. Ramsey McDonald, "American Social Settlements," *Commons,* ii (Feb. 1898), 4–7.

38. John Gavit, "Social Settlements," *Bibliography of College, Social and University Settlements* (Cambridge, 1897), 7; Woods to Miss Dawes, Dec. 20, 1892, Woods MSS.

39. Robert Woods, "The University Settlement Idea," *Philanthropy and Social Progress,* 69; Herman Hegner, "Scientific Value of Social Settlements," *American Journal of Sociology,* iii (Sept. 1897), 171–82.

40. For example see Barnett to Addams, June 9, 1893; Mrs. Barnett to Woods, Aug. 22, 1921, SEH.

41. Taylor, "A Social Center for Civic Cooperation: Chicago Commons," *Commons,* ix (Dec. 1904), 585–94; Mary McDowell, "Social Settlements: A Descriptive Definition," *Commons,* v (Aug. 1900), 5–6.

42. Francis Hackett review of Lillian Wald, *House on Henry Street,* *New Republic,* v (Jan. 8, 1916), 255; Thorstein Veblen, *Theory of the Leisure Class* (New York, Mentor edn., 1959), 224; Sinclair Lewis, *Ann Vickers* (New York, 1932), 224.

43. Robert H. Bremner, *From the Depths,* 37–41.

44. *Ibid.* 51–7; Frank D. Watson, *The Charity Organization Movement in the United States* (New York, 1922), 172–221.

45. William Mathews, "The Settlement House Is Not a Charity," *The Meaning of the Settlement Movement* (Pittsburgh, 1909), 31–2; Vida Scudder, *Socialism and Character,* 16–18.

46. Hunter, "Relations Between Social Settlements and Charity Organizations," NCCC, 1902, 302–14.

47. Addams, "Social Settlements," NCCC, 1897, 338; Mary K. Simkhovitch, "The Case Work Plan," NCCC, 1909, 137–49.

48. F. B. Peabody, "Social Settlements," NCCC, 1897, 329; Leonora O'Reilly, *Asacog Club Year Book,* 1899–1900, O'Reilly MSS.

49. William J. Tucker, "The Work of Andover House in Boston," *The Poor in Great Cities,* 177–93; notes for address, "Charities and Correction," n.d., Riis MSS.

50. "Discussion of Settlement Work at the National Conference," *Charities Review,* iv (Jan. 1895), 562; Graham R. Taylor, "Chicago and the Social Settlements," *Chicago Magazine* (July 1907), 76, clip-

ping, Taylor MSS; "Discussion of Settlements," *NCCC*, 1897, 472.

51. See, for example, Mary McDowell, "The Settlement and Organized Charity," *NCCC*, 1896, 123–7; Lillian Wald to Jacob Schiff, Aug. 29, 1893, Wald MSS.

52. Julia Lathrop, "Hull House as a Sociological Laboratory," *NCCC*, 1894, 313–20; Mary McDowell, "The Settlement and Organized Charity," *NCCC*, 1896, 124; Woods, "The Neighborhood and the Nation," *NCCC*, 1909, 101–6.

53. See, for example, "First Massachusetts State Conference of Charities," *Charities*, xi (Nov. 28, 1903); 483–515; Cornelia Bradford to Lillian Wald, Nov. 24, 1913, Wald MSS.

54. See, for example, Robert Hunter, "The Relation Between Social Settlements and Charity Organization," *NCCC*, 1902, 302; Kennedy, "Initiation to Social Work," *The Family*, xxvii (March 1946), 406.

55. Marcelous Hartley to Stokes, March 24, 1898, Stokes MSS; interview, J. G. Phelps Stokes, Dec. 4, 1958.

56. John Gavit, "Rural Social Settlements," *Commons*, iv (May 1899), 5–6. It seems to me that Morton and Lucia White exaggerate the anti-urbanism of Jane Addams, *The Intellectual Versus the City*, 146–54. Certainly the settlement worker had none of the "intense anti-urban feeling" that George Mowry finds a part of "The Progressive Profile," *Era of Theodore Roosevelt*, 91.

57. See Frances Ingram, "The Settlement Movement in the South," *World Outlook* xxvii (May 1937), clipping, NFS; Bradley Buell, "Eleanor McMain: One of the Pioneers," *Survey Graphic*, xx (Jan. 1, 1931), 374–7, 402–3.

58. Woods and Kennedy, *Handbook*, 20–23; James E. Rogers, "Social Settlements in the San Francisco Disaster," *Charities and the Commons*, xvi (June 2, 1906), 311–13.

59. Of the total number of settlements in 1911, 40% were located in Boston (33), Chicago (34), and New York (82); another more selective list in 1908 put 54% of the settlements in these cities. William I. Cole, *Motives and Results of the Settlement Movement* (Harvard University, Dept. of Social Ethics, Publication No. 2, 1908), 7.

60. Anna Davies, "A Glance at the Philadelphia Settlements," *Commons*, x (May 1905), 299; Woods and Kennedy, *Handbook*, 262–281.

61. James B. Reynolds, "Eight Years at the University Settlement," *USSQ*, ii (July 1, 1906), 36–8.

62. See Records and Minutes of the Boston Social Union, 1908–1915, SEH; Minutes of the Meeting of the Association of Neighborhood Workers, Oct. 1913—Jan. 4, 1916; UNH; Minutes and Records of the National Federation of Settlements, NFS.

63. Josephine Goldmark, *Impatient Crusader: Florence Kelley's Life Story* (Urbana, Illinois, 1953), 68–9.

CHAPTER 2

1. Addams, "The Subjective Necessity for Social Settlements," "The Objective Value of a Social Settlement," *Philanthropy and Social Progress* (New York, 1893), 1–56.
2. Kenneth E. Boulding "Alienation and Economic Development: The Larger Background," *Neighborhood Goals in a Rapidly Changing World* (New York, 1958), 61–71. Richard Hofstadter, *The Age of Reform*, 131–212. Interestingly Hofstadter cites Jane Addams's article on "The Subjective Necessity for Social Settlements," but fails to mention the other article; see page 208. On the larger problem of the motivation of reformers see a perceptive article by Martin Duberman which argues that it is quite possible to have a rational reason for engaging in reform without having a psychological or status deficiency. Martin Duberman, "The Northern Response to Slavery," in Duberman, ed., *The Antislavery Vanguard: New Essays on the Abolitionists* (Princeton, 1965), 394–412.
3. William Dwight Porter Bliss, "The Church and Social Reform Workers," *Outlook*, LXXXII (Jan. 20, 1906), 122–5. Ninety-two per cent of the charity workers and 71% of the other social reformers were active church members.
4. Of 188 settlement workers whose religious affiliation could be determined, 53 were Congregationalist; 42, Presbyterian; 31, Episcopal; 22, Jewish; 13, Unitarian; 9, Methodist; 4, Baptist. This and other information in this chapter was drawn from a career-line study of 274 settlement workers who spent at least six months in a settlement between 1886–1917. I claim no special scientific accuracy for this study. I started with a list of 389 relatively prominent settlement workers compiled from the annual reports and lists of residents of the forty largest settlements. Of this number, fairly complete biographical information was found for 274 (129 men and 145 women), giving the men a somewhat higher proportion than they probably had in most settlements. But these 274 were residents in more than eighty settlements (30% were residents in more than one), and can, I think, be taken as a representative group of settlement workers in the progressive era, though by no means should it be interpreted as a scientific sample.
5. Addams, "The Subjective Necessity," *Philanthropy and Social Progress*, 3; Hofstadter, *The Age of Reform*, 203–10, he makes too much of the Protestant sense of guilt in explaining the reforms of the progressive era.
6. Eleanor Woods, *Robert Woods, Champion of Democracy* (Boston, 1929), 1–43; "Notes on Mr. Woods' Philosophy" prepared by Mrs. Woods, April 12, 1950, SEH.
7. Sheldon Spencer, "Jim Reynolds as I Knew Him at Yale," *James*

Bronson Reynolds, March 17, 1891–January 1, 1924; A Memorial (New York, 1927), 57; sketch, *NCAB*, x, 235–6.

8. Albert J. Nock, "Raymond Robins," *American Magazine*, vii (Nov. 1910), 41.

9. Vida Scudder, *On Journey*, 57 ff; Ellen Gates Starr, "A Bypath into the Great Roadway," *Catholic World*, cxix (May 1924), 177–90; (June 1924), 358–73; James K. Paulding, *Charles B. Stover*, 12 ff.

10. Mark A. DeWolfe Howe to his mother, Feb. 9, 1893, Howe MSS; *SEH Report* (March 1903), 17 ff.

11. Jane Addams, Address, "Proceedings of the Twenty-fifth Anniversary of the University Settlement Society," *University Settlement Annual Report*, 1911, 22–32.

12. Ernest Poole, *The Bridge: My Own Story* (New York, 1940), 66–71. Among the novels written by settlement workers are the following: Florence Converse, *Children of Light* (Boston, 1912); Vida Scudder, *A Listener in Babel* (Boston, 1903); Ernest Poole, *The Harbor* (New York, 1915); Albert Edwards [Arthur Bullard], *A Man's World* (New York, 1912); Isaac Friedman, *By Bread Alone* (New York, 1901); LeRoy Scott, *The Walking Delegate* (New York, 1905).

13. Poole, *The Bridge*, 68–9.

14. Robert A. Woods, ed., *The City Wilderness: A Settlement Study* (Boston, 1898); *Hull-House Maps and Papers* (New York, 1895).

15. Charles H. Cooley, "Settlement Fellowships and the University," *Commons*, v (Oct. 1900), 1–2.

16. Interview David Howie, Jan. 9, 1959; Claude M. Fuess, *Joseph B. Eastman: Servant of the People* (New York, 1952); Frances Hackett, "Hull House—A Souvenir," *Survey Graphic*, lix (June 1, 1925), 275.

17. For one interesting account of life in a settlement see Nicholas Kelley, "Early Days at Hull House," *SSR*, xxviii (Dec. 1954), 424–429.

18. Quotations from Lloyd to Anne Withington, Sept. 13, 1903, Lloyd MSS; Friedman, *By Bread Alone*, 279.

19. Francis Hackett, "Hull-House," *Survey Graphic*, lix (June 1, 1925), 275; Friedman, *By Bread Alone*, 279; Poole, *The Bridge*, 71; Poole in Anna Walling, ed., *William English Walling: A Symposium* (New York, 1938), 24.

20. The median age of one group of abolitionists was 29. David Donald, *Lincoln Reconsidered* (New York, 1956), 26. One group of progressives was under 40, George Mowry, *The California Progressives* (Berkeley, 1951). The median age group of civil service reformers was 48, Ari Hoogenboom, *Outlawing the Spoils: A History of Civil Service Reform, 1765–1883* (Urbana, 1961), 190–97.

21. There were 54 Master's degrees, 32 Ph.D.'s, 27 LL.B.'s. Only 11 had courses in social work.

22. See, for example, David Loth, *Swope of G. E.: The Story of General*

Swope and General Electric (New York, 1958), 32–3; Graham Taylor, *Chicago Commons Through Forty Years* (Chicago, 1936), 8 ff; Philip Davis, *And Crown Thy Good* (New York, 1952), 183 ff.

23. For example see Philip Davis, *And Crown Thy Good*, 81–90; Francis Hackett, "Hull-House," *Survey Graphic*, LIV (June 1, 1925), 275.

24. Nearly 60% of 239 settlement workers came from cities of more than 25,000 in 1880 and nearly 40% came from cities of more than 100,-000 population. Cf. Hofstadter, *Age of Reform*, 175.

25. Vida Scudder, *On Journey*, 38 ff; interview J. G. Phelps Stokes, Dec. 5, 1958; Louis Pink, OHP, 3–4; Simkhovitch, *Neighborhood*, 15–16; Jane Addams, *Twenty Years at Hull House*, 3.

26. Raymond Fosdick, *Chronicle of a Generation, An Autobiography* (New York, 1958), 76.

27. Of 120 settlement workers whose fathers' occupations could be determined, 33 were ministers, 21 were teachers, 15 were lawyers, 14 small businessmen, 7 were doctors. If one compares this group of settlement workers with the business leaders as defined in William Miller, "American Historians and the Business Elite," *Journal of Economic History*, IX (Nov. 1949), 187–218, it is interesting to note that both businessmen and settlement workers came from old stock, middle-class American families. Both groups divided between rural and urban in about the same proportions. But the settlement workers went to college in a much larger number, and their fathers were more often teachers and ministers, while the businessmen's fathers were business and professional men.

28. Fifty-nine of 244 came to settlement work after at least one year of high school or college teaching. Addams, "Subjective Necessity," *Philanthropy and Social Progress*, 15.

29. Vida Scudder, "The Relation of College Women to Social Need," Paper presented at the Association of Collegiate Alumnae, Oct. 24, 1900, BPL; *A Listener in Babel*, 57; Mary B. Sayles, "The Work of a Woman Tenement House Inspector," *Outlook*, LXXV (Sept. 12, 1903), 121; quotation from "In the Social Settlements," *Chicago Evening Post*, clipping, April 1908, Addams MSS.

30. Addams, "Subjective Necessity," 17; "Harold Estabrook," Harvard, Class of 1892, *10th Anniversary Report*, 51; M. A. DeWolfe Howe to his mother, Jan. 1893, Feb. 8, 1893, Howe MSS.

31. Frank Bruno, *Trends in Social Work* (New York, 1948), 133; James Ford, "Social Ethics," Samuel Eliot Morison, ed., *The Development of Harvard University Since the Inauguration of President Eliot* (Cambridge, 1930), 220–30; "Homer Folks," OHP, 41; quotation from *The Confessions of a Reformer* (New York, 1925), 1.

CHAPTER 3

1. Addams, "The Subjective Necessity," 10.
2. Morrison Swift, "Working Populations of Cities and What the Universities Owe Them," *Andover Review*, XIII (June 1890), 589–613; Addams, *Twenty Years at Hull House*, 101; Addams, *My Friend Julia Lathrop*, 50; *Denison House Report*, 1895, 3, 1907, 5; Scudder, *On Journey*, 143–4.
3. Nicholas Kelley, "Early Days at Hull House," *SSR*, XXVII (Dec. 1954), 427; Robert Morss Lovett, *All Our Years* (New York, 1945), 42; Sinclair Lewis, *Ann Vickers*, 157.
4. Ellen Gates Starr, "Art and Labor," *Hull-House Maps and Papers*, 165–82; *Hull House, a Social Settlement: An Outline Sketch*, Feb. 1, 1894; Clarence A. Perry, "School Center History in Chicago," *Journal of Social Forces*, III (Jan. 1925), 292, quoting Burchard's remarks at a National Extension Association Meeting in Chicago, Jan. 1919.
5. "Art and the People," *Harpers Weekly*, XXXVII (April 29, 1893), 394–5; King quoted in A. C. Bernheim, "Results of Picture Exhibition in Lower East Side," *Forum*, XIX (July 1895), 612.
6. Addams, "Art Work Done by Hull House," *Forum*, XIX (July 1895), 614–7; *Chicago Public School Art Society*, 7th Annual Report, 1902.
7. Addams, "Social Education of the Industrial Democracy," *Commons*, V (June 1900), 17; Francis Hackett, "As An Alien Feels," *New Republic*, III (July 24, 1915), 303–6.
8. Woods and Kennedy, *Settlement Horizon*, 43; Francis Lee Maxwell, "Settlement Kindergarten," *USSQ*, II (July 1906), 79–81; Nina C. Vandewalker, *The Kindergarten in American Education* (New York, 1923), 111.
9. Vandewalker, *Kindergarten in American Education*, 12–75; Timothy Smith, "Progressivism in American Education," *Harvard Educational Review*, XXXI (Spring 1961), 178–81.
10. Amalie Hofer, "The Social Settlement and the Kindergarten," *NEA Proceedings*, 1895, 514–25; Vandewalker, *Kindergarten in American Education*, 107–12. On Hall see Lawrence Cremin, *The Transformation of the School* (New York, 1961), 100–5.
11. Hofer, "Social Settlement and the Kindergarten," *NEA Proceedings*, 1895, 520.
12. For example, Graham Romeyn Taylor, "Social Settlements and their Work Among Children," *Chatauquan*, XLIII (June 1906), 364–5.
13. Joseph Lee, "Kindergarten Principles in Social Work," *Charities*, x (Dec. 5, 1903), 532–7.
14. See Oscar Handlin, *The Uprooted* (Boston, 1952), 151 ff; Lillian Wald, *House on Henry Street*, 105–8; Alice Hamilton, *Exploring the Dangerous Trades*, 69–70.

15. Woods and Kennedy, *Handbook,* 59, 127; Eleanor Woods, *Robert Woods,* 178. Susan Forte, "Manual Training in Settlements," *Commons,* VII (June 1902), 11–14; "Settlement Craft on a Business Basis," *Survey,* XXIII (Feb. 26, 1910), 795–6.

16. "Hull House Labor Museum," *Chatauquan,* XXXVIII (Sept. 1903), 60–1; Addams, *The Spirit of Youth in City Streets* (New York, 1911), 127–9.

17. Notes made by Miss Josephine Starr on the life of Ellen Starr, April 1960, Starr MSS; Ellen Starr "Hull House Bookbindery," *Commons,* V (June 1900), 21–2.

18. For example, Henry Moskowitz, "The East Side in Oil and Crayon," *Survey,* XXVIII (May 11, 1912), 271–3; "The Third Monthly Conference," *Charities,* VII (March 29, 1902), 280–6.

19. See Rita Teresa Wallach, "The Social Value of the Festival," *Charities and the Commons,* XVI (June 2, 1906), 315–9; also Blake McKelvey, *The Urbanization of America* (New Brunswick, 1963), 278.

20. Thomas Tapper, "Music and East Side Children: A Story of a Novel Social Settlement," *Outlook,* LXXXVIII (Feb. 22, 1908), 427–32; Henry Moskowitz, "Music School Settlements," *Survey,* XXVI (June 24, 1911), 462–3.

21. Cremin, *Transformation of the School,* 66–75. See also Morris I. Berger, "The Settlement, The Immigrant and The Public School," unpublished Ph.D. thesis (Columbia University, 1956).

22. Woods, "Industrial Education from the Social Worker's Standpoint," *Charities and the Commons,* XIX (Oct. 5, 1907), 852; "Does the Present Trend Toward Vocational Education Threaten Liberal Culture?" *School Review,* XIX (Sept. 1911), 466–76.

23. Woods, "Industrial Education from the Social Worker's Standpoint," *Charities and the Commons,* XIX (Oct. 5, 1907), 855; "Does the Present Trend," *School Review,* XIX (Sept. 1911), 473.

24. Eleanor Woods, *Robert Woods,* 174–94; *SEH Report,* 1904, 41; Paul Kellogg, "The National Society for the Promotion of Industrial Education," *Charities and the Commons,* XVII (Dec. 23, 1905), 363–371. The settlements, of course, did not originate manual training. See McKelvey, *Urbanization of America,* 168–81.

25. Bloomfield to Addams, May 23, 1901, Addams MSS; Philip Davis, *And Crown Thy Good,* 122; "Meyer Bloomfield," *DAB,* XXII, 45–6.

26. Ralph Albertson, unpublished autobiography; Philip Davis to Albertson, Sept. 7, 1905; Bloomfield to Albertson, Jan. 8, 1906, Frank Parsons MSS; Davis, *And Crown Thy Good,* 118–24 ff. For an account of Parsons see Arthur Mann, *Yankee Reformers in an Urban Age* (Cambridge, 1954), 126–44.

27. Philip Davis, *Breadwinners College,* pamphlet n.d.; *And Crown Thy Good;* 173–8; Marris Raphael Cohen, *A Dreamer's Journey* (Boston, 1949), 110–31; Charles Forcey, *The Crossroads of Liberalism,* (New York, 1961), 95.

28. John M. Brewer, *The Vocational Guidance Movement* (New York, 1925), 20–3.

29. Bloomfield, *Vocational Guidance of Youth* (Boston, 1911); *Youth, Schools, and Vocation* (New York, 1915). See also Ruth Beverly Wolf and Ruth Elizabeth Barry, "History of the Guidance-Personnel Movement in Education," unpublished Ed. thesis (Teachers College, Columbia University, 1955).

30. Wald, *House on Henry Street*, 46–53; Wald to Dr. Abbott E. Ketteridge, Oct. 29, 1903, Wald MSS; "Reformatory Influence of Social Service Upon City Politics," *Commons*, vi (March 1902), 3–4.

31. Quotation is from Wald, "The Feeding of the School Children," *Charities and the Commons*, xx (June 13, 1908), 371–4.

32. Wald, *House on Henry Street*, 117–21; J. E. Cutler, "The Social Side of the Public School," *Charities and the Commons*, xx (July 18, 1908), 487–92. On the juvenile court see Ray Ginger, *Altgeld's America* (New York, 1958), 222–5; John C. Burnham, "Psychiatry, Psychology and the Progressive Movement," *American Quarterly*, xii (Winter, 1960), 457–65, especially note on 462.

33. Woods and Kennedy, *Settlement Horizon*, 276; Florence Kelley "Local School Boards and Settlements," *Charities and the Commons*, xv (Oct. 14, 1905), 104–5. Allen F. Davis, "Raymond Robins: The Settlement Worker as Municipal Reformer," *SSR*, xxxiii (June 1959), 131–41. See Chapter 8 for the way educational reform led to political reform.

34. Smith, "Progressivism in American Education," *Harvard Educational Review*, xxxi (Spring 1961), 168–93. He defines progressive education as consisting of a combination of three elements— "education for life," the child-centered school, and social reform.

35. Cremin, *The Transformation of the School*, 63 ff; Addams, "John Dewey and Social Welfare," *John Dewey, The Man and His Philosophy* (Cambridge, 1930), 140–52; *My Friend Julia Lathrop*, 50; Jane Dewey, "Biography of John Dewey," Paul Schilipp, ed., *Philosophy of John Dewey* (New York, 1939), 29–30. See also Lewis S. Feuer, "John Dewey and the Back to the People Movement in American Thought," *Journal of the History of Ideas*, xx (Oct.-Dec. 1959), 545–68, and Christopher Lasch, *New Radicalism in America* (New York, 1965), 158–64.

36. Dewey to Addams, March 29, 1897, Addams MSS; Feuer, "John Dewey and the Back to the People Movement," 545–68.

37. Wald to John Dewey, Oct. 26, 1914, Wald MSS; Addams, "A Toast to John Dewey," *Survey*, lxiii (Nov. 15, 1959), 203.

38. John and Evelyn Dewey, *Schools of Tomorrow* (New York, 1915), Chapter 8.

CHAPTER 4

1. Woods, "Settlement Workers Get Together on Social Problems," *Survey*, xxxi (Oct. 11, 1913), 45; Wald, *House on Henry Street*, 95.

2. Woods and Kennedy, *Settlement Horizon*, 121–30; Addams, *Twenty Years*, 16–7; Charles F. Ernst, "South End House Cady Scheme," *Survey*, xxvii (Oct. 7, 1911), 969–75.

3. Notes by Miss Josephine Starr on Ellen Gates Starr, April 1960, Starr MSS; Woods to Addams, May 23, 1898; Wald to Addams, Dec. 24, 1914, Addams MSS.

4. Simkhovitch, "Fresh Air Organization," *Charities*, x (June 20, 1903), 601–2; William Mathews, "Lillian House: Which Affords Its Guests Fresh Air, Farm Life and Every Country Joy," *Survey*, xxiv (June 4, 1910), 407–19; Woods and Kennedy. *Settlement Horizon*, 127.

5. "On Life's Farm," *Commons*, iii (June 1898), 1–2; "Flower Mission Work," *Commons*, i (July 1896), 12.

6. Elizabeth Thacher Kent, *William Kent* (privately printed, 1950), 95–6; Addams to Kent, March 7, 1910, "Jane Addams," n.d., William Kent MSS.

7. Wald, *House on Henry Street*, 81–4; "Playgrounds for Children," *Charities*, vi (May 11, 1901), 46; Anne O'Hagan Shinn, "Where Barrow Street and Bleecker Meet," *Survey*, xxxix (Dec. 1, 1917), 247.

8. Clarence E. Rainwater, *The Play Movement in the United States* (Chicago, 1922), 13–43; E. Woods, *Robert Woods*, 213 ff; Joseph Lee, *Constructive and Preventive Philanthropy* (New York, 1902); Riis, "Playgrounds for City Schools," *Century*, xlviii (Sept. 1894), 657–66.

9. Stover, "Playground Progress in Seward Park," *Charities*, vi (April 27, 1901), 386; James K. Paulding, *Charles Stover*, 43 ff; J. G. Phelps Stokes, "Narrative," Stokes MSS; *University Settlement Annual Report*, 1896, 16.

10. Stokes, "Narrative"; Outdoor Recreation League letterhead, Stokes MSS.

11. William Potts, "Seward Park Playground," *Charities*, iii (June 17, 1899), 3; quotation from Stover, "Playground Progress in Seward Park," *Charities*, vi (April 27, 1901), 391.

12. "Seward Park at Last a Reality," *Charities*, x (Feb. 7, 1903), 127–133.

13. "Playground Association of America," *Charities and the Commons*, xvi (April 21, 1906), 116–7; Henry Curtis to Stokes, March 2, 1906.

14. Alvan Sanborn, "Anatomy of a Tenement Street," *Forum*, xviii (Aug. 1898), 554–72; Florence Kelley, "Sweating System," *Hull-House Maps and Papers*, 27–45; Ernest Poole, "The Lung Block:

Some Pictures of Consumption in its Stronghold," *Charities,* xi (Sept. 5, 1903), 193–9.

15. Bremner, *From the Depths,* 206–7; *Andover House Circular,* Dec. 1893, 7.

16. Eleanor Woods, *Robert Woods,* 49; Estabrook, *Some Slums of Boston* (Boston, 1898); Anne Withington, "Boston Tenement House Conditions," *Commons,* ix (Sept. 1904), 418.

17. Mary B. Sayles, "Housing Conditions in Jersey City," *Annals,* xx (July 1902), 139–50.

18. "To Improve Pittsburgh's Bad Housing," *Charities and the Commons,* xix (March 28, 1908), 1783; Bessie B. Stoddard, "Courts of Sonoratoun; The Housing Problem as it Is to be Found in Los Angeles," *Charities and the Commons,* xv (Dec. 2, 1905), 295–9; Bradley Buell, "Eleanor McMain: One of the Pioneers," *Survey Graphic,* xx (Jan. 1931), 374–8.

19. "Proposed Budget for City Homes Association," with sketch of founding, 1913–14, Blaine MSS; Robert Hunter, *Tenement Conditions in Chicago: Report of the Investigating Commitee of the City Homes Association* (Chicago, 1901), 16, 162.

20. "To Re-Investigate Chicago Housing Conditions," *Charities and the Commons,* xv (Nov. 18, 1905), 229–30; Addams, "The Housing Problem in Chicago," *Annals,* xx (July 1902), 99–107.

21. Jacob Riis, *The Making of An American* (New York, 1901); Riis, "What Settlements Stand For," *Outlook,* lxxxix (May 9, 1908), 69–72. Here as elsewhere in this chapter, I am indebted to Roy Lubove, *The Progressives and the Slums: Tenement House Reform in New York City, 1890–1917.* (Pittsburgh, 1962).

22. Lawrence Veiller, OHP, 3; "Settlement Contribution to Legislation," *Commons,* v (July 1901), 7; Lubove, *Progressives and the Slums,* 81–149.

23. Veiller, OHP, 11–13; Form letters from De Forest, May 6, 1899, July 19, 1899, Veiller MSS; Veiller, "Tenement House Exhibition of 1899," *Charities Review,* x (March 1900), 19–27.

24. Veiller, OHP, 13–15; Lubove, *Progressives and the Slums,* 117–49.

25. Mrs. Blaine to Veiller, July 29, 1904; Ball to Raymond Robins, Dec. 28, 1903, Blaine MSS; Charles Ball, "The Municipal Museum of Chicago," *Commons,* x (April 1905), 215–20; Veiller, "National Housing Association," *Survey,* xxiii (March 5, 1910), 841–8.

26. Kelley, "The Settlements: Their Lost Opportunity," *Charities and the Commons,* xvi (April 7, 1906), 81; Wald to Harry Van Dyke, July 9, 1908, Wald MSS; Simkhovitch, "Committee on Congestion and City Planning," Nov. 16, 1910, Simkhovitch MSS.

27. Benjamin Marsh, *Lobbyist for the People* (Washington, 1953), 17; *Carola Woerishoffer: Her Life and Work* (Philadelphia, 1912), 13, 59–60; Lubove, *Progressives and the Slums,* 231–4.

28. Kelley, "Congestion and Sweated Labor," *Charities and the Commons*, xx (April 4, 1908), 48–50; John Martin, "The Exhibit of Congestion Interpreted," *Ibid.*, xx (April 4, 1908), 27–39.

29. Simkhovitch, "Committee on Congestion and City Planning," Simkhovitch MSS; Charles M. Robinson, "The City Plan Exhibition," *Survey*, xxii (May 29, 1909), 313–18; Marsh, "The Congestion Exhibit in Brooklyn," *Charities and the Commons*, xx (May 9, 1908), 209–11.

30. Mary Simkhovitch, *Proceedings of the First National Conference on City Planning*, Washington, D.C., May 21, 22, 1909; Hearing Before Senate Committee on District of Columbia; 61st Congress, 2d Session; Senate Document 422, 101–4. See Robert A. Walker, *The Planning Function in Urban Government* (Chicago, 1941), 10–12.

31. Walker, *The Planning Function*, 11–16. On the City Beautiful Movement see John Burchard and Albert Bush-Brown, *The Architecture of America: A Social and Cultural History* (Boston, 1961), 273 ff. From 1913 to 1916 Ford was consultant to the Commission on Building Districts and Restriction, and drafted the New York City Zoning Ordinance, the first such ordinance in America.

32. Stokes, "Narrative," 24–6, Stokes MSS; Hooker, "A Plan for Chicago," *Survey*, xxii (Sept. 4, 1909), 778–90; Kellogg, "The Reconstruction Era in Boston," *Survey*, xxiii (Oct. 2, 1909), 13–14. For a sympathetic account of the Garden City Movement see Lewis Mumford, *Culture of Cities* (New York, 1938), 392–6.

33. Gaylord S. White, "Legislation Opposed by New York Social Workers," *Commons*, ix (April 1904), 144–6; "Mass Meeting at Greenwich House," *Charities*, x (Feb. 21, 1903), *Settlement Journal* (Henry St.) 1 (April 1914), 8–9.

34. James H. Hamilton, "The Winning of the Boulevard," *USSQ*, ii (Dec. 1906), 24–6; Lillian Wald, "The East Side in Danger," *Commons*, x (April 1905), 222; Wald, *Windows on Henry Street* (Boston, 1934), 3–4.

35. Taylor, "Survival and Revival of Neighborhoodship," *Survey*, xxviii (May 4, 1912), 231.

36. *Greenwich House Report*, 1904, 8. See also, Simkhovitch, "The Neighborhood Looks at Planning," March 25, 1944, Simkhovitch MSS.

37. Woods, "Neighborhood in Social Reconstruction," *The Neighborhood and Nation Building* (Boston, 1923), 148–9; "The Recovery of the Parish," *Ibid.*, 133–46; Jane Addams's remark recalled by Albert Kennedy in address, "The Settlement Heritage," at NCSW, June 4, 1953, copy NFS.

38. Dewey, "The School as Social Center," *National Educational Association Journal of Proceedings*, 1902, 381.

39. J. G. Phelps Stokes, "The Schools as Social Centers," *Annals*, xxiii

(May 1904), 460; James K. Paulding, "Public Schools as a Center of Community Life," *Educational Review*, xv (Feb. 1898), 147–54; Simkhovitch, *Neighborhood*, 67.

40. Simkhovitch, *Neighborhood*, 163–7.

41. Simkhovitch, "The Enlarged Function of the Public School," *NCCC*, 1904, 471–86.

42. "Interrelation of School and Neighborhood Work in Speyer School," *Teachers College Record*, iv (May 1904), 244–56; Jesse D. Burks and Edgar A. Joslyn, "The Speyer School Building," *Teachers College Record*, iv (May 1904), 261–5.

43. Woods and Kennedy, *Handbook*, 223–4; "The School as a Social Center," *Charities*, xiv (April 1, 1905), 646; "A School Teachers' Settlement," *Charities*, xii (July 16, 1904), 740.

44. Salter, "Shall the Settlements Merge," *Commons*, vii (April 1903), 18.

45. Simkhovitch, "The Settlement and the Public School," *Commons*, viii (May 1903), 10–12; Hamilton, "Is the Settlement a Permanent Institution," *Charities and the Commons*, xv (Oct. 14, 1905), 102–4.

46. Henry C. Metcalfe and L. Urwick, editors, *Dynamic Administration: The Collected Papers of Mary Parker Follett* (New York, 1945), 9–29; Clarence Perry, *Wider Use of the School Plant* (New York, 1910), 270–1.

47. Perry, *Wider Use*, 270–3; Harriet L. Childs, "The Rochester Social Centers," *American City*, v (July 1911), 18–22; Perry, "The School as a Factor in Neighborhood Development," *NCCC*, 1914, 385–93.

48. Sidney Dillick, *Community Organization for Neighborhood Development: Past and Present* (New York, 1953), 58–60; "Programs of the Social Center Movement," *Survey*, xxxi (July 17, 1914), 473.

49. "The School as a Social Center and Its Relation to Evening Recreation Centers and Other Activities," *Playground*, vi (April 1912), 193; "Field Houses of Chicago and Their Possibilities," *Charities and the Commons*, xviii (Aug. 3, 1907), 535–8; Perry, "School Center History in Chicago," *Social Forces*, iii (Jan. 1925), 291–3.

50. Bessie D. Stoddart, "Recreative Centers of Los Angeles, California," *Annals*, xxxv (March 1910), 426–35; Rainwater, *Play Movement*, 104–9.

51. Louis H. Pink, "Socializing the Public Library," *Survey*, xxix (Feb. 15, 1913), 675; Simkhovitch, "The New York Public Library Assembly Halls," *Charities and the Commons*, xv (March 17, 1906), 885–6.

52. "The Social Halls Association," *Charities*, vi (May 25, 1901), 442–3; Walling, "The Movement for Neighborhood Social Halls," *Commons*, ix (May 1904), 193–8; Wald, *House on Henry Street*, 216–18.

53. James Hamilton, "New York Excise Question," *Commons*, ix (Feb. 1904), 55–7; Woods and Kennedy, *Settlement Horizon*, 260–64. See

also James H. Timberlake, *Prohibition and the Progressive Movement, 1900–1920* (Cambridge, 1963); Raymond Caulkins, *Substitutes for the Saloon* (Boston, 1901).

CHAPTER 5

1. Addams, *Twenty Years at Hull House*, 98; Zueblen, "The Chicago Ghetto," *Hull-House Maps and Papers*, 96.
2. Frederick A. Bushée, "Population," Robert A. Woods, ed., *The City Wilderness*, 38; "Italian Immigrants in Boston," *Ibid.*, 46–7; "Ethnic Factors in the Population of Boston," *American Economic Association Studies*, Series III, Vol. IV, 299–477.
3. *USSQ*, I (July 1905), II (Oct. 1906).
4. (Philadelphia, 1905).
5. Balch, *Our Slavic Fellow Citizen* (New York, 1910); Mercedes M. Randall, *Improper Bostonian: Emily Greene Balch* (New York, 1964), 118–20; Grace Abbott, *The Immigrant and the Community* (New York, 1917); "A Study of the Greeks in Chicago," *American Journal of Sociology*, xv (Nov. 1909), 379–93; Philip Davis, *Immigration and Americanization* (Chicago, 1926).
6. John Daniels, *America Via the Neighborhood* (Boston, 1920), 222–231.
7. Mary Richmond reported Gavit's speech at a Settlement Conference in 1899 in a letter to Florence Kelley, June 3, 1899, reprinted in Ralph E. and Muriel W. Pumphrey, *The Heritage of American Social Work* (New York, 1961), 261–2.
8. Daniels, *America Via the Neighborhood*, 163, 181, 193–202; Vida Scudder, *On Journey*, 259; Simkhovitch, *Neighborhood*, 80–4.
9. Ernest Poole, "The Story of Manual Levine," *Outlook*, LXXXVII (Oct. 26, 1907), 413–19.
10. Davis, *And Crown Thy Good*, 86–8; Francis Hackett, "As an Alien Feels," *New Republic*, III (July 24, 1915), 303–6.
11. Scudder, *On Journey*, 258–68; "Work with Italians in Boston," *Survey*, XXII (April 3, 1909), 47–51; *Denison House Report*, 1907, 15–18.
12. Cahan, *The Rise of David Levinsky* (New York, Harper Torchbook, 1960), 165. See also Chapter 3.
13. Rita Teresa Wallach, "The Social Value of the Festival," *Charities and the Commons*, XVI (June 2, 1906), 315–19; John Higham, *Strangers in the Land* (New Brunswick, 1955), 236; George Cary White, "Social Settlements and Immigrant Neighbors," *SSR*, XXXIII (March, 1959), 55–66.
14. Walter Weyl, *The New Democracy* (New York, 1912), 347; Wald, *House on Henry Street*, 290. Robert Hunter also favored restriction. See *Poverty*, 261–317.

15. Weyl, "Immigration and the Industrial Situation," *USSQ*, I (July 1905), 61–73.

16. Kellogg, "The Minimum Wage and the Immigrant," *NCCC*, 1911, 165–77. See also Hunter, "Immigration the Annihilator of our Native Stock," *Commons*, IX (April 1904), 114–17.

17. Woods, ed., *Americans in Process*, 364; *SEH Annual Reports*, 1900, 1913, 1917. See also Barbara Solomon, *Ancesters and Immigrants* (Cambridge, 1956), 140–3. Mrs. Solomon, it seems to me, exaggerates Woods's racism.

18. Addams, "Immigration: A Field Neglected by the Scholars," *Commons* (Jan. 1905), 9–19; Addams, "Pen and Book as Test of Character," *Survey*, XXIX (Jan. 4, 1913), 420.

19. Graham R. Taylor, "The Cincinnati, Civic Convention," *Survey*, XXII (Dec. 4, 1909), 321–8; Higham, *Strangers in the Land*, 119–23.

20. Wald to H. D. Howard, Feb. 20, 1911, Wald MSS; Edith Abbott, "Grace Abbott and Hull House," *SSR*, XXIV (Dec. 1950), 493–4; Addams, "Pen and Book as Tests of Character," *Survey*, XXIX (Jan. 6, 1913), 419–20.

21. Weyl, "Immigration and the Industrial Situation, *USSQ*, I (July 1905), 61–73; Jane Robbins, "The Immigrant and the College Student," *Charities*, XIV (Sept. 2, 1905), 1637–8.

22. Solomon, *Ancestors and Immigrants*, 143, 196–7.

23. Edith Abbott, "Grace Abbott and Hull House," *SSR*, XXIV (Dec. 1950), 493–518; "Grace Abbott: A Sister's Memories," *SSR*, XIII (Sept. 1939), 351–407.

24. Higham, *Strangers in the Land*, 238–40; Wald, *House on Henry Street*, 293; "New York State to Protect Aliens," *Survey*, XXV (Nov. 5, 1910), 171–2; Robert Fuller to Wald, July 16, 1908, Wald MSS.

25. "Report of the Committee to Study Conditions of Negroes in the Pleasant Street District," Boston Social Union, 1910, SEH; Woods and Kennedy, *Handbook*, 268.

26. Woods and Kennedy, *Handbook;* Sarah Collins Fernandis, "Social Settlement Work Among Colored People," *Charities and the Commons*, XXI (Nov. 21, 1908), 302. There was also an institution that called itself a settlement at Tuskegee, Alabama.

27. "Report of the Committee to Study Conditions of Negroes in the Pleasant Street District," SEH; Frederick A. Bushée, "Population," Robert A. Woods, ed., *The City Wilderness*, 44.

28. Woods seems to have been in favor of something less than equality for the Negro. See Woods, "Introduction" to John Daniels, *In Freedom's Birthplace*, and Woods to Jane Addams, Aug. 7, 1912, Addams MSS. For corroboration of the point that some progressives were pro-Negro, see Gilbert Osofsky, *Harlem: The Making of a Ghetto* (New York, 1966), 53–67.

29. Samuel McCune Lindsay, "Introduction," W. E. Burghardt Du Bois, *The Philadelphia Negro: A Social Study* (Philadelphia, 1899); El-

liot M. Rudwick, *W. E. B. Du Bois: A Study in Minority Group Leadership* (Philadelphia, 1960), 28–34; Susan Wharton to Addams, Oct. 23, 1895, Addams MSS.

30. Ovington, "The Color Line in Social Work," *Charities*, xiv (April 11, 1905), 645; *The Walls Came Tumbling Down*, 3–52; Franz Boas, "Introduction," Ovington, *Half a Man: The Status of the Negro in New York* (New York, 1911); Mary K. Simkhovitch, "Greenwich House," *Commons*, x (March 1905), 169; Ovington to Addams, Jan. 10, 1903, Addams MSS.

31. Frances Kellor, "The Criminal Negro: A Sociological Study," *Arena* (Jan.-June 1901); "Assisted Emigration from the South: The Women," *Charities*, xv (Oct. 7, 1905), 12–13. Also see Osofsky, *Harlem*, 57–8.

32. Woods, "Introduction," Daniels, *In Freedom's Birthplace; South End House Report, 1905*, 32–3. There were a few other studies including Ray Stannard Baker, *Following the Color Line*, 1908, and a book written by a friend of Hull House, Louise De Koven Bowen, *The Colored People of Chicago* (1913). See Osofsky, *Harlem*, 54.

33. "The Negro in the Cities of the North," *Charities*, xv (Oct. 7, 1905), 1–96. Among the contributors were many settlement workers.

34. Daniels, *In Freedom's Birthplace*, 404–20.

35. Ernest Poole, Howard Brubaker, Charles E. Russell sketches, Anna Walling, ed., *William English Walling*, 21–9, 35–45, 75–9; David Shannon, *The Socialist Party of America* (New York, 1955), 43–61; Walling to Eugene Debs, Dec. 14, 1909, Feb. 12, 1910, Walling MSS.

36. Interview Anna Walling, Jan. 22, 1959; Walling, "The Founding of the NAACP," *The Crisis*, xxxvi (July 1929), 226; Walling, "The Race War in the North," *Independent*, lxv (Sept. 3, 1908), 529–34; Mary White Ovington, *How the National Association for the Advancement of Colored People Began* (New York, 1914).

37. Interview Anna Walling, Jan. 22, 1959; Ovington sketch, Anna Walling, ed., *William English Walling*, 80; Walling, "The Founding of the NAACP," *Crisis*, xxxvi (July 1929), 226.

38. See Eric Goldman, *Rendezvous with Destiny*, 177–83, and Osofsky, *Harlem*, 53–67 for accounts which do connect the NAACP with the progressive movement.

39. Wald, *Windows on Henry Street*, 49. On the conference see Elliott M. Rudwick, "The National Negro Committee Conference of 1909," *Phylon Quarterly*, xviii (Jan. 1958), 413–19; Anna Walling to Addams, June 8, 1909, Addams MSS.

CHAPTER 6

1. "As For Trade Unions," *Commons*, iv (June 1897), 12. See also Hamilton, *Exploring the Dangerous Trades*, 62–3.

2. Hamilton, *Exploring the Dangerous Trades,* 80. Of course many settlements played no part in the labor movement, but most of the important settlements were active supporters. Philip Davis, "The Social Settlement and the Trade Union," *Commons,* IX (April 1904), 146–7. Jane Addams, "The Settlement as a Factor in the Labor Movement," *Hull-House Maps and Papers,* 245–87.

3. Quoted in *New York Commissioner of Labor Report,* 1900, 251.

4. Quotation from "They Don't Suit the 'Intellectuals,'" *American Federationist,* XX (Feb. 1913), 132. See also Helen Marot, *American Labor Unions* (New York, 1915), 1–10.

5. Friedman, *By Bread Alone,* 279; *Retrospect and Prospect of Gad's Hill Settlement,* 9.

6. "A Word to Labor Unions," *Commons,* I (Sept. 1896), 7; Addams to Lloyd, Dec. 22, 1895, Lloyd MSS.

7. Quotation from Hamilton, *Exploring the Dangerous Trades,* 62. See also, Addams, "The Present Crisis in Trades-Union Morals," *North American Review,* CLXXIX (Aug. 1904), 178–93.

8. Historians have over-emphasized the paternalistic attitude of most progressives toward labor. At least this interpretation is exaggerated when applied to a large group of settlement workers. See Samuel P. Hays, *The Response to Industrialism, 1885–1914,* 85–6; Hofstadter, *Age of Reform,* 239–40; Mowry, *Era of Theodore Roosevelt,* 99–103. J. Joseph Huthmacher, "Urban Liberalism and the Age of Reform," *MVHR,* XLIX (Sept. 1962), 231–41 and Irwin Yellowitz, *Labor and the Progressive Movement in New York State,* redress the balance somewhat.

9. Hamilton, *Exploring the Dangerous Trades,* passim; "The Social Settlement and Public Health," *Charities and the Commons,* XVII (March 1907), 1037–40.

10. "Union Label," *Commons,* II (May 1897), 10; Woods, "Social Recovery," *City Wilderness,* 282; Taylor to T. M. Anderson, Oct. 15, 1902, Taylor MSS.

11. Addams, "A Modern Lear," *Survey,* XXIX (Nov. 2, 1912), 131–7; Albert Shaw to Addams, Jan. 1896; A. C. Bartlett to Addams, Dec. 5, 1900; "Defense of Unions: Miss Addams Speaks in Behalf of Walking Delegate," *Chicago Post,* Dec. 1, 1900, clipping, Addams MSS.

12. Edith Abbott, "Grace Abbott and Hull House, 1908–1921," *SSR,* XXIV (Sept. 1950), 374–94.

13. "The Tailors' Strike," *Hull House Bulletin,* May 1896, 5; Kelley to Lloyd, March 3, 1896; Starr to Lloyd, March 9, 1896; April 8, 17, 21, 24, 1896; Hamilton, *Exploring the Dangerous Trades,* 62.

14. Hamilton, *Exploring the Dangerous Trades,* 82; quotation from Jacob S. Potofsky, "Happy Birthday to Ellen Gates Starr," *Advance,* 1939, clipping, Starr MSS; Sidney Hillman to Starr, Dec. 22, 1915; Starr MSS.

15. Fitzpatrick open letter to organized labor, Aug. 27, 1908; *Address Delivered by Raymond Robins at the National Protest Meeting of the Chicago Federation of Labor*, April 19, 1908, Robins MSS; *Chicago Tribune*, April 20, 1908; see also Allen F. Davis, "Raymond Robins: The Settlement Worker as Municipal Reformer," *SSR*, xxxiii (June 1959), 131–41.
16. *SEH Report*, 1896, 6–7, 1917, 16–17; Hillman to Starr, Dec. 1, 1915, Starr MSS; Mathew Josephson, *Sidney Hillman, Statesman of American Labor* (New York, 1952), 39–95.
17. Scudder, *On Journey*, 156; Wallace De Wolf to Mary McDowell, Dec. 14, 1903, McDowell MSS; interview Eva White, Aug. 15, 1957; Davis, *And Crown Thy Good*, 137; Edith Abbott, "Grace Abbott and Hull House, 1908–21," *SSR*, xxiv (Dec. 1950), 499.
18. Taylor, "Social Settlement and the Labor Movement," *NCCC*, 1896, 143–9; *Pioneering on Social Frontiers*, 138–73; Simkhovitch, *Neighborhood*, 76; "Memorial Services for James Mullenbach," June 21, 1935; J. M. Williams to Taylor, Aug. 1, 1900; Taylor to Williams, Aug. 2, 1900, Taylor MSS; Taylor, "Between the Unions in Chicago's Industrial Civil War," *Commons*, ix (April 1904), 141–6. See also Wade, *Graham Taylor*, 144–5.
19. John Gavit, "Chicago Commons Free Floor Labor Discussion," *Commons*, v (Oct. 1900), 9–11; "Free Speech Policy Justified," *Commons*, ix (Feb. 1904), 63; Graham Taylor, *Chicago Commons Through Forty Years*, 125–39; *SEH Report*, 1896, 11–12; "Social and Economic Conference, *Commons*, i (Nov. 1896), 15.
20. Hamilton, *Exploring the Dangerous Trades*, 83–6; Wald, *House on Henry Street*, 234–8; John Gavit to Taylor, Sept. 3, 1927, Taylor MSS.
21. Darrow to Addams, Sept. 11, 1901; Addams MSS; Isaacs to Taylor, April 14, 1934, Taylor MSS.
22. Taylor, *Pioneering*, 325–6, quoting *Chronicle; Chicago Evening Post*, March 5, 1908; *Inter-Ocean*, editorial, March 4, 1908, clippings, Addams MSS; Charles Norton to Addams, March 11, 1908, Addams MSS; Addams, "The Chicago Settlements and Social Unrest," *Charities and the Commons*, xx (May 1908), 159. See Wade, *Graham Taylor*, 134–5.
23. David Shannon, *Socialist Party of America*, 45 ff; interview, J. G. Phelps Stokes, Dec. 5, 1958; Kelley to Raymond Robins, June 20, 1907, Robins MSS.
24. "Mary McDowell Discusses Influences that Uplifted Packingtown," *Chicago Daily News*, July 29, 1904, 3; McDowell, "At the Heart of the Packingtown Strike," *Commons*, ix (Sept. 1904), 398.
25. McDowell, "Beginnings" (unpublished autobiography), Introduction, 1–6; Howard E. Wilson, *Mary McDowell: Neighbor*, 25–8; McDowell, "A Quarter of a Century in the Stock Yards District," 1919, 1–5.

26. McDowell, "Civic Experiences," 1914, 1–10, McDowell MSS; John Gavit, "Mary McDowell—Settlement Worker," *Commons*, II (Jan. 1898), 1–2; McDowell to Lloyd, Dec. 4, 1894, Nov. 4, 1896, Lloyd MSS.

27. Donnelly to McDowell, April 25, 1903, McDowell MSS; McDowell, "At the Heart of the Packingtown Strike," *Commons*, IX (Sept. 1904), 400; quotation from Wilson, *Mary McDowell*, 95 (probably about 1902).

28. Nellie F. Mahoney, "The Women Workers in the Stock Yard Strike," *Union Labor Advocate*, V (Sept. 1904), 19; McDowell, "The Story of a Women's Labor Union," *Commons*, VII (Jan. 1903), 1–3; Mollie Daley to McDowell, Aug. 1, 1902; Donnelly to Whom it May Concern, Sept. 19, 1902, McDowell MSS.

29. "The Butchers' Strike," *Outlook*, LXXVI (July 23, 1904), 671–2; "Mary McDowell Discusses Influences that Uplifted Packingtown," *Chicago Daily News*, July 29, 1904, 3.

30. Ernest Poole, "The Meat Strike," *Independent*, LVII (July 28, 1904), 182.

31. McDowell, "The Strike at the Stock Yards," *Union Labor Advocate*, V (Sept. 1904), 20–22; McDowell, "A Quarter of A Century in the Stock Yards District," 15.

32. McDowell, "The Strike at the Stock Yards," *Union Labor Advocate*, V (Sept. 1904), 20–22; Samuel Hopkins Addams, "Meat: A Problem for the Public," *Collier's Magazine*, XXIII (July 20, 1904), 8–10.

33. *Chicago Daily News*, July 21, 1904; the *Inter-Ocean*, July 13, 1904; *Chicago Daily News*, July 20, 1904; "Mary McDowell Discusses Influences that Uplifted Packingtown," *Chicago Daily News*, July 29, 1904, 3; McDowell, "At the Heart of the Packingtown Strike," *Commons*, IX (Sept. 1904), 397–402.

34. Ernest Poole, *The Bridge*, 92–5; Poole, "The Meat Strike," *Independent*, LVII (July 20, 1904), 179–84; Antanos Kaztanskis (Ernest Poole), "From Lithuania to the Chicago Stock Yards: An Autobiography," *Independent*, LVII (Aug. 4, 1904), 241–8.

35. Poole, *The Bridge*, 94; William Hard and Ernest Poole, "The Stock Yard Strike: Competitive Wages and the Right to Live," *Outlook*, LXXXVII (Aug. 13, 1904), 884–9.

36. Upton Sinclair, *The Jungle* (New York: Viking Press, 1946), VII–XI; Hamilton, *Exploring the Dangerous Trades*, 73; Upton Sinclair to Addams, May 29, 1905, Addams MSS; Poole, *The Bridge*, 95.

37. McDowell, "At the Heart of the Packingtown Strike," *Commons*, IX (Sept. 1904), 402; Poole, "The Meat Strike," *Independent*, LVII (July 28, 1904), 180; Graham Taylor, "Chicago's Stake in Settling the Strike," *Daily News*, Aug. 27, 1904; Graham Romeyn Taylor, "Conciliation Winning Its Way," *Commons*, IX (Oct. 1904), 479–86; "The Community's Interest in the Stock Yards' Strike: The Inside View of an Outsider," *Commons*, IX (Sept. 1904), 402–6; William

Hard and Ernest Poole, "The Stock Yard Strike," *Outlook,* LXXVII (Aug. 13, 1904), 889.

38. *Chicago Daily News,* July 21–23, 1904; "Butcher Strike Settled and Reopened," *Outlook,* LXXVII (July 30, 1904), 725–6; Taylor, "Strike Echoes Worth Heeding," *Chicago Daily News,* Aug. 13, 1904; Mary McDowell, "At the Heart of the Packingtown Strike," *Commons,* IX (Sept. 1904), 397–402.

39. *Chicago Daily News,* July 22–Sept. 10, 1904; *Inter-Ocean,* July 22–Sept. 10, 1904; Poole, *The Bridge,* 96–8.

40. McDowell, "A Quarter of a Century," 16–17; McDowell, "Our Proxies in Industry," Caroline M. Hill, ed., *Mary McDowell and Municipal Housekeeping: A Symposium* (Chicago, 1937), 58; "The Story of Dr. DeBey," *Union Labor Advocate,* v (Oct. 1904), 14.

41. "The Stock Yards' Strike," *Union Labor Advocate,* v (Oct. 1904), 18; McDowell, "A Quarter of a Century," 19, McDowell MSS.

42. "Mary McDowell Discusses Influences that Uplifted Packingtown," *Chicago Daily News,* July 29, 1904, 3; *Chicago Tribune,* Aug. 10, 1904. Hard's editorial summarized the articles written by Ernest Poole describing the Lithuanian immigrant; Carroll D. Wright to Theodore Roosevelt, n.d., reprinted *Bulletin of the Department of Labor,* x, No. 56 (Jan. 1905), 1; "Influence of Trade Unions on Immigrants," *Commons,* x (May 1905), 303–7; Ethelbert Stewart to McDowell, Aug. 15, 1904, McDowell MSS.

43. *James Bronson Reynolds: A Memorial,* 14–16, 62–3; Roosevelt to Addams, Jan. 24, 1906, Addams MSS; "Government Inspection of Products of Packing Plants," Jan. 24, 1923, McDowell MSS (Mary McDowell's recollections of the episode).

44. "Government Inspection of Products of Packing Plants," Jan. 24, 1923, McDowell MSS; Roosevelt to James Wadsworth, May 26, 1906, Elting Morrison, ed., *Letters of Theodore Roosevelt* (Cambridge, 1952), v, 282–3.

45. "Government Inspection of Products of Packing Plants," Jan. 24, 1923, McDowell MSS; Reynolds to Addams, June 7, 1906, Addams MSS. See also John Braeman, "The Square Deal in Action: A Case Study in the Growth of the 'National Police Power,'" in John Braeman, Robert H. Bremner, and Everett Walters, eds., *Change and Continuity in Twentieth-Century America* (Columbus, Ohio, 1964), 35–80.

46. Reynolds to Addams, June 7, 1906, Addams MSS; Roosevelt to James Wadsworth, July 8, 1908. Morrison, ed., *Letters of Theodore Roosevelt,* v, 294–6.

CHAPTER 7

1. Addams, *Twenty Years,* 198–9. Quotation from Addams, *My Friend Julia Lathrop,* 116.

2. Addams, *Twenty Years*, 198–200; Kelley, "Hull House," *New England Magazine*, xviii (June 1898), 554–61; Josephine Goldmark, *Impatient Crusader*, 1–23; Florence Kelley Wischnewetzky, "White Child Slavery," *Arena*, i (April 1890), 594–5; "Our Toiling Children," *Our Day*, vi (Sept. 1890), 192–7.

3. Kelley to Lloyd, July 13, Aug. 10, Oct. 10, 1893, Lloyd MSS; Goldmark, *Impatient Crusader*, 26–72; Chester A. Destler, *Henry Demarest Lloyd and the Empire of Reform* (Philadelphia, 1963), 252–5.

4. Addams, *Twenty Years*, 201–2; Woods and Kennedy, *Settlement Horizon*, 185.

5. Kelley to Lloyd, July 13, 1893, Oct. 10, 1893, Lloyd MSS; Goldmark, *Impatient Crusader*, 35–43.

6. Quotation from Kelley to Lloyd, Aug. 20, 1893, Lloyd MSS.

7. Kelley, "Hull House," *New England Magazine*, xviii (June 1898), 561; Kelley to Lloyd, March 2, 1895, Lloyd MSS.

8. Addams to Lloyd, March 16, 1897; Alzina Stevens to Lloyd, March 28, 1897; Hooker to Lloyd, April 5, 1897, Lloyd MSS; *Commons*, ii (Sept. 1897), 9.

9. Addams, "The Operation of the Illinois Child Labor Law," *National Child Labor Committee Proceedings*, ii, 72; "Mary McDowell Discusses Influences that Uplifted Packingtown," *Chicago Daily News*, July 29, 1904, 3; Addams to Alice Haldeman, Feb. 27, 1903, Addams MSS; *Chicago Tribune*, July 12, 1904.

10. Cornelia F. Bradford, "For Jersey City's Social Uplift," *Commons*, x (Feb. 1905), 101–6; Katherine Coman, "The South Park Settlement, San Francisco," *Commons*, viii (Aug. 1903), 710; Kellogg Durland to Lloyd, March 24, 1903, May 7, 1903, Lloyd MSS; Durland, "Child Labor in Pennsylvania," *Outlook*, lxiv (May 9, 1903), 124–7.

11. Philip Davis, "Child Life on the Street," *NCCC*, 1909, 250–4; *Newsboys' Conditions in Chicago*, pamphlet, n.d., Addams MSS; Myron E. Adams and H. Brewster Adams, *The Buffalo Newsboy and the Street Trade Bill* (New York, 1903), 3–12; William Hard, "De Kid Wat Works at Night," *Everybody's Magazine*, xviii (Jan. 1908), 25–37.

12. Helen Marot, "The Child Labor Movement in New York," *Commons*, viii (April 1903), 5; Goldmark, *Impatient Crusader*, 81; interview, J. G. Phelps Stokes, Jan. 22, 1959. See also Jeremy Felt, *Hostages of Fortune: Child Labor Reform in New York State* (Syracuse, 1965).

13. *NCAB*, xiv (New York, 1910), 353–4; interviews, J. G. Phelps Stokes, Dec. 5, 1958, Jan. 22, 1959; Hunter, *Tenement Conditions in Chicago*; Hunter, *Poverty* (New York, 1904). See Peter d'A. Jones, introduction to Harper torchbook edition (New York, 1965).

14. Marot, "The Child Labor Movement in New York," *Commons*, viii

(April 1903), 5–6; interview, J. G. Phelps Stokes, Jan. 22, 1959; biographical sketch, Stokes MSS.

15. V. Everett Macy to Stokes, Jan. 20, 1903, Stokes MSS. *University Settlement Bulletin* (Dec. 1902), clipping, Walling MSS.

16. Goldmark, *Impatient Crusader*, 81–2; Hunter to Stokes, Nov. 22, 1904; Child Labor Committee form letter, Feb. 10, 1904, Stokes MSS.

17. Walling, "Child Labor," *Current Literature*, xxxiv (Feb. 1903), 216; Hunter, *Poverty*, 243; Addams, "Standards of Education for Industrial Life," NCCC, 1911, 162.

18. Florence Kelley, *Some Ethical Gains Through Legislation* (New York, 1905), 99; Edgar Gardner Murphy, "Child Labor as a National Problem," NCCC, 1903, 121–34; "A National Child Labor Committee," *Charities*, xii (April 1904), 409.

19. *New York World*, April 23, 1904; *New York Times*, April 23, 1904, clippings, Addams MSS; Bremner, *From the Depths*, 279.

20. Beveridge to Kelley, Oct. 19, 1907; Kelley to Beveridge, Oct. 31, 1907; Samuel M. Lindsay to Beveridge, Nov. 8, 1907, Albert Beveridge MSS; Wald to Villard, Sept. 27, 1907, Villard MSS; Claude G. Bowers, *Beveridge and the Progressive Era* (Boston, 1932), 250.

21. Goldmark, *Impatient Crusader*, 94–5. Mrs. Kelley made the suggestion in a series of lectures that later were incorporated in *Some Ethical Gains Through Legislation*, 99. Address by Wald, *Proceedings of Conference on Care of Dependent Children*, 1909, 203. See also Wald, "The Idea of the Federal Children's Bureau," NCSW, 1932, 33–7.

22. Roosevelt to Wald, Jan. 5, 1909, Wald MSS; Wald, "The Idea of the Federal Children's Bureau," NCSW, 1932, 33–7.

23. Wald, "The Idea of the Federal Children's Bureau," 35; Wald to James Loeb, May 17, 1912, Wald MSS; Julia Lathrop to Graham Taylor, Dec. 15, 1927, Taylor MSS; Julia Lathrop resigned in 1922 and was replaced by another Hull House resident, Grace Abbott.

24. Mary Kingsbury [Simkhovitch], "The Relation of the Settlement to Women and Children," *Charities*, i (June 1898), 5–7; Mary McDowell, "The Need for a National Investigation into Women's Work," *Charities and the Commons*, xvii (Jan. 5, 1907), 635.

25. Edith Abbott and Sophonisba Breckinridge were already at work in 1905 on a study of women in industry using census data and this reinforced their concern. E. Abbott, *Women in Industry* (New York, 1909), xiii–xiv. Mary McDowell, "The Need for a National Investigation into Women's Work," *Charities and the Commons*, xvii (Jan. 5, 1907), 634–6; McDowell to Mrs. Emmons Blaine, Feb. 9, 1907, Blaine MSS.

26. S. N. D. North to Addams, Dec. 9, 1905, Addams MSS; Howard Wilson, *Mary McDowell*, 124–7; "National Investigation of Women in Industry," *Charities and the Commons* (Nov. 4, 1905), 134.

27. *U. S. Congressional Record,* 59th Congress, 1st Session, 1906, XL, 94; Charles Neill to Jane Addams, Jan. 29, 1906; Neill to Sophonisba Breckinridge, Jan. 29, 1906, Addams MSS.
28. "Annual Report," *National Child Labor Committee Proceedings,* 1908, 150; form leter enclosed McDowell to Mrs. Emmons Blaine, Feb. 9, 1907, Blaine MSS; McDowell, "The Need for a National Investigation," *Charities and the Commons,* XVII (Jan. 5, 1907), 636; *U. S. Congressional Record,* 59th Congress, 2nd Session, 1906–07, XLI, 500, 1457, 2040.
29. McDowell to Mrs. Emmons Blaine, Feb. 9, 1907, Blaine MSS.
30. *United States Commerce and Labor Department Report on the Conditions of Women and Child Wage Earners in the United States,* Senate Documents, LXXVI–CIV (61st Congress, 2nd Session, 1909–10).
31. I lean heavily in this section on a perceptive article by Roy Lubove, "The Progressives and the Prostitute," *Historian,* XXIV (May 1962), 308–30.
32. Michael Gold, *Jews Without Money* (New York, 1930), 15, quoted Lubove, *The Progressives and the Slums,* 69.
33. Wald to Dr. Abbott E. Kittredge, Oct. 29, 1903, Wald MSS.
34. Woods and Kennedy, *The Settlement Horizon,* 260–64; *The Social Evil: With Special Reference to Conditions Existing in the City of New York* (New York, 1902); *The Social Evil in Chicago: A Study of Existing Conditions* (Chicago, 1911); Lubove, "The Progressives and the Prostitute."
35. Louise C. Wade, *Graham Taylor,* 197–202.
36. Jane Addams, *A New Conscience and an Ancient Evil* (New York, 1912), 19–26.
37. *Ibid.,* 69–74; *The Social Evil in Chicago,* 43.
38. Addams, *A New Conscience,* 130–33; Lubove, "The Progressives and the Prostitute."
39. *Ibid.,* 181–219; Lavina L. Dock, *Hygiene and Morality* (New York, 1910).
40. O'Sullivan, "Autobiography," 1–70; Scudder, *On Journey,* 155.
41. Graham Taylor to Addams, Feb. 15, 1913 (quoting Mary Kenny's words when Taylor first met her at the home of Henry Demarest Lloyd), Taylor MSS. See also O'Sullivan, "Autobiography," 62–7; Destler, *Henry Demarest Lloyd,* 253–4.
42. O'Sullivan, "Autobiography," 87; Addams to Lloyd, Nov. 18, Dec. 15, 1891, Jan. 2, 1892, Lloyd MSS; Samuel Gompers, *Seventy Years of Life and Labor* (New York, 1943), I, 490.
43. O'Sullivan, "Autobiography," 88; Scudder, *On Journey,* 155.
44. O'Sullivan, "Autobiography," 88 ff; Scudder, *On Journey,* 155; Gompers, *Seventy Years,* I, 337, 347–8; SEH Report, 1896, 12.
45. Anna Walling, ed., *William English Walling,* 14–36; Walling, "Open

Shop Means the Destruction of the Unions," *Independent,* LVI (May 12, 1904), 1069-73.

46. Walling to Elizabeth Christman, May 11, 1929, WTUL, Box 25; Alice Henry, *Women and the Labor Movement* (New York, 1930), 109.

47. Interview, Anna Walling, Jan. 22, 1959; O'Sullivan, "Autobiography," 200-201; Walling to Elizabeth Christman, May 11, 1929, WTUL, Box 25.

48. Philip Davis, *And Crown Thy Good,* 1-140; Walling to McDowell, Nov. 25, 1903; Alice Henry to Elizabeth Christman, March 12, 1930, WTUL, Box 25.

49. Davis, *And Crown Thy Good,* 140; Gompers, *Seventy Years,* I, 490; O'Sullivan, "Autobiography," 201.

50. Report of Meeting Held for the Purpose of Organizing the Women's Trade League, WTUL, bound volume, Box 1. On Mary Morton Kehew see Randall, *Improper Bostonian,* 112-15.

51. Report of Meetings and Constitution, WTUL, bound volume, Box 1.

52. Report of the Second Meeting of the National Board of the WTUL, WTUL, bound volume, Box 1; Anna Nichols, "The Women's Trade Union League of Illinois," *Union Labor Advocate,* IV (June 1904), 20; Walling to Leonora O'Reilly, Dec. 17, 1903 (with notations in Miss O'Reilly's handwriting), O'Reilly MSS, SL. Mary K. Simkhovitch, "Fifty Years of the Settlements in New York," paper read at fiftieth anniversary of the founding of University Settlement, Dec. 4, 1936, copy, NFS.

53. Walling to Margaret Dreier, Dec. 28, 1904, WTUL, Box 1; Walling to Margaret Dreier, Jan. 17, 1905, WTUL, Box 25; O'Reilly to Gertrude Barnum, Dec. 29, 1905; Barnum to O'Reilly, Oct. 8, 1905, O'Reilly MSS.

54. Walling to Margaret Dreier, Jan. 17, 1905, WTUL, Box 25; *Report of the Third Meeting of the Executive Board,* March 1905, WTUL, bound volume, Box 1; Samuel Gompers's address, Berkley Lyceum, New York, March 24, 1905, WTUL, bound volume, Box 1.

55. Gompers to Gertrude Barnum, Oct. 12, 1905, Nov. 8, 1905; Barnum to Gompers, Nov. 9, 1905, WTUL, bound volume, Box 1; Margaret Robins to Executive Board Members, Dec. 19, 1911, Feb. 21, 1914; Gompers to Margaret Robins, Feb. 21, 1914, WTUL, bound volume, Box 1.

56. Walling to Margaret Dreier, Nov. 1, 1904; Walling to Elizabeth Christman, May 11, 1929, WTUL, Box 25; Mary Dreier, *Margaret Dreier Robins: Her Life, Letters and Work* (New York, 1950), 21.

57. *New York Times,* Nov. 5, 1909; National Women's Trade Union League, *Report of Interstate Conference Held Sept. 26-28, 1908,* 6; quoted in Yellowitz, *Labor and the Progressive Movement,* 65.

58. Raymond Robins to Margaret Dreier, May 8, 1905, Robins MSS;

Mary Dreier, *Margaret Dreier Robins*, 34 ff. See also Allen F. Davis, "Raymond Robins: The Settlement Worker as Municipal Reformer," *SSR*, XXXIII (June 1959), 131-41.

59. See Mary Dreier, *Margaret Dreier Robins*, passim; McDowell, "The Need for a National Investigation," *Charities and the Commons*, XVII (Jan. 5, 1907), 634-6; Mary Anderson (as told to Mary N. Winslow) *Woman at Work: The Autobiography of Mary Anderson* (Minneapolis, 1951), 37-8; Agnes Nester, *Women's Labor Leader: The Autobiography of Agnes Nester* (Rockford, 1954), 66 ff.

CHAPTER 8

1. Quotation from Woods, "Settlement Houses and City Politics," *Municipal Affairs*, IV (June 1900), 396-7; "Are Social Settlers Debarred from Political Work?" handwritten MS, Simkhovitch MSS.

2. Eleanor H. Woods, *Robert A. Woods*, 126, 154, 161; Robert Woods, ed., *Americans in Process; SEH Report*, 1896, 9; 1909, 11; interview, Albert Kennedy, Jan. 13, 1959; interview, David Howie, Jan. 9, 1959; see James Michael Curley, *I'd Do It Again* (Englewood Cliffs, 1957), for a lively though biased account of the struggle for political power in Boston.

3. Woods to Addams, April 28, 1898, Addams MSS; "Roots of Political Power, Robert Woods, ed., *City Wilderness*, 114-47 (Clark is not given credit for the chapter). See Harvard Class of 1893, *Tenth Anniversary Report*, 65.

4. Woods, "Traffic in Citizenship," *Americans in Process*, 147-9, 177-89; interview, Albert Kennedy, Jan. 13, 1959. Woods described Lomasney as "the king of ward eight," and Fitzgerald, "the young Napoleon of the North End." It was Fitzgerald who threatened suit; Woods to Addams, April 28, 1898, Addams MSS.

5. Interview, Eva White, Aug. 15, 1957. See Lincoln Steffens, *The Autobiography of Lincoln Steffens* (New York, 1931), 615-27, for a sketch of Lomasney; Durland to Lloyd, May 7, 1903, Lloyd MSS; Curley, *I'd Do It Again*, 63. Curley claims that Durland gave up because he discovered that Curley's Tammany Club was doing more than a settlement could for the neighborhood.

6. Anna Davies, "A Glance at the Philadelphia Settlement," *Commons*, X (May 1905), 299; Charles Bernheimer, "Social Workers and Philadelphia Political Reform," *Charities and the Commons*, XV (March 17, 1906), 889-90; "From 'Lady Bums' to Ward Grafters," *Charities and the Commons*, XV (Feb. 3, 1906), 574-5.

7. For example see J. Salwyn Schapiro, "Henry Moskowitz: A Social Reformer in Politics," *Outlook*, CII (Oct. 26, 1912), 446-9; "Settlements in Politics," *Commons*, IV (June 1899), 9.

8. *Hull-House Maps and Papers*, 15-19; *Chicago Tribune*, Jan. 24,

1898, 9; quotation from Ray Stannard Baker, "Hull House and the Ward Boss," *Outlook*, LVIII (March 28, 1898), 770.

9. Kelley, "Hull House," *New England Magazine*, XVIII (June 1898), 565; quotation from Baker, "Hull House and the Ward Boss," *Outlook*, LVIII (March 28, 1898), 769–70.

10. Addams, *Twenty Years*, 315; Kelley, "Hull House," *New England Magazine*, XVIII (June 1898), 554–5.

11. Kelley to Lloyd, Sept. 26, 1898, Lloyd MSS; Addams, "The Objective Value of a Social Settlement," *Philanthropy and Social Progress*, 49.

12. Addams to Mary Smith, Feb. 24, 1895, Addams MSS; Kelley, "Hull House," *New England Magazine*, XVIII (June 1898), 556; Addams, *Twenty Years*, 284.

13. Addams to Mary Smith, Aug. 8, 1895, Addams MSS; Addams, *Twenty Years*, 285; *Chicago Tribune*, March 21, 1895, 3.

14. In Chicago each ward elected two aldermen for terms of two years, but scattered so that only one alderman was elected each year. Powers had been re-elected in 1894. Addams, *Twenty Years*, 315–16; Lawler, Independent, polled 3044 votes to 2842 for the Democratic party's candidate, 1974 for the Republican candidate, and 319 for a People's party's candidate. In the same election, the 19th ward gave 4395 votes to the Democratic candidate for mayor and 3937 to the Republican candidate; Jane Addams, "Political Reform," *Democracy and Social Ethics* (New York, 1902), 274–8.

15. Addams to Lloyd, Dec. 22, 1895, Lloyd MSS.

16. *Ibid.*; Addams, *Twenty Years*, 322; *Chicago Tribune*, April 4, 1896.

17. Addams to Lloyd, Dec. 22, 1895, Lloyd MSS; *Hull House Bulletin*, March 1896, 4–5.

18. *Chicago Tribune*, March 25, 1896; *Hull House Bulletin*, March 1896, 5; Kelley, "Hull House," *New England Magazine*, XVIII (June 1898), 565. Powers's majority was cut from 2700 in 1894 to 1100 in 1896. See Chapter 9 for a discussion of the Municipal Voters' League.

19. Addams, "Political Reform," *Democracy and Social Ethics*, 249–63; *Chicago Tribune*, April 4, 1896; Addams, "Ethical Survivals," *International Journal of Ethics*, VIII (April 1898), 289.

20. Addams, "Ethical Survivals," 276–85.

21. Quotation from *Chicago Evening Post*, Feb. 19, 1896, clipping, Addams MSS.

22. Addams, "Political Reform," *Democracy and Social Ethics*, 243–8.

23. Baker, "Hull House and the Ward Boss," *Outlook*, LVIII (March 28, 1898), 770. Chicago Commons had helped elect James Walsh in the 17th ward. See below.

24. Kelley, "Hull House," *New England Magazine*, XVIII (June 1898), 556.

25. *Chicago Tribune*, Jan. 23, Jan. 24, 1898.

26. "The Alderman's Pull," *Commons,* ii (March, 1898), 6; Woods to Addams, April 28, 1898, Addams MSS.
27. Addams, "Ethical Survivals," *International Journal of Ethics,* viii (April 1898), 276, 282.
28. *Ibid.,* 277–88.
29. *Chicago Tribune,* Jan. 24, 1898; *Hartford Times,* March 8, 1898, clipping, Addams MSS; *Chicago Tribune,* March 7, 1898.
30. *Chicago Chronicle,* Jan.–April 1898; Addams, *Twenty Years,* 318; Addams to Mary Smith, March 28, 1898; "A Voter" to Addams, Jan. 17, 1898, Addams MSS.
31. *Hull House Bulletin,* Nov. 1897, 1, March 1898, 1; *Chicago Tribune,* Jan. 24, Feb. 18, March 18, 1898.
32. Addams to Mary Smith, March 26, 28, 1898, Addams MSS; *Chicago Tribune,* Jan. 26, March 7, 1898, editorial quoting Harlan.
33. *Chicago Tribune,* April 6, 1898, 6.
34. Baker, "Hull House and the Ward Boss," *Outlook,* lviii (March 28, 1898), 770; Addams to O'Sullivan, April 3, 1898, Addams MSS.
35. Powers's quotation in *Chicago Tribune,* April 6, 1898, 6; Kelley to Lloyd, Sept. 26, 1898, Lloyd MSS.
36. Kelley, "Hull House," *New England Magazine,* xviii (June 1898), 566.
37. See interview with Addams, *Chicago Tribune,* Feb. 19, 1900; Addams, "Ethical Survivals," 290. See also Anne F. Scott, "Saint Jane and the Ward Boss," *American Heritage,* xii (Dec. 1960), 12–17, 94–9.
38. "Minutes of the Seventeenth Ward Council of the Civic Federation," 1895–97, Taylor MSS. The 17th ward Civic Federation was informally connected with the Chicago Civic Federation which was founded in 1894. See Chapter 9; also, Louise Wade, *Graham Taylor,* 129–33.
39. Taylor, *Chicago Commons through Forty Years,* 9; "Minutes," Feb. 1, 1895; Taylor, *Chicago Commons,* 67; Taylor, "Ward Politics: Good and Bad Challenge," *Daily News,* March 5, 1910.
40. "Minutes," March 15, 29, April 13, 1895; "Civic Federation," *Commons,* i (April 1896), 2.
41. "Minutes," Jan. 10, March 21, 1896; *Inter-Ocean,* March 27, 1896, clipping, Addams MSS.
42. *Chicago Times-Herald,* April 14, 1897, clipping, Taylor MSS; "Minutes," April 8, 1897; "Record of Mass Meeting of Citizens of 17th Ward held April 12, 1897, to take action concerning alleged frauds," Taylor MSS.
43. "Chicago's Great Crisis," *Commons,* iii (Nov. 1898), 1; handbill, n.d. (1898), scrapbook, Taylor MSS; "Constitution of the Seventeenth Ward Municipal Club," n.d., Taylor MSS; "New Hope in Our Ward Politics," *Commons,* vi (April 1901), 15; *Commons,* vi (May 1901), 14–15.

44. Taylor, *Chicago Commons*, 68; "17th Ward Community Club Constitution," n.d. (1902), Taylor MSS.
45. Interview, Albert Kennedy, Jan. 13, 1959. For an account of Taylor and Chicago Commons, see Louise Wade, *Graham Taylor*.
46. Taylor, *Chicago Commons*, 9; John Palmer Gavit, scrapbook, NFS; Taylor to William Kent, April 12, 1913, Taylor MSS; Taylor, "Mediator of Social Justice," *Chicago Daily News*, April 20, 1935.
47. Taylor, *Chicago Commons*, 260; Taylor, "Raymond Robins: Civic Patriotism," 1932, Taylor MSS. "Raymond Robins," *The Public*, x (Sept. 21, 1907), 578–85; William A. Williams, "The Outdoor Mind," *Nation*, CLXXIX (Oct. 30, 1954), 384–5.
48. Taylor to Robins, Dec. 20, 1902, Robins MSS; Taylor, *Chicago Commons*, 71; William Dever, "Address at 25th Anniversary of Chicago Commons, April 25, 1919," Taylor MSS; "The Aldermanic Election in Chicago," *Commons*, VII (April 1902), 18. In 1901 Republican Smulski won by 1300 votes while the ward gave the Democratic candidate for mayor a majority of six hundred. In 1902, Democrat Dever won by 1819 votes.
49. "City Politics at the Settlement," *Commons*, VII (March 1903), 16; "First Gun of the Aldermanic Campaign," March 27, 1903, Taylor MSS; handbills, placards, circulars, scrapbook, Taylor MSS.
50. Northwestern Settlement was included in the 17th ward when the wards were reorganized in 1900; Graham R. Taylor, "Chicago Settlements and Ward Politics," *Charities and the Commons*, XVI (May 1906), 184.
51. Interview, Roy C. Tibbets with Christ Anderson, May 19, 1925, Taylor MSS; Alfred Johnson to William Dever, Feb. 15, 1906, Dever MSS; Taylor to Avery Connley, April 4, 1913, Taylor MSS. In 1923 Dever became mayor of Chicago; see Chapter XI.
52. Taylor to Robins, Dec. 20, 1902, Robins MSS.
53. Robins's nominating speech for John J. McManaman, with Robins's penciled notes, n.d. (1905), Robins MSS; Taylor to Robins, Aug. 22, 1902, Robins MSS.
54. Graham R. Taylor, "Chicago Still Fighting On," *Commons*, IX (Nov. 1904), 557–9; *Chicago Tribune*, Oct. 19, 1904, 6; Robins to Mrs. Blaine, Oct. 8, Nov. 1, 1904, Blaine MSS; *Chicago Tribune*, Nov. 9, 1904.
55. See, for example, Simkhovitch, "Friendship and Politics," *Political Science Quarterly*, XVII (June 1902), 189–205.

CHAPTER 9

1. Simkhovitch, *Neighborhood*, 85; Hamilton, *Exploring the Dangerous Trades*, 73–4; Brander Mathews, "In Search of Local Color," *Vignettes of Manhattan* (New York, 1894), 69.
2. See Albion W. Small, "Fifty Years of Sociology in the United

States," *American Journal of Sociology,* xxi (May 1916), 771; George A. Lundberg, ed., *Trends in American Sociology* (New York, 1929), 267–70. See almost any early issue of *American Journal of Sociology* or *American Political Science Quarterly.*

3. "Charles Zueblin," *NCAB,* xiv (New York, 1910), 454–5. On Goodnow see John M. Gaus, "The Politics of the City Neighborhood," *The Public,* xxi (June 15, 1919), 758; Ely to Addams, Feb. 3, 1898; Dec. 16, 1910; Addams MSS; John Commons, *Myself* (New York, 1934), 56, 68. See Chapter iii for a discussion of Parsons.

4. Frederick C. Howe, *Confessions of a Reformer,* 75–9; statement of Charles Beard, *Settlements 60th Anniversary, 1886–1946,* Pamphlet, NFS.

5. G. R. Taylor, "The Standard for a City's Survey," *Charities and the Commons,* xxi (Jan. 2, 1909), 508; Taylor, *Satellite Cities* (New York, 1915). The Boston study, lost for years, has recently been discovered and published. See Robert A. Woods and Albert S. Kennedy, *The Zone of Emergence,* abridged and edited by Sam B. Warner, Jr. (Cambridge, 1962).

6. See Bremner, *From the Depths,* 67–85, 140–63.

7. Edward T. Devine, *When Social Work Was Young* (New York, 1939), 110–12; Kellogg, "Social Engineer in Pittsburgh," *Outlook,* xciii (Sept. 25, 1909), 165.

8. Woods, "A City Coming to Itself," *Charities and the Commons,* xxi (Feb. 6, 1909), 785–800; William H. Mathews, *Adventures in Giving* (New York, 1939); Jane Addams, *Second Twenty Years at Hull House* (New York, 1929), 10; Bremner, *From the Depths,* 155–7.

9. Jane Robbins, "The Settlement and the Immigrant," *College Settlement Association Quarterly,* i (June 1916), 7.

10. Woods, "The Settlement Houses and City Politics," *Municipal Affairs* iv (June 1900), 395–7; Woods to Miss Dawes, Dec. 20, 1892, Woods MSS.

11. Eleanor Woods, *Robert A. Woods,* 119–20; Woods to M. A. DeWolfe Howe, Dec. 9, 1898, Howe MSS.

12. Woods to Howe, Dec. 9, 1898, Howe MSS; Woods to Addams, May 17, 1897, Addams MSS; M. A. DeWolfe to Allen F. Davis, Feb. 11, 1959. (Howe married Quincy's daughter.)

13. Eleanor Woods, *Robert Woods,* 120–24; William R. Woodbury, "Boston's Municipal Gymnasiums," *Commons,* ix (Oct. 1904), 1468–1473; Josiah Quincy, "Municipal Progress in Boston," *Independent,* lii (Feb. 1900), 424–6. See also Richard M. Abrams, *Conservatism in a Progressive Era; Massachusetts Politics, 1900–1912* (Cambridge, 1964); Geoffrey T. Blodgett, "Josiah Quincy, Brahmin Democrat," *New England Quarterly,* xxxviii (Dec. 1965), 435–53.

14. Woods, "Settlement Houses and City Politics," *Municipal Affairs*, IV (June 1900), 397.
15. Anne Withington, "Boston's Public School Campaign," *Commons*, X (Jan. 1905), 35–6; "History of the Good Government Association," *City Affairs*, I (March 1905), 1–2.
16. Woods, ed., *Americans in Process*, 177–89, SEH Report, 1906, 3; 1907, 15; Woods, "Settlement Houses and City Politics," *Municipal Affairs*, IV (June 1900), 395.
17. *SEH Report*, 1907, 15; William Clark, "The Roots of Political Power," *City Wilderness*, 114–24; Woods, "Traffic in Citizenship," *Americans in Process*, 147–89; A. Chester Manford, "City Government," Elizabeth M. Herlihy, ed., *Fifty Years of Boston* (Boston, 1932), 95.
18. Hanford, "City Government," Herlihy, ed., *Fifty Years of Boston*, 99–102. See also Richard M. Abrams, *Conservatism in a Progressive Era*, 146–8.
19. *SEH Report*, 1908, 3–4; *Boston Evening Transcript*, Dec. 8, 1909.
20. Hanford, "City Government," Herlihy, ed., *Fifty Years of Boston*, 102–6.
21. "Men of Boston, Control Your Own City, Vote for Plan No. 2," Advertisement, *Boston Evening Transcript*, Nov. 1, 1909; also *Transcript*, Nov. 2; Henry G. Pearson, *James J. Storrow: Son of New England* (Boston, 1932), 82–3.
22. *Transcript*, Nov. 10–18, 1909.
23. Pearson, *Storrow* 1–73; Jacob M. Burns, *West End House: The Story of a Boys' Club* (Boston, 1934), 28–9.
24. *SEH Report*, 1910, 6.
25. Pearson, *Storrow*, 80; *Transcript*, Nov. 19, 1909; Eleanor Woods, *Robert Woods*, 72, 101; interview, David Howie, Jan. 9, 1959.
26. Interview, David Howie, Jan. 9, 1959 (Howie recalled Lomasney's remark). Curley apparently had a somewhat higher opinion of Bottomley. See James M. Curley, *I'd Do It Again*.
27. *SEH Report*, 1904, 31; 1910, 6; *Transcript*, Jan. 4, 1910; interview, Howie, Jan. 9, 1959.
28. *Transcript*, Jan. 1–10, 1910; *SEH Report*, 1910, 6; Ward nine gave 1584 votes to Storrow, 1269 to Fitzgerald in 1910. In 1907 the same ward had given 825 votes to Hibbard and 274 to Fitzgerald.
29. Esther G. Barrows, *Neighbors All: A Settlement Notebook* (Boston, 1929), 172–3; *SEH Reports*, 1910–14.
30. Reynolds, "The Settlement and Municipal Reform," *NCCC*, 1896, 140–42.
31. Reynolds, "Eight Years at University Settlement," *USSQ*, II (July 1906), 34–45; *James Bronson Reynolds: A Memorial*, 45.
32. Form letter, April 17, 1897; John Clark to Seth Low, Sept. 8, 1897, Low MSS; "Saving a City," *Commons*, II (Sept. 1897), 5–6.

33. Benjamin R. Low, *Seth Low* (New York, 1925), 37–63; Reynolds to Low, June 3, 1897; Low to Richard Watson Gilder, Sept. 8, 1897, Low MSS.

34. Low to William Beebe, Sept. 6, 7, 1897; Reynolds to Low, Aug. 17, 20, 25, Sept. 10, 21, 24, Nov. 5, 1897; Low to Reynolds, Sept. 22, Oct. 14, 1897, Low MSS.

35. Wald to Low, Oct. 27, 1897; Josephine Shaw Lowell to Low, Oct. 17, 1897, Low MSS; Lillian Betts, *The Leaven in a Great City* (New York, 1903), 192; *James B. Reynolds: A Memorial*, 39–40; *East Side House Annual Report*, 1901; Jane E. Hitchcock, "A Reminiscence," *Settlement Journal*, Nov. 1906, 1–3.

36. Gustavous Myers, *The History of Tammany Hall* (New York, 1917), 282; Reynolds to Low, Nov. 5, 1897, Low MSS.

37. The Committee of Fifteen, which investigated vice in New York, grew directly out of the work and the agitation of several people connected with the settlements in New York. See John L. Elliot, "Public Opinion and New York Politics," *Commons*, VI (March 1902), 1–3.

38. Memo, Nov. 20, 1901; Carl Mead to Everett P. Wheeler, Nov. 6, 1901; O. Gould Wilkie to Wheeler, Nov. 9, 1901; William Timm to Wheeler, Nov. 8, 1901, Everett P. Wheeler MSS. The inspectors sometimes did not challenge the Tammany ballots, because they found more discrepancies in the reform ballots.

39. J. Salwyn Schapiro, "Henry Moskowitz: A Social Reformer in Politics," *Outlook*, CII (Oct. 26, 1912), 446–9. On Ingersoll see sketch, *NCAB* (New York, 1941), XXIX, 500–501.

40. Meyers, Tammany Hall, 295; *Commons*, VI (Jan. 1902), 2.

41. Herbert Parsons, "James Bronson Reynolds, Citizen," *Reynolds—A Memorial*, 60–61; "Reformatory Influences of Social Service upon City Politics," *Commons*, VI (March 1902), 3–4.

42. Riis, "Has Reform Made Good," *Outlook*, LXXV (Sept. 5, 1903), 18–23; Edward T. Devine, "Municipal Reform and Social Welfare in New York," *Review of Reviews*, XXVIII (Oct. 1903), 433–48.

43. Lincoln Steffens, *The Shame of the Cities* (New York, 1957), 199; "Glimpses of a Great Campaign," *World's Work*, VII (Dec. 1903), 4255–9; Steven C. Swett, "The Test of a Reformer: A Study of Seth Low," *New York Historical Society Quarterly*, XLIV (Jan. 1960), 5–41.

44. Most of the settlement workers opposed Sunday closing of the saloon. Simkhovitch, "The New York City Election," *Commons*, VIII (Dec. 1903), 7; "Glimpses of a Great Campaign," *World's Work*, VII (Dec. 1903), 4255–9. See also Charles Garrett, *The LaGuardia Years: Machine and Reform Politics in New York City* (New Brunswick, 1961), 40–41.

45. Moskowitz, "A Settlement Followup," *Survey*, XXV (Dec. 1910), 439–40; "The Political Settlement," *Survey*, XXIV (May 14, 1910),

279–80; Jane Robbins, "Political Influence in Neighborhood Civic Life," *Neighborhood*, I (Jan. 1928), 29–35.

46. See, for example, Wald to Commissioner William H. Edwards, July 14, 1911; Wald to Governor Dix, March 15, 1912; Wald to Martin Glynn, Jan. 15, 1914, Wald MSS.

47. *New York Times*, June 17, 1909; "The New York Campaign, The Outcome," *Outlook*, XCIII (Nov. 13, 1909), 572–3; "Raymond V. Ingersoll," *NCAB*, XXIX, 500–501.

48. "Mayor Gaynor's New Appointments," *Survey*, XXIII (Jan. 15, 1910), 508–9, James K. Paulding, *Charles B. Stover*, 45–8.

49. For this aspect of municipal reform see Samuel Haber, *Efficiency and Uplift: Scientific Management in the Progressive Era, 1890–1920* (Chicago 1964), 99–116.

50. "Henry Bruère," OHP, 10–17.

51. Henry Bruère, "Efficiency in City Government," *Annals*, XCI (May 1912), 3–22; "Effective Light in New York," *Outlook*, LXXXVII (Dec. 21, 1907), 837.

52. Raymond B. Fosdick, *Chronicle of a Generation*, 65–77, 79–107; Fosdick to Wald, Feb. 5, 1912, Wald MSS.

53. "Trained Social Workers Take Charge of New York City Government," *Survey*, XXXI (Jan. 1, 1914), 33–43; "Henry Bruère," OHP, 89–94.

54. Steffens, *The Shame of the Cities*, 164.

55. Reynolds to Addams, Feb. 5, 1893; Woods to Addams, June 26, 1893, Addams MSS. For the civic reform movement in Chicago before 1893 see Sidney I. Roberts, "Businessmen in Revolt: Chicago 1874–1900; unpublished Ph.D. thesis (Northwestern University, 1960).

56. Albion Small, "Civic Federation of Chicago," *American Journal of Sociology*, I (July 1895), 79–103; quote from Frederick Whyte, *The Life of W. T. Stead* (New York 1925), II, 42; memo on organizational meeting for the Civic Federation, n.d., Taylor MSS. See also Joseph O. Baylen, "A Victorian's Crusade in Chicago, 1893–1899," *JAH*, LI (Dec. 1964), 418–34.

57. Civic Federation form letter, Nov. 6, 1895, Lloyd MSS; *Civic Federation Annual Reports*, 1894–1903.

58. Edwin Burnett Smith, "Council Reform in Chicago," *Municipal Affairs*, IV (June 1900), 347–62; Wade, *Graham Taylor*, 131–3, 188–190. See also Chapter 8.

59. Addams, *Twenty Years*, 332; Taylor, Pioneering, 56–7; Steffens, *Shame of the Cities*, 168–70; Wade, *Graham Taylor*, 131–3.

60. Smith, "Council Reform in Chicago," *Municipal Affairs*, IV (June 1900), 347–62; *Chicago Tribune*, April 4, 1896; *Chicago Daily News*, April 4, 1901; *Municipal Voters' League Annual Report*, 1900.

61. Steffens, *Shame of the Cities*, 162–94.

62. "Why Municipal Reform Succeeds in New York and Fails in Chicago," *Independent*, LVI (April 14, 1904), 832–5.
63. Edward Bemis to Lloyd, April 4, 1903, Lloyd MSS; *Hiram House Reports*, 1896–1904; Reynolds, "The Settlement and Municipal Reform," *NCCC*, 1896, 138–42; Woods and Joseph Eastman, "The Boston Franchise Contest," *Outlook*, LXXXII (April 14, 1906), 835–841.
64. For example see Alzina Stevens to Lloyd, March 15, 1897; Addams to Lloyd, March 21, 1897. For the story of the street railway franchises, see Ray Ginger, *Altgeld's America*, 173–82.
65. George Hooker to Lloyd, July 5, 1903; Lloyd to Bemis, July 30, 1903, Lloyd MSS; "Chicago's Public Ownership Vote," *Commons*, IX (May 1904), 170–71.
66. "Outline of Plan to Function Independent Citizens in Practical Politics," n.d., Robins MSS; Taylor to Robins, Nov. 24, 1904, Nov. 7, 1905, Robins MSS; Robins to Mrs. Blaine, March 3, 1905, Blaine MSS.
67. "Municipal Ownership in the Chicago Election," *Commons*, X (April 1905), 197–200; Allen T. Burns to Robins, March 18, 1905, Robins MSS; Harold L. Ickes, *The Autobiography of a Curmudgeon* (New York, 1943), 107.
68. Ickes, *Autobiography*, 107; Robins to Edward F. Dunne, May 8, 1905, Robins MSS; *Chicago Tribune*, Feb. 18, 1906.
69. *Chicago Tribune*, Feb. 18, 20, 1906; *Chicago Record-Herald*, Feb. 18, 1906.
70. Ickes, *Autobiography*, 107–8; Margaret Haley to Robins, Dec. 11, 1905; George Schilling to Robins, Dec. 29, 1905, Robins MSS; Edward F. Dunne, "Our Fight for Municipal Ownership," *Independent*, LXI (Oct. 18, 1906), 927–30.

CHAPTER 10

1. See for example, Addams, "The Steps by which I Became a Progressive," syndicated article (1912), Addams MSS; Robins to Margaret Robins, Feb. 3, 1910, Jan. 17, 1912, Robins MSS; "The Political Settlement," *Survey*, XXIV (May 14, 1910), 439–40.
2. Most historians have interpreted the campaign of 1912 as an elaborate debate between the philosophies of New Freedom and New Nationalism, or they have seen the Progressive party as merely the vehicle for the personal revolt of Roosevelt against the Republican Stalwarts. See, for example, Arthur Link, *Woodrow Wilson and the Progressive Era, 1910–17* (New York, 1954); Forcey, *The Crossroads of Liberalism*, 121 ff; Goldman, *Rendezvous with Destiny*, 188–216; Mowry, *Theodore Roosevelt and the Progressive Movement* (Madison, 1946), 220–55; John M. Blum, *The Republican: Roosevelt* (Cambridge, 1954), 149.

3. For the relationship between charity organizations and the settlements, see Chapter 1.
4. *NCCC*, 1911, 148–213; *NCCC*, 1912, 564; Owen Lovejoy, "Standards of Living and Labor," *NCCC*, 1912, 375.
5. "Social Standards for Industry, *NCCC*, 1912, 388–95; Lovejoy, "Standards of Living and Labor," *NCCC*, 1912, 376.
6. Kellogg, "The Industrial Platform of the New Party," *Survey*, XXVIII (Aug. 24, 1912), 668–70; Kellogg to Robins, July 10, 1912, Robins MSS.
7. Moskowitz to Wald, Aug. 2, 1912, Wald MSS; Kellogg to Addams, Oct. 10, 1912 (enclosing memo based on the Cleveland report, which Kellogg had given to Roosevelt), Addams MSS; quotation from Kellogg to Addams, Feb. 9, 1929, SAP, also used in Addams, *The Second Twenty Years*, 27.
8. Moskowitz to Wald, Aug. 2, 1912, Wald MSS; Kellogg to Addams, Feb. 9, 1929, SAP. For the text of Roosevelt's speech see *The Works of Theodore Roosevelt*, ed., Hermann Hagedorn (New York, 1926), XVII, 254–99.
9. Kellogg, "The Industrial Platform," *Survey*, XXVIII (Aug. 24, 1912), 668–70. For the Progressive party platform see *National Party Platforms, 1840–1956*, ed., Kirk H. Porter and Donald B. Johnson (Urbana, Ill., 1956), 175–83.
10. William Allen White, *Autobiography of William Allen White* (New York, 1946), 484–5; Mary Dreier, *Life and Letters of Margaret Dreier Robins*, 88–9; Addams, *Second Twenty Years*, 28–9; Kellogg to Robins, July 10, 1912, Robins MSS; *New York Times*, Aug. 6–8, 1912.
11. William Allen White Syndicated Column, *Chicago Record-Herald*, Aug. 8, 1912; *Chicago Tribune*, Aug. 8, 1912; Eugene Lies to Robins, Aug. 8, 1912, Robins MSS.
12. Telegram, Roosevelt to Addams, Aug. 9, 1912, Addams MSS. Roosevelt seems to have changed his mind about the need of woman suffrage for political reasons. See Roosevelt to Addams, Oct. 31, 1911, Addams MSS.
13. Mary Dreier to Wald, n.d., Wald MSS; Stephen Wise to Wald, Aug. 24, 1912 (quoting letter he has written to Henry Morgenthau), Wald MSS. Despite his enthusiasm for the platform, Wise finally supported Wilson during the campaign.
14. Jane Addams, "My Experiences as a Progressive Delegate," *McClure's*, XL (Nov. 1912), 13.
15. George E. Mowry, *Theodore Roosevelt and the Progressive Movement*, 266–9; Jane Addams, "The Progressive Party and the Negro," *The Crisis*, V (Nov. 1912), 30–31; *New York Times*, Aug. 6, 1912, 2; Aug. 7, 1912, 2; Mary Child Nerney to Addams, Aug. 13, 1912, Addams MSS.
16. Cornelia Bradford to Addams, Aug. 10, 1912, Addams MSS.

17. For example, Wald to Henry Morgenthau, Aug. 12, 1912, Wald MSS. She did not actively support the Progressives until after the campaign of 1912 and then accepted a position on the New York Progressive Committee.
18. Moskowitz to Wald, Aug. 2, 1912, Wald MSS.
19. Robins to Clarence Barbour, Sept. 16, 1912; Robins to Paul Strayer, Sept. 16, 1912, Robins MSS.
20. Kellogg, "The Industrial Platform of the New Party," *Survey,* xxviii (Aug. 24, 1912), 668–70; Sophonisba Breckinridge to Addams, Sept. 7, 1912, Breckinridge MSS; Marsh to Robins, July 26, 1912, Robins MSS; David Shannon, *Socialist Party of America,* 43–61.
21. Moskowitz to Wald, Aug. 2, 1912, Wald MS; Taylor, "The Man and Movement of the Hour," *Chicago Daily News,* Oct. 12, 1912, Taylor Daily News Scrapbook, Taylor MSS; Jean Gordon to Addams, Aug. 10, 1912, Addams MSS.
22. Robins to Clarence Barbour, Sept. 16, 1912, Robins MSS; Leo Arnstein to Wald, Aug. 6, 1912, Wald MSS; Moskowitz to Wald, Aug. 2, 1912, Wald MSS.
23. J. Salwyn Schapiro, "Henry Moskowitz; A Social Reformer in Politics," *Outlook,* cii (Oct. 26, 1912), 446–9; "Dr. Moskowitz and his Campaign," *Settlement Journal* (Nov. 1912), 1–3. Moskowitz polled 25% of the vote in a losing cause.
24. Addams to Wald, Aug. 15, 1912; Frances Kellor to Wald, Aug. 29, 1912, Wald MSS; Kellor to Jane Addams, n.d. (1912), Sophonisba P. Breckinridge MSS.
25. Moskowitz to Wald, Aug. 2, 1912, Wald MSS; Mary Dreier to Wald, n.d. (1912), Wald MSS; Kellogg to Addams, Oct. 10, 1912; Devine to Emily Balch, Sept. 2, 1912 (enclosed in Devine to Addams, Sept. 2, 1912), Addams MSS; Almy to Robins, Sept. 19, 1912, Robins MSS; Simkhovitch, *Neighborhood,* 175; Forcey, *Crossroads of Liberalism,* 150.
26. John Kingsbury to Robins, July 24, 1912, Sept. 18, 1912, Robins MSS; Kingsbury to Addams, Aug. 15, 1912, Addams MSS; Kingsbury to Robins, Oct. 9, 1912, Kingsbury MSS.
27. Philip Davis, *And Crown Thy Good,* 220 ff; Eleanor Woods, *Robert A. Woods,* 257–8; Woods to Addams, Aug. 7, 1912, Addams MSS; quotation from Robins to Clarence Barbour, Sept. 16, 1912, Robins MSS; Margaret Robins to Robins, June 21, 1912; Ickes to Robins, July 17, Aug. 17, Oct. 18, 1912, Robins MSS.
28. Dreier, *Margaret Robins,* 89–91; Margaret Robins to Addams, Oct. 31, 1912, Addams MSS; Taylor to Daniel Howe, Oct. 9, 1912, Taylor MSS; Taylor, "Humanizing Politics," *Survey,* xxix (Oct. 5, 1912), 10–11.
29. Addams to S. P. Breckinridge, July 19, Sept. 5, 1912, Breckinridge MSS; Addams to Harold Ickes, Sept. 27, 1912, Harold Ickes MSS;

MSS articles by Jane Addams: "The Progressive Party and the Needs of Children," "The Progressive Party and the Protection of Immigrants," "The Progressive Party and the Class of Disinherited," "The Progressive Party and Safeguards for Working Girls," "The Progressive Party and Organized Labor," "The Progressive Party and Woman's Suffrage."

30. Chairman of the Speakers' Bureau to Jane Addams, Oct. 2, 1912 (enclosing itinerary for her speaking tour), Addams MSS; Dr. Anna Howard Shaw, "Campaigning for Suffrage in the West," *The American* (Trenton, New Jersey), clipping, n.d., Addams MSS.

31. McDowell to Addams, Aug. 16, 1912; Kellogg to Addams, Oct. 10, 1912, Addams MSS; Henry Morgenthau to Lillian Wald, Aug. 8, 1912; Wald to Morgenthau, Aug. 12, 1912, Wald MSS. Miss Wald refused to support Wilson publicly.

32. She probably received the most criticism for her refusal to take a stand in the school board crisis in Chicago in 1907. See Allen F. Davis, "Raymond Robins: The Settlement Worker as Municipal Reformer," *SSR*, xxxiii (June 1959), 131–41. Addams to Wald, Aug. 15, 1912, Wald MSS; Edith Abbott, "Grace Abbott of Hull House, 1908–1921," *SSR*, xxiv (Dec. 1950), 504.

33. Edward T. Devine, "Politics and Social Work," *Survey*, xxix (Oct. 5, 1912), 9.

34. *New York Sun*, Aug. 18, 1912, clipping, Addams MSS; Addams, "Pragmatism in Politics," *Survey*, xxix (Oct. 5, 1912), 12.

35. Quotation from Moskowitz to Wald, Aug. 2, 1912, Wald MSS; Addams, "Pragmatism in Politics," *Survey*, xxix (Oct. 5, 1912), 12; Kellogg to Kingsbury, July 1, 1912, SAP; Robins to Clarence Barbour, Sept. 16, 1912, Robins MSS; Donald R. Richberg, *Tents of the Mighty* (New York, 1930), 38.

36. Addams, *The Second Twenty Years*, 40–41; Taylor to Daniel Howe, Oct. 9, 1912, Taylor MSS; Notes for Address, n.d. (after the election, 1912), Robins MSS.

37. Kellor, "A New Spirit in Party Organization," *North American Review*, cxix (June 1914), 835; Addams, *Second Twenty Years*, 40–41; Richberg, *Tents of the Mighty*, 40. Quotation from Frances Kellor article, "Something New In Politics," enclosed in Kellor to Addams (Dec. 24, 1912), Addams MSS; *The Progressive Service of the National Progressive Party*, Jan. 25, 1913, pamphlet.

38. *The Progressive Service of the National Progressive Party*, Jan. 25; Addams, *Second Twenty Years*, 40–41. See also John A. Garraty, *Right Hand Man: The Life of George W. Perkins* (New York, 1960), 296.

39. Progressive Service form letter, Jan. 16, 1913, Addams MSS; Kellogg to Mrs. Joseph Bowen, April 12, 1913; memo, "Progressive Service," n.d. (1913), Addams MSS.

40. Memo, Jan. 18, 1913, Addams MSS; Kellor, "A New Spirit in Party Organization," *North American Review*, CXCIX (June 1914), 887; Richberg, *Tents of the Mighty*, 41.
41. Katherine Coman to Addams, Jan. 1, Jan. 6, 1913, Addams MSS; *Settlement Journal* (Nov. 1912), 3; Wald to William Hotchkiss, Nov. 15, 1912, Wald MSS.
42. For a discussion of the McNamara case see: John Commons and Associates, *History of Labor in the United States, 1896–1932* (New York, 1935), IV, 318–21; Devine, *When Social Work Was Young*, 117; telegram, Mrs. Blaine to Kellogg, Dec. 17, 1911, Blaine MSS; "To Survey Readers and Survey Associates," *Survey*, XXIX (Nov. 23, 1912), 1–8; "The Larger Bearings of the McNamara Case: A Symposium," *Survey*, XXVII (Dec. 30, 1911), 1412–19.
43. "The Larger Bearings of the McNamara Case," 1412–19; Graham Taylor, "The McNamara Confessions," *Survey*, XXVII (Dec. 9, 1911), 1339–40.
44. "A Communication to Hon. William Howard Taft," Dec. 30, 1911, pamphlet, Blaine MSS; "Federal Commission on Industrial Relations," *Survey*, XXVII (Jan. 13, 1912), 1563. For the story in more detail see Allen F. Davis, "The Campaign for the Industrial Relations Commission, 1911–1913," *Mid-America*, VL (Oct. 1963), 211–228.
45. Memo, Graham R. Taylor to Mrs. Blaine, n.d., Blaine MSS; *U. S. Congressional Record*, 62nd Congress, 2nd Session, 1661–2.
46. "To Survey Readers and Survey Associates," *Survey*, XXIX (Nov. 23, 1912), 5. The Children's Bureau finally became a reality in April 1912; "Movement Under Way for Industrial Commission," *Survey*, XXVII (March 2, 1912), 1821–2.
47. "Allen T. Burns' New Appointment," *Survey*, XXII (April 10, 1909), 89–90; "Personals," *Survey*, XXXII (July 18, 1914), 421; Burns, obituary, *New York Times*, March 10, 1953.
48. Memo Graham R. Taylor, n.d., Blaine MSS; Notes taken by Mrs. Blaine at City Club Meeting, Feb. 3, 1912, Blaine MSS.
49. Graham R. Taylor to Mrs. Blaine, Feb. 16, 1912; Taylor to Chicago Committee, March 29, 1912, Blaine MSS; Devine, "Hughes-Borah Bill," *Survey*, XXVII (March 9, 1912), 1898–9.
50. *Hearing before the Committee on Labor of the House of Representatives on the Bill H.R. 21094 to create an Industrial Commission*, March 22, 1912 (Washington, 1912); Graham R. Taylor to Mrs. Blaine, April 27, May 14, 1912, Blaine MSS; *House of Representatives Reports* 6132, 62nd Congress, 2nd Session, IV, Report 726 (May 16, 1912).
51. Mrs. Blaine to Julius Rosenwald, June 12, 1912; Graham R. Taylor to Chicago Committee, June 19, July 12, 1912, Blaine MSS.
52. Stephen Wise to Addams, Sept. 3, 1912, Breckinridge MSS; Lindsay to Committee, Sept. 3, 1912, Addams MSS; Taylor to Ethelbert

Stewart, Sept. 7, 1912; Taylor to Charles Nagel, Sept. 12, 1912; Stephen Wise to Addams, Sept. 16, 1912, Addams MSS.

53. "Statement adopted at meeting of Committee on Industrial Relations," Dec. 18, 1912, copy Blaine MSS; Lindsay to Committee, Dec. 23, 1912; G. R. Taylor to Mrs. Blaine, Dec. 19, 1912, Blaine MSS.

54. Kellogg to Mrs. Bowen, April 12, 1913; Kellor to Kellogg, July 17, 1913, Addams MSS; Richberg, *Tents of the Mighty*, 42.

55. Kingsbury to Addams, Jan. 17, 1913, Addams MSS.

56. Robins to Kellor, Nov. 20, 1913, Robins MSS; Garraty, *Right Hand Man*, 285–308. Kingsbury to Addams, Dec. 23, 1912, Jan. 17, 1913, Addams MSS. See George Mowry, *Theodore Roosevelt and the Progressive Movement*, 291–4; Amos E. Pinchot, *History of the Progressive Party, 1912–16*, edited by Helene Maxwell Hooker (New York, 1958), 182–225.

57. Kingsbury to Addams, Dec. 23, 1912; Addams to Robins, Feb. 20, 1914, Robins MSS; Telegram, Kellor to Robins, n.d. (1913), Robins MSS; William Draper Lewis to Addams, Feb. 17, 1914; Ickes to Addams, April 19, 1914, Addams MSS.

58. Richberg, *Tents of the Mighty*, 48; Garraty, *Right Hand Man*, 298–300; Robins to Addams, March 9, 1914; Robins to Perkins, March 9, 1914; Robins to Kellor, Sept. 13, 1913, Robins MSS; Robins to Roosevelt, Aug. 3, 1914, Roosevelt MSS.

59. Roosevelt to Robins, Aug. 13, 1914; Elting Morrison, ed., *The Letters of Theodore Roosevelt*, VII, 767; Roosevelt to Perkins, Aug. 23, 1913, *Letters of Theodore Roosevelt*, VII, 742–3. "Social Workers and the Extra Session," *Survey*, XXX (April 5, 1913), 3–4; "Governor Wilson and the Social Workers," *Survey*, XXIX (Feb. 8, 1913).

60. Robins to Walter Weyl, Sept. 19, 1914; Robins to Taylor, Nov. 7, 1914, Robins MSS. *Address of Raymond Robins as Temporary Chairman of the Progressive National Convention*, June 7, 1916, Robins MSS.

61. Mark Perlman, *Labor Union Theories in America* (Evanston, Illinois, 1958), 284–92; John A. Fitch, "Field Investigations of the Industrial Relations Commission," *Survey*, XXXIII (Feb. 27, 1915), 578–82.

62. "Changes in the Industrial Relations Commission," *Survey*, XXXIII (March 27, 1912), 686; United States Commission on Industrial Relations, *Industrial Relations Final Report and Testimony*, 11 vols. (Washington, 1916).

CHAPTER 11

1. John Haynes Holmes, "War and the Social Movement," *Survey*, XXXII (Sept. 26, 1914), 630; Wald quoted in R. L. Duffus, *Lillian Wald*, 148.

2. Wald to William Dean Howells, Sept. 22, 1914, Wald MSS; Kellogg to Addams, Sept. 11, 15, 1914, Addams MSS. See also Donald Johnson, *The Challenge to American Freedoms: World War I and the Rise of the American Civil Liberties Union* (Lexington, 1963), 1–25.

3. Hamilton, *Exploring the Dangerous Trades*, 164; *A Heart that Held the World: An Appraisal of the Life of Helena Stuart Dudley and A Memorial to Her Work* (Boston, 1939), 11–12.

4. Addams, *Second Twenty Years*, 131–4; Hamilton, *Exploring the Dangerous Trades*, 161–82.

5. Johnson, *Challenge*, 4; "Committee to Fight 'Huge War Budget,'" *Survey*, xxxv (Jan. 1, 1916), 370.

6. Wald, *Windows*, 296; Duffus, *Wald*, 155–60.

7. Minutes of the Meetings of the Association of Neighborhood Workers, Oct. 1913-Jan. 4, 1916, UNH; Weinstein, *The Ardent Eighties*, 112; Arthur Link, *Wilson: The New Freedom* (Princeton, 1956), 255–7; "Why Wilson: A Statement by Social Workers," Oct. 1916, SAP.

8. Robins to George Perkins, March 9, 1914, Robins MSS; McDowell, "The Settlement and Politics," McDowell MSS; Addams to Kellogg, Oct. 25, 1916, SAP; Kellogg, "Progressivism," *Survey*, xxxvii (June 17, 1916), 304.

9. Kellogg, "The Fighting Issue," *Survey*, xxxvii (Feb. 17, 1917), 572–7; "War Resolutions Adopted by the Settlements," *Survey*, xxxviii (June 16, 1917), 265; Helena Dudley to Jane Addams, April 10, 1917, Addams MSS; Mrs. Simkhovitch quoted in Linn, *Jane Addams*, 330–31.

10. Addams, *Second Twenty Years*, 142; Taylor to Victor Lawson, Oct. 4, 1917, Taylor MSS; "Social Settlements and the War," *Survey*, xxxviii (April 7, 1917), 29–30; Bruno Lasker to Wald, April 14, 1917, Wald MSS.

11. Devine, "Social Forces in Wartime," *Survey*, xxxviii (July 7, 1917), 316.

12. John Andrews to Paul Kellogg, Oct. 6, 1917, SAP.

13. John Commons and Associates, *History of Labor in the United States*, iii, 200–205, 321–5, 341–5; "How Workingmen Fare at Washington," *Survey*, xxxix (Feb. 23, 1918), 575; quotation from John Fitch, "Stretching the Pay Envelope: Some New Methods of Fixing Wages," *Survey*, xxxix (Jan. 12, 1918), 411.

14. John B. Andrews, "Federal Government to Uphold Labor Standards," April 21, 1917, SAP; "Planning a New Child Labor Law," *Survey*, xl (June 15, 1918), 323; Baker quoted in Kelley, "The War and Women Workers," *Survey*, xxxix (March 9, 1918), 628–631.

15. Bruno Lasker, "The Housing of War Workers: Lessons from British

Experience for Fulfillment of an Urgent Task," *Survey*, xxxix (Jan. 1918), 390–97; Roy Lubove, "Homes and a Few Well-Placed Fruit Trees: An Object Lesson in Federal Housing," *Social Research*, xxvii (Winter 1960), 469–86.

16. Julia C. Lathrop, "The Military and Naval Insurance Act," *Nation*, cvi (Feb. 7, 1918), 157–8; "Soldiers and Sailors Insurance Law," *Survey*, xxxix (Oct. 13, 1917), 39–40.

17. Alice Hamilton and Gertrude Seymour, "The New Public Health," *Survey*, xxxviii (April 21, 1917), 59–62; Owen R. Lovejoy, "A War Program for Peace," *NCSW*, 1919, 664–5.

18. Wald to Joseph Girdansky, July 7, 1917; Wald to Elizabeth Farrell, June 19, 1918, Wald MSS.

19. P. P. Claxton, "Effect of the War on Schools," *National Municipal Review*, vi (Sept. 1917), 571–2; "School Centers and War Work," *Christian Science Monitor*, April 11, 1918, clipping, Eva W. White MSS; Sidney Dillick, *Community Organization for Neighborhood Development*, 71–6; Roy Lubove, *The Professional Altruist: The Emergence of Social Work As a Career* (Cambridge, 1965), 178, 189–92.

20. Eleanor Flexner, *Century of Struggle: The Woman's Rights Movement in the United States* (Cambridge, Mass., 1959), 288–93; Mary Dreier, *Margaret Dreier Robins*, 132–5; Chambers, *Seedtime of Reform*, 9–10; "War-Time Gains of the Suffragists," *Survey*, xxxviii (April 28, 1917), 97.

21. Fosdick, *Chronicle of a Generation*, 142–86; Eva W. White, "War Activities as they Have Affected Housing, Health and Recreation," *NCSW*, 1919, 496–502.

22. "Social Workers Stand for Prohibition," *Survey*, xxxix (March 23, 1918), 687–8; Devine quoted by Arthur Kellogg, "The National Conference of Social Work," *Survey*, xxxviii (June 16, 1917), 255; Woods, "Prohibition and its Social Consequences," *NCSW*, 1919, 763–4.

23. Fosdick, *Chronicle of a Generation*, 144–8; Newton Baker to Fosdick, Sept. 20, 1917, quoted in Frederick Palmer, *Newton D. Baker: America at War*, 2 vols. (New York, 1931), I, 311; Fosdick, "The Program of the Commission on Training Camp Activities with Relation to the Problem of Venereal Disease," *Social Hygiene*, iv (Jan. 1918), 71–6; Arthur Kellogg to Charles W. Eliot, Aug. 30, 1917, SAP.

24. "War-Camp Community Service," *Playground*, xi (1917), 509–10; John Hope Franklin, *From Slavery to Freedom: A History of American Negroes* (2nd ed., New York, 1961), 444–68; Higham, *Strangers in the Land*, 202–3, 302–3; "For a Constructive Law on Immigration," *Survey*, xl (Feb. 23, 1918), 575; Kellogg to Grace Abbott, Feb. 15, 1918, SAP.

25. Woods quoted by Winthrop Lane, "National Conference of Social Work," *Survey*, XL (June 1918), 256–7; Addams, *The Second Twenty Years*, 144–52; Kellogg to Addams, Sept. 20, 1918, SAP.

26. Kellogg, "To the Unfinished Work," *Survey*, XLII (July 5, 1919), 513–14.

27. John L. Elliot, "Ten Days in Vienna," *Survey*, XLV (Oct. 2, 1920), 33–46; "Settlements Overseas," *Survey*, XLV (Oct. 9, 1920), 52–3; Elliott to Addams, Aug. 20, 1922, Addams MSS; Isabelle Dubroca, *Good Neighbor: Eleanor McMain of Kingsley House*, 122–31.

28. Addams quote from Lovett, *All Our Years*, 154–5; Wald, "Public Health in the Soviet Union," *Survey*, LIII (Dec. 1, 1924), 270–74; Wald, *Windows on Henry Street*, 251–84; Christopher Lasch, *American Liberals and the Russian Revolution* (New York, 1962). For Mrs. LaFollette's statement see Lewis Feuer, "American Travelers to the Soviet Union, 1917–32: The Formation of a Component of New Deal Ideology," *American Quarterly*, XIV (Summer 1962), 119–49.

29. David A. Shannon, *Between the Wars: America, 1919–1941* (Boston, 1965), 3–30; I am especially indebted here and other places in this chapter to Chambers, *Seedtime of Reform*.

30. Addams, *Second Twenty Years*, 153–87; Charles Cooper to Taylor, Jan. 27, 1921, Taylor to Cooper, Feb. 14, 1921, Taylor MSS.

31. *A Heart That Held the World*, 14; "Settlements," *Survey*, XXXII (May 30, 1914), 1246–7.

32. Johnson, *Challenge*, 10–14; 145–8; Cooper to Addams, Aug. 30, 1922, Addams MSS.

33. Cornelia Bradford to Woods, Feb. 20, 1917, NFS; Graham Taylor to Rev. E. L. Benson, Aug. 16, 1915, Taylor MSS; interview, Albert Kennedy, Jan. 13, 1959; Chambers, *Seedtime*, 119–20.

34. Cooper to Taylor, Jan. 27, 1921; Taylor to Kellogg, Sept. 9, 1932, Taylor MSS; John Gaus to Woods, Jan. 2, 1924, SEH.

35. Vida Scudder, "An Old Friend with A New Name," *Survey*, XXXVIII (June 2, 1917), 219–20; Woods to Ernest Hopkins, Feb. 21, 1923, SEH.

36. Nathan E. Cohen, *Social Work in the American Tradition* (New York, 1958), 137–9; Abraham Epstein, "The Soullessness of Present Day Social Work." *Current History*, XXVIII (June 1928), 390–95; Chambers. *Seedtime of Reform*, 87–128. On the development of social work as a profession, see Lubove, *The Professional Altruist*.

37. Henry F. Pringle, *Alfred E. Smith: A Critical Study* (New York, 1927), 61–73.

38. Taylor, *Pioneering*, 239–45; Chicago Commission on Race Relations, *The Negro in Chicago: A Study of Race Relations and a Race Riot* (Chicago, 1922); Chambers, *Seedtime*, 132–3.

39. "Neighbors," *Survey*, L (June 1923), 293–4; Howard Wilson, *Mary McDowell*, 187–209.

40. "Neighborhood and Nation," *Survey*, XLII (June 21, 1919), 465; "Neighborhood and Settlement," *Survey*, XLVI (July 16, 1921), 511.
41. Cooper to Addams, Aug. 30, 1922, Addams MSS.
42. Kellogg, "New Beacons in Boston," *Survey*, LXIV (July 15, 1930), 341; Cooper to John L. Elliot, Sept. 2, 1927, copy Addams MSS.
43. "A Quarter Century of the College Settlement," *Survey*, XXXIII (Nov. 14, 1914), 170.
44. Sidney Dillick, *Community Organization*, 67–94; Clarence Perry, "School Center History in Chicago," *Journal of Social Forces*, III (Jan. 1925), 291–3; Ernest W. Burgess, "Can Neighborhood Work Have a Scientific Basis," Robert Park *et. al.*, *The City* (Chicago, 1925), 142–55.
45. Isabel Taylor, "New Settlement Leadership," *Neighborhood*, I (July 1928), 19–24; "Settlement Faith and Practice; A Symposium by Headworkers Who Have Taken Office Since 1915," *Neighborhood*, III (Sept. 1930), 101–19.
46. Woods and Kennedy, *Settlement Horizon;* interview, Kennedy, Jan. 13, 1959.
47. Kennedy, "The Visual Arts in Twenty-Eight Settlements," Albert J. Kennedy, Kathryn Fara and Associates, *Social Settlements in New York City* (New York, 1933), 179–236; Kellogg, "Semi-Centennial of the Settlements," *Survey Graphic*, XXIV (Jan. 1935), 30–32; Marjorie McFarland, "Settlement For Sale," *Survey*, LXIII (March 15, 1930), 707, 733.
48. Kellogg to Kennedy, Feb. 17, 1938, Kennedy to Kellogg, April 17, 1928, NFS; Kellogg to Addams, April 17, 1928, SAP; Kellogg, "The Unsettling Settlements," *Survey*, LX (May 15, 1928), 281.
49. Martha Bensley Bruère, ed., *Does Prohibition Work?* (New York, 1927), quotation from 304. Kennedy, "The Saloon in Retrospect and Prospect," *Survey Graphic*, XXII (April 1933), 203–6.
50. Kellogg to Kennedy, Feb. 17, 1928, NFS; Kellogg to Addams, April 17, 1928, SAP.
51. After four years of publication *Neighborhood* collapsed in 1932.
52. *Case Studies of Unemployment* (Philadelphia, 1930); Clinch Calkins, *Some Folks Won't Work* (New York, 1929); Helen Hall and Irene H. Nelson, "How Unemployment Strikes Home," *Survey*, LXIII (April 1, 1929), 51–6; *Helen Hall Settlement Papers: A Descriptive Bibliography* (New York, 1959), forward; Kellogg to Addams, Jan. 23, 1931, SAP.
53. Gertrude Springer, "Shock Troops to the Rescue," *Survey*, LXIX (Jan. 1933), 11.
54. Mary H. Simkhovitch, *Here is God's Plenty: Reflections on American Social Advance* (New York, 1949), 39; "United Neighborhood Houses, 1900–1958: Fifty-Eight Years of Service," UNH; J. M. Flagler, "The Public Be Served," *New Yorker*, XXXV (Dec. 12, 1959), 59 ff (Dec. 19, 1959), 41 ff; Stuart Patrick, "Some Legis-

lative Contributions of the Settlement Houses to Modern Urban Society," Unpublished B.A. thesis (Princeton, 1961).

55. See, especially, Roy Lubove, "New Cities for Old: The Urban Reconstruction Program of the 1930's," *Social Studies*, LIII (Nov. 1962), 203–14; Clarence S. Stein, "A New Venture in Housing," *American City*, XXXII (March 1925), 277–81; Elliot, "Alexander M. Bing," *Neighborhood*, I (Oct. 1928), 3–8.

56. Clarence A. Perry, "Neighborhood and Community Planning: *Regional Survey of New York and Its Environs*," VIII (New York, 1929); James Dahir, *The Neighborhood Unit Plan: Its Spread and Acceptance* (New York, 1947).

57. Simkhovitch to Geoffry Parson, Oct. 23, 1945; Simkhovitch, "A Woman's View of Housing," Simkhovitch MSS; Simkhovitch, *Here is God's Plenty*, 25–47; Timothy L. McDonnell, *The Wagner Housing Act: A Case Study of the Legislative Process* (Chicago, 1957), 51–87.

58. "A Dutchman's Farm," *Survey Graphic*, XXVIII (June 1939), 389–94.

59. See especially Chambers, *Seedtime*, 253–67. Also, "United Neighborhood Houses, 1900–1958," UNH.

60. Scudder, *On Journey*, 160–61; James G. Stevens to William Cole, Jan. 11, 1912, SEH; *Report On the Questions Drawn Up By Present Residents in Our College Settlements and Submitted to Past Residents* (Publication of the Church Social Union, Sept. 15, 1896), 14–20; Bruno Lasker, OHP, 196.

61. Hunter to Addams, Dec. 19, 1910, Addams MSS; Fosdick, *Chronicle of a Generation*, 291; Davis, *And Crown Thy Good*, 220–22; Louis Pink, OHP, 6–8.

62. Anne Withington to William Cole, Jan. 24, 1912, SEH.

63. Albert Kennedy to Thomas Turley, March 16, 1945, NFS.

64. Claud M. Fuess, *Joseph Eastman*; Joseph Eastman to Miss Blood, Nov. 23, 1933, SEH.

65. William Mathews, *Adventures in Giving*, 71 ff, especially 182–241.

66. See Arthur M. Schlesinger, Jr., *The Crisis of the Old Order*, 25; David Loth, *Swope of G.E.: The Story of Gerard Swope and General Electric in American Business* (New York, 1958), 31 ff; Wald to Addams, Dec. 19, 1934, Addams MSS.

Index

Morris, William, 5, 7; influence on American settlement workers, 23, 47

Moskowitz, Belle, 232

Moskowitz, Henry, 30, 43, 186, 232; and Industrial Relations Commission, 208; and investigation of prostitution, 136; and local politics, 151; and organized labor, 108; and municipal reform, 183–5; and organization of NAACP, 101; and Progressive party, 197–201, 205, 207; sketch, 183

Motivation of settlement workers, xi, 26–39, 269, note 2; Jane Addams on, 26–9; career-line study of, 269, note 4

Mott, John, 225

Mowry, George, xi

Mullenbach, James, 108, 166

Municipal Arts Society (New York), 72

Municipal Museum (Chicago), 69

Municipal ownership, 190–92

Municipal reform, 170–93; Boston, 174–80; Chicago, 187–93; New York, 180–87; settlement workers' relation to businessmen in, 174–6, 188

Municipal Voters' League (Chicago), 155, 165, 167–8, 189–91

Murphy, Edgar Gardner, 131

Murphy, Governor Franklin, 66

Music education, 49–50

Nation, 102

National Association for the Advancement of Colored People (NAACP), 97–102, 194, 199. *See also* Negroes

National Association of City Planning, 72

National Child Labor Committee, 25, 123, 131–4, 194, 223, 234

National City Planning Conference, 73

National Civic Federation, 188, 212

National Committee for Constructive Immigration Legislation, 227

National Community Center Association, 80–81, 235

National Conference of Charities and Correction, 19, 91; Jane Addams president of, 21, 195; becomes National Conference of Social Work, 226; and child labor, 130–31; and congestion exhibit, 72; and Progressive party plat-

form, 195–8; *Proceedings* of, 21; favors prohibition, 225–6; relation to settlements, 21, 195, 234

National Conference on City Planning, 194

National Conference of Social Work, *see* National Conference of Charities and Correction

National Conference on Vocational Guidance, 54

National Consumers' League, 25, 131, 234

National Education Association, 51, 77

National Federation of Settlements, 25, 195, 234–8; records of, 248

National Federation of Women's Clubs, 133

National Housing Association, 69

National Industrial Recovery Act, 241

National League for the Protection of Negro Women, 97

National League on Urban Conditions Among Negroes, 98, 233

National Playground Association of America, 64, 194, 225

National Progressive Committee, 201–2. *See also* Progressive party

National Progressive Service, 206–8, 213–16. *See also* Progressive party

National Society for the Promotion of Industrial Education, 52

National Vocational Guidance Association, 54

National War Labor Board, 222

National Women's Trade Union League, 99, 101, 115, 123, 133, 194, 203, 234; organization of, 138–46; purpose of, 142–3, relation to American Federation of Labor, 142–5. *See also* Margaret Dreier Robins, Leonora O'Reilly, Mary Kenny O'Sullivan, William English Walling

Nature, settlement workers' attitude toward, 60–61. *See also* Anti-urbanism, Cities

Negroes: 94–102, 118; and Progressive party, 198; during World War I, 226–7; in 1920's, 230, 232–3. *See also* National Association for the Advancement of Colored People

Neighborhood, 238

Neighborhood Guild (New York), 9–12, 14, 32, 40, 43, 63, 183. *See also* University Settlement